ESTIMATING TABLES FOR HOME BUILDING

by

Paul I. Thomas

CRAFTSMAN

Craftsman Book Company
6058 Corte del Cedro, P.O. Box 6500, Carlsbad, CA 92008

Library of Congress Cataloging-in-Publication Data

Thomas, Paul I.
  Estimating tables for home building.

  Reprint. Originally published: Handbook of tables and
formulas for home construction estimating.   Englewood
Cliffs, N.J. : Prentice-Hall, c1979.
  Includes index.
  1. House construction--Estimates.   I. Title.
TH437.T45   1986   692'.5   86-4404
ISBN 0-934041-10-5

CONTENTS

CONTENTS

CONTENTS

How This Handbook Will Assist You

This handbook of Tables and Formulas presents an original and completely new approach to estimating the quantities of materials and the labor for the construction of one-family dwellings, garages and small commercial buildings. The main objective—to simplify and speed up the work of the estimator.

Most of the Tables have been created by the author specifically for this book.* They are the result of several years of research and more than 100,000 separate calculations. Starting with the materials in the footings and foundations of various dimensions, the Tables follow the logical order of constructing a building from floor slabs; floor, wall and roof framing; finish floors; sheathing and siding; brickwork (veneer and solid); roofing; and interior and exterior decorating.

The Tables accommodate buildings that have *ground-floor* areas up to 3,000 square feet. The Formulas, which are nothing more than simple arithmetical rules, supplement the Tables. They apply to buildings that have *ground-floor* areas in excess of 3,000 square feet.

Materials used in the installation of electrical wiring, plumbing, heating and air conditioning are much too varied in kind and in specifications to be adapted to Tables or Formulas. Therefore, they are not included in the text although labor Tables are furnished for most of these specialized building trades to guide the estimator in figuring labor costs.

Each Table is prefaced by a full step-by-step explanation of how it is to be used, followed by illustrative examples of its application.

Twenty-five Labor Tables for estimating the number of hours required to apply or install materials and perform various kinds of operation are included to guide the estimator. The production hours in these Tables represent averages under normal working conditions. They are the result of special studies that have been made on many construction jobs.

Under the heading Estimating Labor and Material, there is a thorough and comprehensive presentation of the fundamentals of estimating labor and material. The material is organized in a manner not usually found in other texts on the subject. For example, sixteen judgment factors are listed and analyzed and should be taken into consideration when estimating labor. Thirteen common errors that are made in estimating are listed and described. The charges that enter into overhead costs are outlined. Three different methods of estimating are shown by

---

*Some of the tables included in this Handbook have appeared previously in HOW TO ESTIMATE BUILDING LOSSES AND CONSTRUCTIONS COSTS, Third Edition, Prentice-Hall, Inc., 1976.

example, and several illustrations are given for developing *unit costs* of labor and material.

The book is visually highlighted with photographic illustrations of typical buildings to which the Tables and Formulas apply. There are several detailed estimates to illustrate the application of the Tables and Formulas.

The principles underlining the Tables are founded on the knowledge that the quantities of major construction materials for dwellings and garages, in fact, practically all buildings, are related to the square-foot area occupied by the structure or to the lineal feet of its perimeter. For example, materials, the quantity of which is a function of the square-foot area occupied by the dwelling (referred to in this text as the *ground-floor* area), would encompass such items as floor slabs, floor framing, rough and finish floors, ceilings, roof framing, roof sheathing and roofing, plaster and drywall ceilings, and ceiling tile and decorations. Materials, the quantity of which is a function of the perimeter, include items such as footings, foundation walls, exterior wall framing, sheathing, siding, plaster and lath or drywall of exterior walls, exterior painting, brick veneer and solid masonry walls, stucco and concrete block.

A few speculative, rule-of-thumb assumptions must necessarily be made in compiling Tables of this kind. For example, there is no fixed rule as to the lineal feet of partition in relation to the ground-floor area of a dwelling. All dwellings do not have the same ceiling heights and the same exterior wall heights. Nor do all dwellings have the same shape, i.e., the ratio of its length to its width. Therefore it is necessary to permit a certain amount of license to establish "norms" for these indeterminates. The text outlines appropriate adjustments wherever these "norms" are at significant variance with the building under consideration. It will be found that in most cases such adjustments are minor.

As a result of a study of numerous dwellings, five assumptions have been made to establish the following "norms."

1. Length-to-width ratio of the building.
2. Exterior wall heights.
3. Interior wall heights.
4. Lineal feet of partition per square foot.
5. Roof pitch when gable areas are included in Table quantities.

Length-to-width ratio of a building is a prime consideration. A study has led to the conclusion that the most common ratio was in the neighborhood of two-to-one. In other words, the length was twice the width. It was also found that this ratio lends itself to a quick, easy adjustment in Table quantities when the ratio is other than two-to-one. This adjustment will be found in Table A, page 25. *The adjustment applies only to materials of construction that are a function of the perimeter.* No length-to-width adjustment is necessary for garages. One-car garages have a ratio of two-to-one. Two-car garages have a ratio of one-to-one.

Exterior wall heights, from the top of the foundation to the top of the uppermost plate or eaves line, are assumed to be 9 feet for a one-story dwelling, 15 feet for a one-and-one-half story dwelling, and 18 feet for a two-story dwelling. Table B shows how the quantities in the Tables may be adjusted where exterior wall heights are other than those assumed. All garage exterior wall heights are assumed to be 8 feet.

Interior wall heights from floor to ceiling, are assumed to be 8 feet. Where they are other than 8 feet, the Table quantities may be adjusted by dividing them by 8 and multiplying by the wall height in feet of the dwelling under consideration.

The *Lineal feet of partition* in dwellings is assumed to be:

10% of the ground-floor area in a 1-story dwelling
15% of the ground-floor area in a 1 1/2-story dwelling
20% of the ground-floor area in a 2-story dwelling

This means that a 1-story dwelling with a *ground-floor* area of 1,500 square feet is assumed to have 150 lineal feet of partition. A 1-1/2 story dwelling with 1,500 square feet of *ground-floor* area is assumed to have 225 lineal feet of partition. A two-story dwelling with 1,500 square feet of *ground-floor* area is assumed to have 300 lineal feet of partition. Floor layouts vary from one dwelling to the other. Where the exact number of feet of partition is desired, it should be scaled from the plan or sketch of the building.

Roof pitch is assumed to be 1/4 (6″ rise-per-foot-of-run) unless otherwise stated in the Table. This is significant only in those Tables that include gable materials. Otherwise, quantities in the Tables for rafters, roof decking, roofing, and trusses are for roof pitches that range from 1/8 (3″ rise-per-foot-of-run) to 1/2 (12″ rise-per-foot-of-run).

Window and door openings have not been deducted in establishing Table quantities with the exception of garages that are attached or detached. A 9-foot wide door is assumed for all one-car garages, and a 16-foot door is assumed for all two-car garages. The actual area of window and door openings should be deducted to determine the quantity of materials to be deducted.

Estimating, by definition, means "approximating"; it is not an exact science in most cases. This does not imply that it can be approached carelessly. There is no excuse for taking wrong measurements, guessing at dimensions, overlooking items, and using bad judgment. No system for estimating suits every occasion; no system is foolproof. All factors that apply to a given situation must be considered. Whatever method is used, it is only as good as the person using it.

HOW THIS BOOK CAN HELP IN ESTIMATING

1. The quantities of materials of construction in the average dwelling, garage and commercial building can quickly be determined from the book by finding the *ground-floor* area and referring to the appropriate Tables and Formulas.

2. A contractor or an architect can, while discussing the construc-

tion of a building, approximate differentials in the cost of construction as the *ground-floor* area of the building is increased or decreased.

3. A builder or a subcontractor can quickly determine the cubic yards of concrete in the footings, foundation or slab of a building by reading directly from the Tables.

4. The number of concrete blocks in a foundation wall, the number of bricks in a 4-inch veneer wall, or in a 12-inch solid wall can be read right from the Tables.

5. A builder or a carpenter can read off the quantity of framing in the entire dwelling, or individual quantities for studding, floor joists, rafters, etc.

6. Appraisers of dwellings for mortgage and tax purposes, or for the amount of insurance to be carried, can very quickly approximate replacement costs.

7. A subcontractor of drywall, plastering, and painting can read off area and quantities.

8. Insurance adjusters, particularly those working on losses after catastrophes, will find the Tables and Formulas excellent for estimating and checking estimates.

Paul I. Thomas

General Instructions

These Tables are designed for conventional 1-, 1-1/2- and 2-story dwellings and for 1- and 2-car attached and detached garages. They show quantities of most of the structural building materials for dwellings with *ground-floor* areas from 200 to 3,000 square feet, and for attached and detached garages that have *ground-floor* areas from 200 to 1,000 square feet. Photographs of typical buildings to which these Tables apply are shown on pages 81-89 and 128-133.

COMPUTATION OF AREAS

The quantities in the major Tables are based on the *ground-floor* square foot area of the dwelling and garage. A few supplemental Tables provide alternate methods for estimating certain construction materials based on vertical heights of walls. For example, Table 2A shows the cubic yards of concrete per lineal foot of wall 1 to 12 feet high and 6 to 12 inches thick. Table 3A shows the number of 8″ × 16″ concrete blocks in walls 8 inches to 10 feet high. Also, there are supplemental Tables and Formulas that provide alternate methods for estimating quantities of certain materials based on the vertical or horizontal square foot area of the walls and floors.

The *ground-floor* area of a dwelling or a garage is computed by direct measurement or from a plan or sketch. Include in this area all extensions and projections, off-sets and recessed areas that are *actually* a part of the main dwelling or garage under consideration. See pages 22 to 24 for illustrative examples.

Do Not Include the Following Areas:

    (a) An attached garage to the main dwelling
    (b) A carport
    (c) Porches, patios and breezeways.

ALTERNATE AREA COMPUTATION FOR ROOF FRAMING,
DECKING AND ROOFING MATERIALS
IN TABLES 11, 12, 13 and 15 THROUGH 26

When the horizontal area covered by the roof of a dwelling is approximately the same as the *ground-floor* area of the dwelling itself, except for the average or normal overhang, or for minor setbacks, the *ground-floor* areas of dwellings in Tables 11, 12, 13 and 15 through 26 should be used. These are the Tables that show quantities of Rafters, Roof Decking and Roofing materials.

When the horizontal area of a roof, i.e., the horizontal area covered by the roof, extends over carports, breezeways, driveways, open decks and porches, and other areas outside of the perimeter of the main dwelling, a more accurate estimate of the materials in the above mentioned Tables can be made by computing the horizontal area covered by the roof structure. A sketch and an illustrative example of a roof of this type are shown on pages 116 and 117. Since the framing, decking and roofing material quantities are a function of the square foot area covered by the roof, regardless of its pitch, there is no need for any adjustment for the length-to-width ratio.

PERIMETER MEASUREMENT

Compute the lineal feet of perimeter from the perimeter that encloses the *ground-floor* area of the dwelling or garage developed under Computation of Areas, above, but do not include the perimeters of (a), (b) or (c) which are described under Computation of Areas, page 17.

Illustrative examples or perimeter measurement are shown on pages 22 to 24.

FINISHED ATTIC ROOMS

A 1-story dwelling that has two or more finished rooms and bath above the first floor should be treated as a 1-1/2- or 2-story dwelling as the case may be. If there is only one finished room and no bath, treat that as a 1-story dwelling. Then estimate the additional construction materials for the extra room.

BASEMENTS

Tables 1, 2, and 3 show the quantities of material for basement footings, foundations and floors. If the basement is partial, that is, it does not extend under the entire dwelling, use the *ground-floor* area of the partial basement section to estimate footings, foundations and concrete floor. Use the *ground-floor* area of the unexcavated part to estimate the footings and any foundation above those footings. (See basement garages below.)

GARAGES

Basement Garages

A garage in the basement of a dwelling requires no more consideration in estimating than if there were no garage, with two exceptions as a rule. The square foot area in the foundation wall taken up by the garage door should be deducted from the foundation construction material using the shortcut formula for Foundations page 154, 165 and 259. The other exception is adding any material necessary if there is a partition separating the garage from the rest of the basement.

Attached Garages

A one-story attached garage is one that adjoins the main dwelling and has no living quarters. The roof may be a continuation of the dwelling roof or it may have a separate roof. The construction materials are estimated using the ground-floor area and applying the appropriate Tables under Attached Garages or using the available formulas.

Detached Garages

A one-story detached garage is one independent of the main dwelling, but may be connected by a breezeway or covered patio. Like attached garages, it may be one-, two- or three-car. The construction materials are estimated using the ground-floor area and applying the appropriate Tables for Detached Garages, or using the formulas provided.

PORCHES, PATIOS AND BREEZEWAYS

To estimate the construction materials for porches, patios and breezeways, compute the ground-floor area and apply the appropriate Tables or formulas provided according to the specifications of the particular structure involved. Footings and foundation walls above the footings should be estimated by using the formulas provided, rather than the Tables. These will be found under Footings, page 148, and under Foundation Walls—Concrete, and under Foundation Walls—Concrete Block.

Concrete slabs should be estimated using Table 5 for areas under 500 square feet, and Table 4 for areas over 500 square feet.

For floor framing, rafter framing, wood flooring, roof decking, roofing, etc. the appropriate Tables should be used based on the ground-floor area and specifications. Formulas may be used also.

Examples of estimating materials for breezeways and porches are shown on pages 118-126.

INTERPOLATING IN THE TABLES

Not all dwellings have *ground-floor* areas of even-hundred square feet. Therefore, it may be desirable to interpolate between two *ground-floor* areas in the Tables.

How to Interpolate

Assume that a dwelling has a *ground-floor* area of 1860 square feet which lies in between 1,800 and 1,900 square feet in the Tables. If Table 24 is being used to estimate the quantity of asphalt shingles on a roof with a 1/4 pitch, it shows 2,214 square feet of shingles for a dwelling of 1,800 square foot *ground-floor* area, and 2,337 square feet of shingles for a dwelling with *ground-floor* area of 1,900 square feet. The difference is 123 square feet. A dwelling with a *ground-floor* area of 1,860 square feet would require:

$$\text{Dwelling 1,800 sq ft area} = 2{,}214 \text{ sq ft shingles}$$
$$\frac{.60 \times 123}{100} = 74 \text{ sq ft shingles}$$
$$\text{Dwelling 1,860 sq ft area} = 2{,}288 \text{ sq ft shingles}$$

It is a matter of discretion with the estimator as to whether interpolation is sufficiently important when rather insignificant differences are involved. Some will prefer to use the nearest 100 square feet; others will use the next highest 100 square feet to provide a factor of safety.

TABLE A

Lineal Feet of Perimeter of Dwellings with Various Length-to-Width Ratios

As the shape of a building elongates, that is, departs from the shape of a square, building materials related to the perimeter of the building increase in quantity if the *ground-floor* area remains constant.

For example, a dwelling that has a *ground-floor* area of 2,000 square feet will have the following lineal feet of perimeter for the length-to-width ratios shown.

Length-to-width ratio	1:1	Perimeter	179 lin ft
" " " "	2:1	"	190 " "
" " " "	3:1	"	207 " "
" " " "	4:1	"	224 " "
" " " "	5:1	"	240 " "

It is apparent that building materials based on perimeter measurement such as footings, foundations, exterior wall framing, sheathing, masonry, etc. will increase in quantity, although materials based on the square foot area will not change in quantity. This also explains why a square building is less costly than a similar one with the same area but longer and narrower.

These Tables are based on a length-to-width ratio of two-to-one (L:W = 2:1) for dwellings and 1-car garages; and on a length-to-width ratio of one-to-one (L:W = 1:1) for 2-car garages. Where quantities of building materials are derived in part or in whole from perimeter measurements, appropriate notation is made in those Tables for adjusting the quantities where the length-to-width ratio is other than two-to-one.

It will be found that in most cases such adjustments are minor as shown in Table A and whether they are necessary is a matter for the estimator to decide in each case. To illustrate, a dwelling with a *ground-floor* area of 1,800 square feet is 60 ft long and 30 ft wide. The length-to-width ratio is 2:1. If this was a square building of the same area, Table A shows that 5 percent should be *deducted* from the quantities in the Tables that are based on the perimeter measurements. If this was a long narrow dwelling with a 3:1 length-to-width ratio, Table A shows that 9 percent should be *added* to the quantities in the Tables that are based on the perimeter measurements.

The length-to-width ratio of a building does not affect the quantity of construction materials that are based on the *ground-floor* area and NO ADJUSTMENT IS TO BE MADE IN THE TABLES WHERE THESE MATERIALS ARE CONCERNED REGARDLESS OF THE SHAPE OF THE BUILDING.

L:W (LENGTH-TO-WIDTH) ADJUSTMENT TABLE

If L:W ratio is 1:1	*deduct* 5% from Tables
If L:W ratio is 2:1	(basis of Tables)
If L:W ratio is 3:1	*add* 9% to Tables
If L:W ratio is 4:1	*add* 18% to Tables
If L:W ratio is 5:1	*add* 25% to Tables

HOW TO USE THIS TABLE

1. Measure or compute the lineal feet of perimeter of your dwelling following the method outlined under Perimeter Measurement in General Instructions.

2. From Table A select the *ground-floor* area of your dwelling and read across to the lineal feet shown that is closest to the perimeter of your dwelling. The length-to-width (L:W) ratio at the top of that column is one to be used.

Illustrative Example No. 1

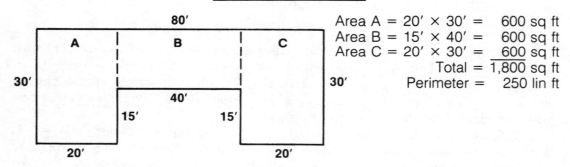

Area A = 20′ × 30′ =   600 sq ft
Area B = 15′ × 40′ =   600 sq ft
Area C = 20′ × 30′ =   600 sq ft
Total = 1,800 sq ft
Perimeter =   250 lin ft

From Table A, the nearest perimeter to 250 lin ft for a *ground-floor* area of 1,800 sq ft is 228 lin ft. The column in which this appears shows a length-to-width ratio of 5:1 for this dwelling.

If the building was a rectangle it would measure 18.97′ × 94.85′ = 1,800 sq ft. This is a length-to-width ratio of 5:1 which is the basis on which the Table A is figured.

Illustrative Example No. 2

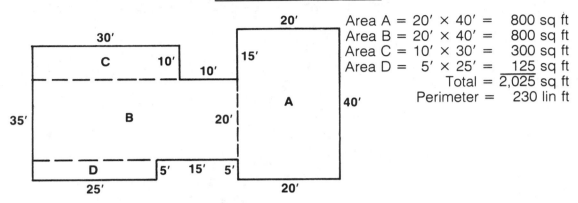

Area A = 20′ × 40′ =   800 sq ft
Area B = 20′ × 40′ =   800 sq ft
Area C = 10′ × 30′ =   300 sq ft
Area D = 5′ × 25′ =   125 sq ft
Total = 2,025 sq ft
Perimeter =   230 lin ft

From Table A, the nearest perimeter to 230 lin ft for a *ground-floor* area of 2,000 sq ft is 224 lin ft. For a *ground-floor* area of 2,100 sq ft the nearest perimeter shown to 230 lin ft is 229 lin ft. Interpolating, the nearest perimeter to 230 lin ft for a *ground-floor* area of 2025 sq ft would be 25% of the difference between 229 lin ft and 224 lin ft plus 224 lin ft.

$$.25 (229 - 224) = 1 + 224 = 225 \text{ lin ft}$$

This falls within the column showing a length-to-width ratio of 4:1 for this dwelling.

If this was a rectangular building it would measure 22.5′ × 90′ = 2,025 sq ft. This is a length-to-width ratio of 4:1 which is the basis on which the Table A is figured.

Illustrative Example No. 3

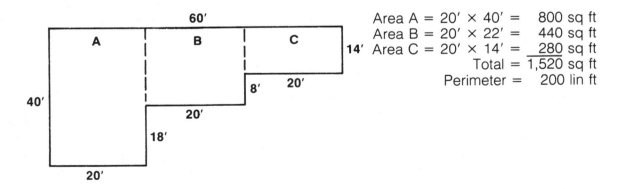

Area A = 20′ × 40′ =   800 sq ft
Area B = 20′ × 22′ =   440 sq ft
Area C = 20′ × 14′ =   280 sq ft
Total = 1,520 sq ft
Perimeter =   200 lin ft

From Table A, the nearest perimeter to 200 lin ft for a *ground-floor* area of 1,500 sq ft is 194 lin ft. For a *ground-floor* area of 1,600 sq ft the nearest perimeter is

200 lin ft. Interpolating, the nearest perimeter to 200 lin ft for a *ground-floor* area of 1,520 sq ft would be 20% of the difference between 200 lin ft and 194 lin ft plus 194 lin ft.

$$.20 \,(200 \,-\, 194) = 1.2 + 194 = 195.2 \text{ lin ft}$$

This falls within the column showing a length-to-width ratio of 4:1 for this dwelling.

If this was a rectangular building on which the Table A is based, it would measure 19.5′ × 78′ = 1,521 sq ft which is a length-to-width ratio of 4:1.

Illustrative Example No. 4

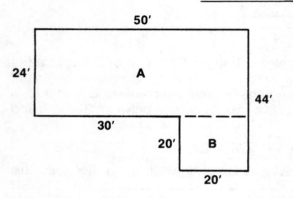

Area A = 24′ × 50′ = 1,200 sq ft
Area B = 20′ × 20′ = 400 sq ft
Total   1,600 sq ft
Perimeter =   188 lin ft

Table A shows the nearest perimeter to 188 lin ft for a *ground-floor* area of 1,600 sq ft is 185 lin ft. This appears in the column that shows a length-to-width ratio of 3:1.

If this was a rectangular building, on which the Table A is based, it would measure 23.1′ × 69.3′ = 1,600 sq ft. This a length-to-width ratio of 3:1.

TABLE A

LINEAL FEET OF PERIMETER OF DWELLINGS
FOR VARIOUS LENGTH-TO-WIDTH RATIOS SHOWN

(For rectangular dwellings divide the length by the width to obtain
the L:W ratio. For irregular shaped dwellings, use this Table)

Ground Floor Area	LENGTH TO WIDTH RATIO				
	1 to 1 Perimeter Lin Ft	2 to 1 Perimeter Lin Ft	3 to 1 Perimeter Lin Ft	4 to 1 Perimeter Lin Ft	5 to 1 Perimeter Lin Ft
200	57	60	66	71	76
300	69	74	80	87	93
400	80	85	92	100	107
500	89	95	103	112	120
600	98	104	113	123	131
700	106	112	122	132	142
800	113	120	131	141	152
900	120	127	139	150	161
1000	126	134	146	158	170
1100	133	141	153	166	178
1200	139	147	160	173	186
1300	144	153	166	180	193
1400	150	159	173	187	201
1500	155	164	179	194	208
1600	160	170	185	200	215
1700	165	175	190	206	221
1800	170	180	196	212	228
1900	174	185	201	218	234
2000	179	190	207	224	240
2100	183	194	212	229	246
2200	188	199	217	235	252
2300	192	203	222	240	257
2400	196	208	226	245	263
2500	200	212	231	250	268
2600	204	216	236	255	274
2700	208	220	240	260	279
2800	212	224	244	265	284
2900	215	228	249	269	289
3000	219	233	253	274	294

TABLE B

Exterior Wall-Height Adjustment

The exterior wall-height from the top of the foundation to the upper plate or eaves line, assumed in developing these Tables is

9 feet in a 1-story dwelling
15 feet in a 1 1/2-story dwelling
18 feet in a 2-story dwelling

The materials of construction that are used in exterior walls are related to, and quantities are based on, the perimeter of the building. The quantities in *specifically designated* Tables may be adjusted if the exterior wall-height of your dwelling is greater than or less than those assumed above.

Select the quantity from the Table and multiply it by the factor shown in Table B to make the adjustment. Adjusting for exterior wall heights is more significant in some materials than in others when considering cost. For illustration, if the wall height of a 1-story dwelling with a *ground-floor* area of 1,600 square feet is 10 ft rather than 9 ft used in the Tables, the quantities should be multiplied by 1.11. If we are estimating the number of brick in an 8-inch wall, Table 31 shows 21,420 bricks. Multiplying that by 1.11 gives 23,776 bricks . . . a difference of 2,356 bricks. If the bricks cost $75 per 1,000 delivered, the difference is $75 × 2.356 = $176. However, if the item being estimated is insulation board, Table 30 shows 1,870 sq ft. Multiplying that by 1.11 gives 2,076 sq ft, a difference of 206 sq ft. If insulation board is $120 per 1,000 sq ft, the difference is $24.72.

As the difference in the wall height increases, the greater the difference in the quantities of the materials. If and when an adjustment is to be made is up to the individual. If many construction materials are being estimated, or an entire dwelling, the difference of one foot in the wall height makes a substantial difference and the cost differential becomes accumulative.

KEEP IN MIND THAT THIS ADJUSTMENT APPLIES ONLY TO TABLES FOR MATERIALS IN THE EXTERIOR WALLS AND TO NO OTHERS.

TABLE B

EXTERIOR WALL HEIGHT ADJUSTMENT

(Applies only when noted in the Tables)

ONE-STORY DWELLINGS—TABLES BASED ON 9' HEIGHT

For wall height of 7'	Multiply Table quantity by .78
For wall height of 8'	Multiply Table quantity by .89
For wall height of 10'	Multiply Table quantity by 1.11
For wall height of 11'	Multiply Table quantity by 1.22
For wall height of 12'	Multiply Table quantity by 1.33
For wall height of 13'	Multiply Table quantity by 1.44
For wall height of 14'	Multiply Table quantity by 1.56

ONE- & ONE-HALF STORY—TABLES BASED ON 15' HEIGHT

For wall height of 12'	Multiply Table quantity by .80
For wall height of 13'	Multiply Table quantity by .87
For wall height of 14'	Multiply Table quantity by .93
For wall height of 16'	Multiply Table quantity by 1.07
For wall height of 17'	Multiply Table quantity by 1.13
For wall height of 18'	Multiply Table quantity by 1.20

TWO-STORY DWELLINGS—TABLES BASED ON 18' HEIGHT

For wall height of 14'	Multiply Table quantity by .78
For wall height of 15'	Multiply Table quantity by .83
For wall height of 16'	Multiply Table quantity by .89
For wall height of 17'	Multiply Table quantity by .94
For wall height of 19'	Multiply Table quantity by 1.06
For wall height of 20'	Multiply Table quantity by 1.11
For wall height of 21'	Multiply Table quantity by 1.17

Note: Use multiples of these factors for higher wall heights. For example, if a one-story building has an exterior wall height of 16 feet, multiply the factor for 8 feet by two (.89 × 2 = 1.78). If a two-story building has an exterior wall height of 24 feet, multiply the factor for 16 feet by one and one half (.89 × 1.5 = 1.335).

TABLES C1 and C2

Gable Areas

These two Tables show the total square feet in *both gables* of gable roofs that have roof pitches of 1/8 to 1/2, for buildings with L:W ratios of 1:1 to 5:1. These gables are assumed to be at the shorter or narrow end of the building.

SIMPLIFIED FORMULA

To quickly compute the square feet in a gable or the gables of a roof, obtain the pitch of the roof, the length-to-width ratio (L:W), and the *ground-floor* area of the building. Multiply the factor in the table below by the *ground-floor* area.

Illustrative Example

A dwelling 25′ × 75′ has a *ground-floor* area of 1,875 sq ft and a L:W ratio of 3:1. Assume a roof pitch of 1/3 which is a rise of 8″ per foot of run. The factor in the formula is .111. 1,875 × .111 = 208 sq ft in both gables.

Roof Pitch	Length-To-Width-Ratio								
	1:1	1.5:1	2:1	2.5:1	3:1	3.5:1	4:1	4.5:1	5:1
1/8	.125	.083	.063	.050	.042	.036	.031	.028	.025
1/6	.167	.111	.083	.067	.056	.048	.042	.037	.033
5/24	.208	.139	.104	.083	.069	.059	.052	.046	.042
1/4	.250	.167	.125	.100	.083	.071	.063	.056	.050
1/3	.333	.222	.167	.133	.111	.095	.083	.074	.067
1/2	.500	.333	.250	.200	.167	.143	.125	.111	.100

For *rectangular shaped dwellings* use the above length-to-width ratio nearest to the dwelling you are estimating. The L:W of your dwelling is the length divided by the width. Example: A dwelling 60′ × 40′ has a L:W of 60 = 1.5 : 1.

For *irregular shaped dwellings* determine the L:W from Table A, pages 21-25.

28

IF GABLE IS AT THE LONG SIDE OF BUILDING

Occasionally a gable is at the long side of a building or a porch, as shown in Figures 3 and 5. When this occurs the gable areas can be determined (1) by computing the area as in a triangle (1/2 base × height) or (2) by multiplying the factor in the formula or the square feet in Tables C1 and C2 when the L:W ratios apply, as noted below:

When L:W Ratio Is:	Multiply Factor in Formula or Table C1 and Table C2 areas by:
1:1	1.0
1.5:1	2.25
2:1	4.0
2.5:1	6.25
3:1	9.0
3.5:1	12.25
4:1	16.0

Illustrative Example

A porch is 30′ long and 12′ wide. The L:W ratio is $\frac{30}{12}$ = 2.5:1. With a roof pitch of ¼, the factor in the formula is .100. That factor must be multiplied by 6.25 as shown above when the L:W ratio is 2.5:1.

$$6.25 \times .100 \times 360 \text{ sq ft} = 225 \text{ sq ft}$$

Treated as a triangle the area of both gables is:

15′ run × 6″ rise per foot = 7′ 6″

$\frac{7.5}{2}$ × 30′ × 112.5 sq ft for one gable

Area of both gables is 112.5 × 2 = 225 sq ft

ADJUSTING GABLE AREAS AND QUANTITIES

The Tables throughout this book are based on a roof pitch of 1/4. If a dwelling or a garage has a roof pitch greater or less than 1/4 it may be desirable to make an adjustment. The following procedure is recommended.

1. Use those Tables that state *Gables Excluded*.
2. Determine the area of both gables from Table C1 or C2, or using the formula on page 28.
3. From Table 14 A obtain the factor the area is to be multiplied by to get the FBM of actual framing, which is .50 for 2″ × 4″ − 16″

on center and .333 for $2'' \times 4'' - 24''$ on center. Add cutting, fitting and blocking—usually 20 to 25 percent.

From Table 30–38 A obtain the factor for the material per sq ft to finish the gable and multiply the gable area by that factor.

4. Add the quantity developed in step 3 to the quantity in step 1 to obtain the total quantity including the gable. Use one half the gable area in the Table C1 and C2 if only one gable is involved as in an attached garage.

Illustrative Example

A one-story dwelling $30' \times 60'$ has a *ground-floor* area of 1,800 sq ft and a gable roof with a pitch of $\frac{1}{2}$. Estimate the exterior wall and partition framing where studs are $2'' \times 4'' - 16''$ on center. From Table 6 there is 2,394 FBM of framing *excluding* gables. From Table C2 there is 450 sq ft in both gables. Table 14 A shows .50 FBM per sq ft for $2'' \times 4'' - 16''$ on center.

$$450 \times .50 = 225 \text{ FBM}$$

$$225 + 2,394 = 2,619 \text{ FBM total framing for exterior studs and partition}$$
studs, including gables.

TABLE C1

GABLE AREAS OF DWELLINGS

NUMBER OF SQUARE FEET IN BOTH GABLES
FOR GROUND FLOOR AREAS SHOWN

Ground Floor Area	ROOF PITCH 1/8					ROOF PITCH 1/6					ROOF PITCH 5/24				
	Length-to-Width Ratio					Length-to-Width Ratio					Length-to-Width Ratio				
	1:1	2:1	3:1	4:1	5:1	1:1	2:1	3:1	4:1	5:1	1:1	2:1	3:1	4:1	5:1
200	26	12	8	6	5	34	17	11	8	7	43	21	14	11	8
300	37	19	13	10	8	50	25	17	13	10	62	32	21	16	13
400	50	25	17	13	10	67	34	22	17	13	84	42	28	21	17
500	62	31	21	16	13	82	42	28	21	17	103	52	35	26	21
600	75	38	25	19	15	100	50	33	25	20	125	63	42	32	25
700	88	44	29	22	17	117	58	39	29	23	147	73	49	37	29
800	100	50	34	25	20	133	67	45	34	27	167	84	56	42	34
900	113	56	38	28	23	150	75	50	38	30	188	94	63	47	38
1000	124	62	42	31	25	165	83	56	42	34	207	105	70	52	42
1100	138	69	46	35	28	184	92	61	46	37	230	115	76	58	46
1200	150	75	50	38	30	201	100	67	50	40	252	126	84	63	50
1300	162	81	54	41	32	216	108	72	54	43	270	135	90	68	54
1400	176	88	59	44	35	234	117	78	59	47	293	147	98	73	59
1500	188	94	63	47	38	250	124	84	63	50	313	156	105	79	63
1600	200	100	67	50	40	267	134	89	67	54	334	167	112	84	67
1700	213	107	71	53	42	284	142	94	71	56	355	178	118	89	71
1800	226	113	75	56	45	301	150	100	75	60	377	188	125	94	75
1900	236	118	78	59	47	315	158	105	78	63	394	198	132	99	78
2000	250	125	84	63	50	334	167	112	84	67	417	209	140	105	84
2100	262	131	88	66	53	349	174	117	88	70	436	218	147	110	88
2200	276	138	92	69	55	368	183	123	92	74	460	229	154	115	92
2300	288	144	96	72	57	384	191	128	96	76	480	239	160	120	96
2400	300	150	100	75	60	400	200	133	100	80	500	250	167	125	100
2500	313	156	104	78	62	417	208	139	104	83	521	260	174	130	104
2600	325	162	109	81	65	434	216	145	109	87	542	270	182	136	109
2700	338	168	113	85	68	451	224	150	113	90	564	280	188	141	113
2800	351	174	116	88	70	468	232	155	116	93	585	290	194	147	116
2900	361	181	121	91	73	482	241	162	121	97	602	301	202	151	121
3000	375	188	125	94	75	500	251	167	125	100	625	314	209	157	125

TABLE C2

GABLE AREAS OF DWELLINGS

NUMBER OF SQUARE FEET IN BOTH GABLES
FOR GROUND FLOOR AREAS SHOWN

Ground Floor Area	ROOF PITCH 1/4					ROOF PITCH 1/3					ROOF PITCH 1/2				
	Length-to-Width Radio					Length-to-Width Ratio					Length-to-Width Radio				
	1:1	2:1	3:1	4:1	5:1	1:1	2:1	3:1	4:1	5:1	1:1	2:1	3:1	4:1	5:1
200	51	25	17	13	10	68	34	22	16	14	102	50	34	26	20
300	74	38	25	19	15	99	50	34	26	20	148	76	50	38	30
400	100	50	33	25	20	134	68	44	34	26	200	100	67	50	40
500	124	62	42	31	25	164	84	56	42	34	248	124	84	62	50
600	150	75	50	38	30	200	100	66	50	40	300	150	100	76	60
700	176	88	58	44	35	234	116	78	58	46	352	176	116	88	70
800	200	100	67	50	40	266	134	90	68	54	400	200	134	100	80
900	225	112	75	56	45	300	150	100	76	60	450	224	150	112	90
1000	248	124	83	62	50	330	166	112	84	68	496	248	166	124	100
1100	276	138	92	69	55	368	184	122	92	74	552	276	184	138	110
1200	302	151	100	75	60	402	200	134	100	80	604	302	200	150	120
1300	324	163	108	81	65	432	216	144	108	86	648	326	216	162	130
1400	352	176	117	88	70	468	234	156	118	94	704	352	234	176	140
1500	376	187	124	94	75	500	248	168	126	100	752	374	248	188	150
1600	400	200	134	100	80	534	268	178	134	108	800	400	268	200	160
1700	425	212	142	107	85	568	284	188	142	112	850	424	284	214	170
1800	450	225	150	113	90	602	300	200	150	120	900	450	300	226	180
1900	473	238	158	118	95	630	316	210	156	126	946	476	316	236	190
2000	500	250	167	125	100	668	334	224	168	134	1000	500	334	250	200
2100	523	262	174	131	105	698	348	234	176	140	1046	524	348	262	210
2200	552	275	183	138	110	736	366	246	184	148	1104	550	366	276	220
2300	576	286	191	144	115	768	382	256	192	152	1152	572	382	288	230
2400	600	300	200	150	120	800	400	266	200	160	1200	600	400	300	240
2500	625	312	208	156	125	834	416	278	208	166	1250	624	416	312	250
2600	650	325	216	162	130	868	432	290	218	174	1300	650	432	324	260
2700	676	338	224	168	135	902	448	300	226	180	1352	676	448	336	270
2800	700	350	232	174	140	936	464	310	232	186	1400	700	464	350	280
2900	722	361	241	181	145	964	482	324	242	194	1444	722	482	362	290
3000	750	376	251	188	150	1000	502	334	250	200	1500	752	502	376	300

Mensuration: Shortcut Mathematics
to Speed up Construction Estimating

A sound working knowledge of elementary arithmetic and simple geometry is necessary to calculate quantities and costs in estimating building losses. Unless a person is regularly or frequently called upon to add, subtract, multiply, and divide whole numbers, fractions, and decimals, the principles are forgotten, mistakes are easily made, and estimates become unreliable. A knowledge of the formulas used in calculating the areas of simple figures, and the volumes of ordinary solids, is of equal importance.

FRACTIONS

A fraction is part of a whole number, for example: 1/2, 1/3, 1/4, 1/8. The number above the line is called the *numerator;* the number below the line is called the *denominator*. The line itself signifies that the top number is to be divided by the bottom number

$$\frac{1}{2} = \frac{numerator}{denominator}$$

The fraction 3/4 means that we are dealing with three parts of a whole unit which has been divided in four equal parts. It indicates that 3 is to be divided by 4. When the division indicated by a fraction is performed, the result is the *decimal equivalent* of the fraction.

$$\frac{3}{4} = .75, \text{ or } \frac{1}{2} = .5$$

TABLE D1

COMMON FRACTIONS WITH DECIMAL EQUIVALENTS

$1/64$	0.015625	$1/7$	.1428
$1/32$	.03125	$1/6$	.1666
$1/16$	.0625	$1/5$	.2
$1/12$	.0833	$1/4$	.25
$1/10$	.1	$1/3$	.333
$1/9$	.1111	$1/2$	.5
$1/8$	.125	1	1.0

Any fraction less than a whole unit as 1/2, 1/6, 4/5, and so forth is called a *proper fraction*.

A fraction equal to or greater than a whole unit, as 3/3, 5/2 or 8/6, is called an *improper fraction*.

Any number that includes a whole number and a fraction, as 1-1/2, is referred to as a *mixed number*.

A mixed number may be converted to a fraction by multiplying the denominator by the whole number and adding the numerator. This result is placed over the denominator of the fraction.

Illustrative Example

$$3^1/_2 = 2 \times 3 + 1 = {}^7/_2$$
$$6^2/_3 = 3 \times 6 + 2 = {}^{20}/_3$$

A fraction may be reduced to its lowest terms by dividing both the numerator and the denominator by a common number, or numbers, until they no longer can be divided by a common number.

Illustrative Example

$${}^{12}/_{30} \div {}^3/_3 = {}^4/_{10}$$
$${}^4/_{10} \div {}^2/_2 = {}^2/_5$$

In this example both the top and bottom are first divided by 3. The top and bottom of the resultant fraction 4/10 is then divided by 2, reducing the fraction to its lowest terms. The same result is obtained if the numerator and denominator of 12/30 are divided by 6.

Adding and Subtracting Fractions

Fractions may be added or subtracted only if they have a common (the same) denominator.

Illustrative Example

Add:		Subtract
$^3/_4 = {}^3/_4$		$^3/_4 = {}^3/_4$
$+^1/_2 = {}^2/_4$		$-^1/_2 = {}^2/_4$
$^5/_4$		$^1/_4$

When adding or subtracting fractions, the numerators only are added or subtracted, and the result is placed over the common denominator.

Multiplication of Fractions

To multiply two fractions, first multiply the numerators, then multiply the denominators. Reduce the resultant fraction to its lowest terms by dividing numerator and denominator by a common number.

Illustrative Example

$$^3/_4 \times {}^1/_3 = {}^3/_4 \times {}^1/_3 = {}^3/_{12} = {}^1/_4$$
(or by cancellation)
$$\not{3}/_4 \times {}^1/\not{3} = {}^1/_4$$

To multiply mixed numbers, first reduce them to improper fractions.

$$1^1/_2 \times 3^1/_4 =$$
$$^3/_2 \times {}^{13}/_4 = {}^{39}/_8 = 4^7/_8$$

Division of Fractions

To divide one fraction by another, invert the divisor and proceed as in multiplication.

Illustrative Example

Divide:
$$^4/_7 \text{ by } {}^1/_2 =$$
$$^4/_7 \times {}^2/_1 = {}^8/_7 = 1^1/_7$$
Expressed another way
$$^4/_7 \div {}^1/_2 = {}^4/_7 \times {}^2/_1 = {}^8/_7 \times 1^1/_7$$

Cancellation is useful in solving problems involving the multiplication or division of two or more fractions (it cannot be used for addition or subtraction).

Illustrative Example

Multiply
$$^2/_4 \times {}^3/_8 \times {}^5/_{10} \times {}^4/_9$$

$$\frac{3 \times 8 \times 4 \times 2}{12}$$

(or)

$$\frac{\overset{1}{\not{3}} \times 8 \times \overset{}{\not{4}} \times 2}{\underset{\not{3}}{\not{12}}} = 16$$

$$\overset{1}{\not{2}}/_4 \times \overset{1}{\not{3}}/\not{8} \times \overset{1}{\not{5}}/\not{10} \times \overset{1}{\not{4}}/\not{9} = {}^1/_{24}$$
$$2 2 3$$

SOME APPLICATIONS OF FRACTIONS IN ESTIMATING

Board Feet—To compute the quantity of board feet in lumber, divide the number of pieces times the dimensions by 12.

Illustrative Example

To obtain the number of board feet in 10 pieces of 2″ × 4″ that are 12 feet long.

$$\frac{10 \times 2 \times 4 \times \cancel{12}}{\cancel{12}} = \quad 80 \text{ FBM}$$

Number of Rafters, Joists or Studs—To find the number of joists, rafters or studs required in a given space, divide the length of the space in feet by the distance in feet, center to center between joists, rafters or studs. Add one unit for the end.

Illustrative Example

Find the number of rafters placed 16 inches on center in a flat roof 36 feet long:
(16 inches = ⁴/₃ feet)

$$36 \div \frac{4}{3} = \overset{9}{\cancel{36}} \times {}^3/\cancel{4} = 27 \text{ plus } 1 = 28 \text{ rafters}$$

Obtain the number of studs placed 20 inches on center in a partition 30 feet long:
(20 inches = ⁵/₃ feet)

$$30 \div \frac{5}{3} = \overset{6}{\cancel{30}} \times {}^3/\cancel{5} = 18 \text{ plus } 1 = 19 \text{ studs}$$

SURFACE MEASUREMENT

A *polygon* is a plane figure bounded by straight-line sides. A three-sided polygon is called a *triangle;* a four-sided polygon is a *quadrilateral.* The figures following illustrate various types of polygons.

In discussing the properties of any polygon in a vertical plane, the *base* is the bottom side, and the *height* or altitude is the perpendicular distance from the highest point to the base. The symbol for the *base* is "b" and the symbol for the height is "h."

The *area* of a polygon is the measurement of its surface without regard to its thickness. In estimating buildings, the calculation of areas of polygons has to do principally with the surfaces of floors, ceilings, interior and exterior walls, and of roof surfaces.

The *perimeter* of a polygon is the sum of the length of its sides. It is the distance around the figure.

RECTANGLES

The area of a rectangle equals the base multiplied by the height. If the rectangle is horizontal, as the floor or ceiling of a room, the area equals the length (1) multipled by the width (w).

RHOMBOIDS, PARALLELOGRAMS

The area of a rhomboid equals the base multiplied by the height. All opposite sides of a rhomboid are parallel.

Area = b × h
Area = 10 × 8 = 80

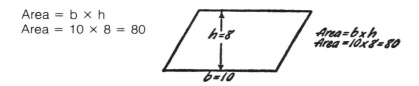

TRAPEZOIDS

The area of a trapezoid equals one-half of the sum of the top and bottom multipled by the height. Only the top and bottom sides are parallel.

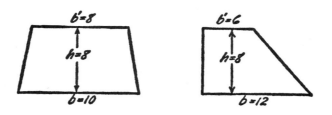

$$\text{Area} = \tfrac{1}{2}(b + b') \times h$$

$$\text{Area} = \frac{8 + 10}{2} \times 8 = 72 \qquad \text{Area} = \frac{6 + 12}{2} \times 8 = 72$$

IRREGULAR POLYGONS

The areas of trapeziums or irregular polygons can only be determined by breaking the figures up into triangles, or regular polygons, and obtaining the areas separately.

Illustrative Example

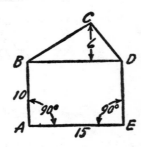

Area ABDE =   10 × 15 = 150
Area   BCD =   ¹/₂(6 × 15) = 45
                              Total   195

TRIANGLES

The area of any triangle equals one-half of the base times the height. (The height is the perpendicular distance from the base to the highest point.)

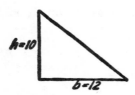

$$\text{Area} = \frac{12 \times 10}{2} = 60$$

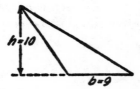

$$\text{Area} = \frac{9 \times 10}{2} = 45$$

Hero's Formula for Area of a Triangle

The area of any triangle may also be computed by the following formula where "s" equals one-half of the sum of the sides of the triangle.

Illustrative Example

s = ¹/₂ (10 + 6 + 8) = 12
Area = $\sqrt{s(s-a)\ (s-b)\ (s-c)}$
Area = $\sqrt{12(12-10)\ (12-6)\ (12-8)}$
    = $\sqrt{12(2)\ (6)\ (4)}$
    = $\sqrt{576}$
    = 24

This formula is advantageous where no angular or other measurements of the triangle are available except the length of the three sides.

Rule of Pythagoras for Right Triangles

The square of the length of the hypotenuse is equal to the sum of the squares of the lengths of the other two sides.

Illustrative Example

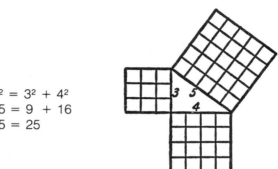

$5^2 = 3^2 + 4^2$
$25 = 9 + 16$
$25 = 25$

By means of this formula if any two sides of a right triangle are known, the other side can be computed.

$$c = \sqrt{a^2 + b^2}$$
$$a = \sqrt{c^2 - b^2}$$
$$b = \sqrt{c^2 - a^2}$$

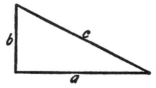

Illustrative Example

$a = 3$ $b = 4$ $c = 5$
Known a and b — find c.
$c = \sqrt{3^2 + 4^2}$
$= \sqrt{9 + 16}$
$= \sqrt{25}$
$= 5$

Illustrative Example

$a = 3$ $b = 4$ $c = 5$
Known: c and b — find a.
$a = \sqrt{5^2 - 4^2}$
$= \sqrt{25 - 16}$
$= \sqrt{9}$
$= 3$

Illustrative Example

$a = 3$ $b = 4$ $c = 5$
Known: c and a — find b.
$b = \sqrt{5^2 - 3^2}$
$= \sqrt{25 - 9}$
$= \sqrt{16}$
$= 4$

Extracting the Square Root of a Number

(A) Extract the square root of 1764.

```
   |17'64 (42 answer)
82 |16
   |164
   |164
```

(B) Extract the square root of 576.

```
   |5'76 (24 answer)
44 |4
   |176
   |176
```

Steps to Take:

1. Begin at right side of number and point off the digits in pairs, ending at left side with one digit (if there is an odd number) or with a pair (if there is an even number of digits).

2. Find the largest square equal to or less than the first digit or pair of digits in the number (*16* in Example A, *4* in Example B). The square root of *that* number is the first digit in your answer (*4* in Example A, *2* in Example B).

3. Subtract this square as shown.

4. Bring down the next two digits in the number and place alongside the remainder.

5. Double the root already found (*4* in Example A, *2* in Example B) and place out on left side as shown.

6. Divide this *doubled root* into the first two digits of your remainder (*8* into *16* in Example A, *4* into *17* in Example B). The quotient is placed alongside the dividend and also it becomes the next digit in the answer.

7. Multiply the quotient obtained by the entire dividend (*2* times *82* in Example A, *4* times *44* in Example B).

8. The process continues in this manner for larger numbers.

Square Root from Table

Table D-2 gives the root and the square beginning with number ten. The nearest root shown may be used or for greater accuracy interpolate.

TABLE D2

SQUARE ROOTS OF NUMBERS

Number	Square Root	Number	Square Root	Number	Square Root	Number	Square Root
100	10.00	150	12.25	200	14.14	250	15.81
101	10.05	151	12.29	201	14.18	251	15.84
102	10.10	152	12.33	202	14.21	252	15.87

TABLE D2

SQUARE ROOTS OF NUMBERS

Number	Square Root	Number	Square Root	Number	Square Root	Number	Square Root
103	10.15	153	12.37	203	14.25	253	15.91
104	10.20	154	12.41	204	14.28	254	15.94
105	10.25	155	12.45	205	14.32	255	15.97
106	10.30	156	12.49	206	14.35	256	16.00
107	10.34	157	12.53	207	14.39	257	16.03
108	10.39	158	12.57	208	14.42	258	16.06
109	10.44	159	12.61	209	14.46	259	16.09
110	10.49	160	12.65	210	14.49	260	16.12
111	10.54	161	12.69	211	14.53	261	16.16
112	10.58	162	12.73	212	14.56	262	16.19
113	10.63	163	12.77	213	14.59	263	16.22
114	10.68	164	12.81	214	14.63	264	16.25
115	10.72	165	12.85	215	14.66	265	16.28
116	10.77	166	12.88	216	14.70	266	16.31
117	10.82	167	12.92	217	14.73	267	16.34
118	10.86	168	12.96	218	14.76	268	16.37
119	10.91	169	13.00	219	14.80	269	16.40
120	10.95	170	13.04	220	14.83	270	16.43
121	11.00	171	13.08	221	14.87	271	16.46
122	11.05	172	13.11	222	14.90	272	16.49
123	11.09	173	13.15	223	14.93	273	16.52
124	11.14	174	13.19	224	14.97	274	16.55
125	11.18	175	13.23	225	15.00	275	16.58
126	11.23	176	13.27	226	15.03	276	16.61
127	11.27	177	13.30	227	15.07	277	16.64
128	11.31	178	13.34	228	15.10	278	16.67
129	11.36	179	13.38	229	15.13	279	16.70
130	11.40	180	13.42	230	15.17	280	16.73
131	11.45	181	13.45	231	15.20	281	16.76
132	11.49	182	13.49	232	15.23	282	16.79
133	11.53	183	13.53	233	15.26	283	16.82
134	11.58	184	13.56	234	15.30	284	16.85
135	11.62	185	13.60	235	15.33	285	16.88
136	11.66	186	13.64	236	15.36	286	16.91
137	11.70	187	13.67	237	15.39	287	16.94
138	11.75	188	13.71	238	15.43	288	16.97
139	11.79	189	13.75	239	15.46	289	17.00
140	11.83	190	13.78	240	15.49	290	17.03
141	11.87	191	13.82	241	15.52	291	17.06
142	11.92	192	13.86	242	15.56	292	17.09
143	11.96	193	13.89	243	15.59	293	17.12
144	12.00	194	13.93	244	15.62	294	17.15
145	12.04	195	13.96	245	15.65	295	17.18

TABLE D2

SQUARE ROOTS OF NUMBERS

Number	Square Root	Number	Square Root	Number	Square Root	Number	Square Root
146	12.08	196	14.00	246	15.68	296	17.20
147	12.12	197	14.04	247	15.72	297	17.23
148	12.17	198	14.07	248	15.75	298	17.26
149	12.21	199	14.11	249	15.78	299	17.29
300	17.32	350	18.71	400	20.00	450	21.21
301	17.35	351	18.73	401	20.02	451	21.24
302	17.38	352	18.76	402	20.05	452	21.26
303	17.41	353	18.79	403	20.07	453	21.28
304	17.44	354	18.81	404	20.10	454	21.31
305	17.46	355	18.84	405	20.12	455	21.33
306	17.49	356	18.87	406	20.15	456	21.35
307	17.52	357	18.89	407	20.17	457	21.38
308	17.55	358	18.92	408	20.20	458	21.40
309	17.58	359	18.95	409	20.22	459	21.42
310	17.61	360	18.97	410	20.25	460	21.45
311	17.64	361	19.00	411	20.27	461	21.47
312	17.66	362	19.03	412	20.30	462	21.49
313	17.69	363	19.05	413	20.32	463	21.52
314	17.72	364	19.08	414	20.35	464	21.54
315	17.75	365	19.10	415	20.37	465	21.56
316	17.78	366	19.13	416	20.40	466	21.59
317	17.80	367	19.16	417	20.42	467	21.61
318	17.83	368	19.18	418	20.45	468	21.63
319	17.86	369	19.21	419	20.47	469	21.66
320	17.89	370	19.24	420	20.49	470	21.68
321	17.92	371	19.26	421	20.52	471	21.70
322	17.94	372	19.29	422	20.54	472	21.73
323	17.97	373	19.31	423	20.57	473	31.75
324	18.00	374	19.34	424	20.59	474	21.77
325	18.03	375	19.36	425	20.62	475	21.79
326	18.06	376	19.39	426	20.64	476	21.82
327	18.08	377	19.42	427	20.66	477	21.84
328	18.11	378	19.44	428	20.69	478	21.86
329	18.14	379	19.47	429	20.71	479	21.89
330	18.17	380	19.49	430	20.74	480	21.91
331	18.19	381	19.52	431	20.76	481	21.93
332	18.22	382	19.54	432	20.78	482	21.95
333	18.25	383	19.57	433	20.81	483	21.98
334	18.28	384	19.60	434	20.83	484	22.00
335	18.30	385	19.62	435	20.86	485	22.02
336	18.33	386	19.65	436	20.88	486	22.05
337	18.36	387	19.67	437	20.90	487	22.07

TABLE D2

Number	Square Root	Number	Square Root	Number	Square Root	Number	Square Root
338	18.38	388	19.70	438	20.93	488	22.09
339	18.41	389	19.72	439	20.95	489	22.11
340	18.44	390	19.75	440	20.98	490	22.14
341	18.47	391	19.77	441	21.00	491	22.16
342	18.49	392	19.80	442	21.02	492	22.18
343	18.52	393	19.82	443	21.05	493	22.20
344	18.55	394	19.85	444	21.07	494	22.23
345	18.57	395	19.87	445	21.10	495	22.25
346	18.60	396	19.90	446	21.12	496	22.27
347	18.63	397	19.92	447	21.14	497	22.29
348	18.65	398	19.95	448	21.17	498	22.32
349	18.68	399	19.97	449	21.19	499	22.34
						500	22.36

APPLICATION OF SURFACE MEASUREMENT TO ESTIMATING

Measurement of Floor and Ceiling Areas

The floor or ceiling area of a room is obtained by multiplying the length by the width.

Illustrative Example

Area = 14′ × 16′ = 224 sq ft

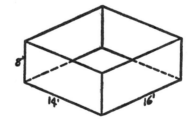

Measurement of Sidewall Areas of Rooms

The sidewall area of a room including the window or door openings is equal to the perimeter times the height from the floor to the ceiling.

Illustrative Example

Perimeter = 2(14′ + 16′) = 60 lin ft
Area   = 60′ × 8′   = 480 sq ft

Another method is to obtain the area of the walls separately and add them together to get the total wall area.

$$2 \text{ walls} = 2(16' \times 8') = 256 \text{ sq ft}$$
$$2 \text{ walls} = 2(14' \times 8') = \underline{224 \text{ sq ft}}$$
$$480 \text{ sq ft}$$

Measurement of Exterior Wall Areas

The exterior areas of buildings may be obtained either by computing each wall area separately and adding them together, or by taking the perimeter of a building and multiplying by the height of the wall. Gable ends, dormers, extensions, and so forth, should be figured separately and added.

Illustrative Example

Perimeter = $2(20' + 30')$ =   100 lin ft
$$\times 10$$
$$\overline{1,000 \text{ sq ft}}$$

Plus Gables = $\dfrac{2(8' \times 20')}{2}$ = $\underline{160}$

Total 1,160 sq ft

Measurement of Rafter Lengths

When the *rise* of a roof is known, and also the *run* (one half the span), the length of the rafter may be calculated from the "Rule of Pythagoras." (See also Table 11-12C, page 191.

Rise = 6 ft
Span = 16 ft
Run = $\dfrac{16}{2}$ = 8 ft

Rafter AC or BC = $\sqrt{6^2 + 8^2}$
$$= \sqrt{36 + 64}$$
$$= \sqrt{100}$$
$$= \quad 10 \text{ ft}$$

Note: To this length must be added any existing overhang.

PROPERTIES OF CIRCLES

The *circumference* of a circle is the distance around its exterior.

The *diameter* is a line from one side of the circumference to the opposite side and passing through the center of the circle.

The *radius* of a circle is a line from the center of the circle to any point on the circumference, and, therefore equals one-half the diameter.

In any circle the circumference when divided by the diameter will always equal the same number called *pi* with symbol π. Its value is approximately 3.1416, or 3 1/7. In other words, the circumference of a circle is about 3 1/7 times as long as its diameter.

$$\frac{\text{Circumference}}{\text{Diameter}} = \pi = 3.1416$$
$$= 3 \ 1/7$$

The circumference of a circle equals π times the diameter. This is expressed as $C = \pi D$, *or* $C = \pi \ 2R$ (also 3 1/7 × diameter).

The diameter of a circle equals the circumference divided by π. This is expressed as
$$D = \frac{C}{\pi}$$

The area of a circle in terms of its radius is π times the radius squared. This is expressed as $A = \pi R^2$ *or* 3 1/7 × R^2.

Illustrative Example

The diameter of a sprinkler tank is 20 feet. What is the area of its base?

$$A = \pi R^2$$
$$= 3.1416 \times 10^2$$
$$= 3.1416 \times 100$$
$$= 314.16 \text{ sq ft}$$

If the height "h" of the tank is 30 feet, what is the exterior wall area? It would be the circumference of the base multiplied by the height.

Wall surface area of a tank	$= \pi$ D h
Circumference	$= \pi$ D
Circumference	= 3.1416 × 20′
Circumference	= 62.832 lin ft
Surface area	= 62.832 × 30′
Surface area	= 1,884.96 sq ft

VOLUME MEASUREMENT

In the measurement of volume three dimensions are considered, namely length, width and height. Volume is expressed in terms of cubic units of inches, feet, and so forth.

Rectangular Solids

The rectangular solid is commonly encountered in estimating.
The formula for the volume of a rectangular solid is:
$$V = LWH$$

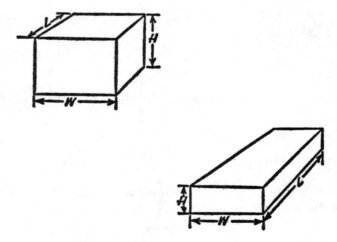

Illustrative Example

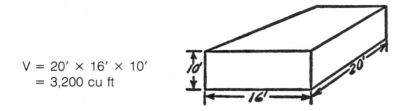

V = 20′ × 16′ × 10′
= 3,200 cu ft

Cylinders

The cylinder is another common type of solid encountered in estimating, and generally its volume in terms of gallons capacity is required.

The cubic volume of a cylinder may be found by multiplying the area of its base by the height or length of the tank. The formula would be expressed: $V = \pi R^2 H$

Illustrative Example

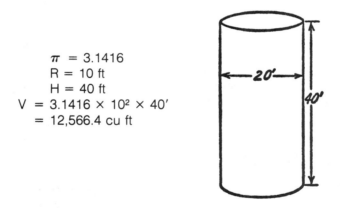

π = 3.1416
R = 10 ft
H = 40 ft
V = 3.1416 × 10² × 40′
= 12,566.4 cu ft

To convert the contents in cubic feet to gallons multiply the number of cubic feet by 7.4805 the number of gallons in one cubic foot.

12,566.4 × 7.4805 = 94,003 gallons

TABLE D3

TABLE OF WEIGHTS AND MEASURES

Linear Measure

12 inches	= 1 foot
3 feet	= 1 yard
5 1/2 yards	= 1 rod
320 rods	= 1 mile
5,280 feet	= 1 mile

Surface Measure

144 square inches	= 1 square foot
9 square feet	= 1 square yard
30 1/4 square yards	= 1 square rod
160 square rods	= 1 acre
43,560 square feet	= 1 acre
640 acres	= 1 square mile or one section

Volume

1,728 cubic inches	= 1 cubic foot
27 cubic feet	= 1 cubic yard
128 cubic feet	= 1 cord
(A cord of wood	= 4′ × 4′ × 8′)

Liquid Measure

4 gills	= 1 pint
2 pints	= 1 quart
4 quarts	= 1 gallon
231 cubic inches	= 1 gallon
31 1/2 gallons	= 1 barrel
63 gallons	= 1 hogshead
7.4805 gallons	= 1 cubic foot
32 ounces	= 1 quart

Dry Measure

2 pints	= 1 quart
8 quarts	= 1 peck
4 pecks	= 1 bushel

Weight Measure

16 ounces	= 1 pound
100 pounds	= 1 hundred weight
2,000 pounds	= 1 ton
2,240 pounds	= 1 long ton

TABLE D4

METRIC CONVERSION TABLE

Metric System

10 millimeters (mm)	=	1 centimeter	(cm)	= 0.3937	inches
10 centimeters	=	1 decimeter	(dm)	= 3.9370	inches
10 decimeters)	=	1 meter	(m)	= 39.37	inches
100 centimeters)				= 3.28	feet
10 meters	=	1 dekameter	(dkm)	= 393.7	inches
10 dekameters	=	1 hectometer	(hm)	= 328.08	feet
10 hectometers	=	1 kilometer	(km)	= 0.62137	miles
10 kilometers	=	1 myriameter	(mym)	= 6.2137	miles

METRIC CONVERSION FACTORS

To Convert From	To	Multiply By
acres	square feet	43,560.0
acres	square meters	4,047.0
acres	square yards	4,840.0
board feet	cubic inches	144.0
centimeters	feet	0.03281
centimeters	inches	0.3937
cubic feet	cubic centimeters	28,317.0

METRIC CONVERSION FACTORS

To Convert From	To	Multiply By
cubic feet	cubic meters	0.028317
cubic feet	cubic yards	0.03704
cubic feet	gallons (U.S.A.)	7.481
cubic feet	gallons (Imperial)	6.22905
cubic feet of water	pounds	62.37

TABLE D4

METRIC CONVERSION TABLE

To Convert From	To	Multiply By
cubic inches	cubic centimeters	16.38716
cubic yards	cubic meters	0.764559
fathoms	feet	6.0
feet	centimeters	30.48
feet	meters	0.304801
gallons (U.S.A.)	cubic centimeters	3,785.0
gallons (U.S.A.)	cubic feet	0.13368
gallons (U.S.A.)	Imperial gallons	0.832702
gallons (Imperial)	gallons (U.S.A.)	1.20091
gallons (U.S.A.)	cubic inches	231.0
gallons (U.S.A.)	liters	3.78543
gallons (U.S.A.)	ounces	128.0
horsepower (U.S.A.)	horsepower (metric)	1.01387
inches	centimeters	2.54001
inches	meters	0.0254001
inches	millimeters	25.4001
liters	cubic feet	0.03532
liters	gallons (U.S.A.)	0.26418
miles (statute)	kilometers	1.60935
miles (statute)	miles (nautical)	0.8684
miles (nautical)	feet	6,080.204
miles (nautical)	miles (statute)	1.1516
pounds (avoirdupois)	grams (metric)	453.592
pounds (avoirdupois)	kilograms	0.453592
square centimeters	square feet	0.0010764
square feet	square centimeters	929.0
square feet	square meters	0.0929034
square inches	square centimeters	6.452
square yards	square meters	0.83613
tons (metric)	tons (short)	1.1023
tons (long)	pounds	2,240.0
tons (short)	pounds	2,000.0
tons (metric)	pounds	2,204.6
yards	meters	0.91442
degrees F	degrees celsius	F°-32 × .5556

Estimating Labor and Material

As was stated in the Preface, estimating by definition means *approximating* and therefore cannot be considered an exact science. It is made up basically of two parts, (1) estimating the materials required and (2) estimating the hours of labor to apply or install those materials. It is the second part, labor, that causes the total estimating of cost to be an inexact science as will be demonstrated later. But first a statement of certain qualifications for a consistently successful estimator.

THE ESTIMATOR'S QUALIFICATIONS

Experience and Study

A person who estimates construction costs need not be a builder or a contractor, but he or she should have a thorough knowledge of the materials, operations and labor time-studies of the particular project involved. This calls for both *experience* and constant *study*. The *experience* increases as the estimator checks the adequacy of the estimates by comparing them with the actual cost of the completed project or operation. The more estimates that are checked against the cost of the completed work, the more valuable experience is added to the estimator's competency. *Study* of actual, on-the-job conditions and the performance of labor is important to support the estimate. Also, a *study* of all authoritatively written reference material on the subject, in books and pamphlets, will broaden the estimator's knowledge and enable him or her to better refine and evaluate the labor factor.

Attention to Detail

The approach to perfection is said to be the sum of a large number of perfect details. The estimator cannot afford to be careless, superficial or general in preparing an estimate. While attention to detail is necessary, one should also guard against over-detailing which, as will be explained later, may tend to increase costs.

50

Mathematics

A successful estimator has a good foundation in basic arithmetic and simple geometry (See Mensuration, pages 33-49). The ideal tool for today's estimator is the electronic calculator with a printed tape record.

Methodical Take-off

The estimator should develop a standard procedure for the methodical take-off of materials and operations whether from a plan or at a job site. That procedure will depend on the specific project. On new construction it generally begins with excavation for footings and foundation and proceeds upward to the finished roof. One should avoid jumping from one operation to another which is unrelated. While there are no rules that can apply to the order of take-off, whatever method followed should conform to a logical, easy-to-follow sequence.

FUNDAMENTALS OF ESTIMATING

The fundamentals of estimating construction costs may be reduced to five considerations: (1) Specifications, (2) Materials, (3) Labor, (4) Overhead and (5) Profit.

Specifications

The estimator usually works from a set of plans and written *specifications*. The plans are a part of the specifications and, in addition to showing dimensions, generally have numerous notations as to kind of materials, sizes; location of windows, doors, stairs; plumbing, heating and electrical layout; etc. Each estimator of a job works with identical plans and specifications, therefore, in theory, each should produce an identical estimate of the materials required.

Estimating Materials

The important factors to consider in taking off materials are the *quantity*, *size* and *quality*. Where the quality or size is in doubt, clarification should be sought from the architect, owner or other party responsible. For example, when a door is specified it should include a description of the number of panels (or lites of glass), the kind of wood, the width, height and thickness. The exact type of hardware should be noted as there is considerable difference in the price of materials, styles and grades.

The pricing of materials should be done at local sources unless the person preparing the estimate has knowledge of an outside source that can furnish materials to the job site at a lower cost. Some contractors, particularly those doing a large volume with supply yards and material houses, have a buying leverage over smaller contractors and in this regard can often obtain certain materials at a slightly lower cost.

Estimating Labor

Estimating labor consists of approximating the length of time that it will take a man or a crew of men, to perform a specific job or operation. The cost of the labor is obtained by multiplying the number of man-hours by the hourly wage scale.

There are many factors which influence every estimator's judgment when he is considering the hours of labor required to install or apply materials or to perform specific operations. Most of these may be found within the following classifications which will serve as a checklist, if the person making the estimate will ask himself these questions:

1. Are there any special or unusual conditions which the workmen will encounter?

2. Is the physical area being worked in confined, or is it open so that the workmen can move about freely?

3. Can labor-saving machines or equipment be used?

4. What experience have the men with the particular type of work they are to do?

5. Is the quality of workmanship required high or average?

6. Will the work have to be done from ladders or scaffolds?

7. Are the lighting conditions adequate?

8. Will the supervision of the men be close or loose?

9. What are the probable weather conditions under which the men will be working?

10. What is the productivity of the individual workman?

11. Are the wages that are being paid standard or substandard?

12. Is smoking permitted on the job?

13. Are there any special union regulations limiting production?

14. Is the job near to or far from a source of labor?

15. Is the supply of labor good or not good?

16. Is it necessary to protect the contents or occupants of the premises while working?

1. *Unusual Conditions.* Special working conditions of a particular job require careful analysis and visualization by the person making the estimate. The estimate may specify the painting and decorating of a room of a given size. This could be a room which was vacant and unoccupied. The work needed to prepare the wall surface might be trifling or nothing, so that all a painter would have to do is walk in and start painting.

A second situation might involve the living room of a palatial home which is furnished and occupied. The painter would be called upon to move furniture, protect the wall-to-wall carpeting, remove and rehang pictures, sandpaper woodwork, remove and reset a radiator, or even wash the walls and woodwork prior to decorating.

A third supposition might be that this room was an office in which two or three persons worked who could not be moved out. The painter might have to work around them and also be very careful not to spatter them or the contents with paint.

Each situation presents circumstances that are peculiar to the particular job. Actually none are serious *per se*, but additional time must be given the painters where their rate of work performed is reduced by physical conditions. If it is known that a painter will average a given number of square feet an hour under conditions similar to those outlined in the first situation, then it is possible to approximate the additional time that must be allowed to meet the conditions described in the other two situations.

2. *Physical Area.* The physical area in which a person is working will affect his efficiency. In confined and cramped quarters such as closets or blind-attics, a mechanic's movements are hampered and he consequently slows down. In wide open areas, without restrictions, efficiency reaches its highest point, everything else being equal.

3. *Labor-Saving Equipment.* The types of work tools and equipment that are used have an appreciable effect on the rate of speed with which work is done. The use of portable electric saws and drills, electric or pneumatic hammers, aluminum ladders, scaffold brackets, paint spray guns, and other modern devices greatly improves working conditions and reduces cost through higher rates of production.

4. *Experience of Men.* The experience and familiarity of the workman with the job he is assigned to affects his rate of production. A roofer who puts on asphalt shingles every day of the week, or a floorlayer who lays hardwood floors as a specialty, will turn out nearly twice as much work per hour as a carpenter who performs these tasks only occasionally. Experienced paperhangers will put on more rolls of paper per hour than a painter who has hung paper only a few times. A carpenter who has never laid out or built a winding staircase will take hours longer than a stair builder who has built many.

5. *Quality of Workmanship.* The quality of workmanship required directly affects the time required to do the work. The higher the quality, the more time will be needed, because it takes more time to do a good job. High grade painting on

trim, where successive coats are hand rubbed takes more hours than 2-coat work in less expensive residences. Cabinet work, or paneling of the highest grade, requires many more hours per unit or square foot than inexpensive cabinetmaking or paneling.

6. *Work Done from Ladders.* Operating from a scaffold, or from a ladder, slows a man down compared to his rate for similar work done on the ground. He not only works with regard for his personal safety when on a scaffold or ladder, but he is also hampered by lack of freedom of movement.

7. *Lighting Conditions.* The lighting conditions in the area where work is being done will affect performance, for a man naturally works faster when he can clearly see at all times exactly what he is doing. When it is apparent that lighting conditions will be poor, or where portable lights have to be shifted about as the work is done, some consideration must be given to a reasonable increase in the time normally allowed.

8. *Supervision.* The type of individual who organizes and lays out the work, and who constructively supervises operations will have a decided effect on the cooperation and efficiency of the workmen. The more experienced the supervisor, and the more capable he is in handling people, the lower will be his unit labor costs, compared with those of a loosely supervised job or one which is given little or no supervision.

9. *Weather Conditions.* Weather conditions will influence the length of time it takes to perform work operations. Where the work involves the exterior of a building, the workmen will do more in pleasant weather than in cold winter months when they keep outside fires going to warm themselves, or go inside occasionally to escape the cold. They work with lighter clothing and can move about more freely. In winter months it is often necessary to provide temporary protection for materials, and allow time for shoveling away snow, especially in northern climates.

Conversely, in extremely hot humid seasons or climates, particularly some of the far southern sections, workmen slow down, especially when working directly in the sun and heat.

10. *Productivity of Workmen.* The individual productivity of workmen varies. Some mechanics do excellent work, but are slow; others do mediocre work, but turn out large quantities. Many persons develop a fixed rate at which they work, others are naturally lazy, talkative, or clock watchers. Construction workmen are no different from persons engaged in factories, offices, or mercantile establishments. They possess all of the human perfections and imperfections. A contractor who knows the individual characteristics of his men and estimates accordingly has an advantage over his competitor who is unfamiliar with the productiveness of the men who will do the job.

11. *Wages Paid.* The old adage that "a laborer is worthy of his hire" has a certain amount of truth to it. Where a man is aware that he is being paid less than others who are doing similar work, or less than the prevailing wage, he tends to turn out the irreducible minimum of work.

12. *Is Smoking Permitted?* Where smoking is prohibited in such occupancies as hazardous manufacturing plants or department stores, workmen who are making repairs will take time out to smoke outside of the prohibited ares. Such time breaks, particularly on small jobs, can increase labor costs.

13. *Union Regulations.* Local union regulations, which limit or restrict the amount of work a man may do during a work day, naturally govern the basis for estimating labor costs. Such restrictions may stipulate the number of bricks a bricklayer can lay, or may prohibit a plasterer from taking on a second job at another location, if he has completed one small job within one work day. Other limitations may require the presence of a foreman, even if only one workman is needed, or may pertain to the use of labor-saving equipment such as paint sprayers or rollers. When such customs are known to exist, the person making the estimate should become thoroughly acquainted with the regulations, in order to give proper consideration when preparing his figures.

14. *Source of Labor.* When a job is located many miles from the source of labor, the estimate may have to include a provision for transportation. Workmen are not expected, in certain jurisdictions, to travel great distances to and from work on their own time or at their own expense.

15. *Supply of Labor.* Labor is a commodity and follows the laws of supply and demand. Where the supply is ample or greater than the demand, the wage rate may be lower and the production is frequently higher. Where the supply is less than the demand, the opposite is often the case.

16. *Necessary to Protect the Contents or Occupants.* When it is necessary for workmen to protect the contents or the occupants of a building, the labor costs increase depending upon the degree of care required. Painting or plastering, for example, in an office building or a retail store during working hours reduces considerably the rate at which a man works, for he must be cautious not to damage the contents, and usually works around the occupants who are intent on performing their own regular jobs.

Prevailing local wage rates should be the basis for estimating the cost of labor. The rate should include such items as *basic rate, insurance, pension, vacation pay,* and any other contributions by employers under programs for holiday pay and unemployment fund.

Overhead

Contractors usually consider two types of overhead to be included in their estimate.

1. Specific overhead, chargeable to each job for which an estimate is being prepared.
2. General overhead, not chargeable to each specific job.

Overhead Charged to Specific Jobs:

       Foreman and/or Superintendent wages
       Watchman wages
       Rubbish removal, clean up costs
       Temporary buildings and structures
          Office (trailer, etc.)
          Tool and/or storage sheds
          Toilet facilities
          Fences, guardrails, etc.
          Signs
       Building permits
       Utilities
          Temporary heat, light and power
          Temporary water
          Temporary telephone
          Out of town jobs
             Travel cost
             Premium labor rates
             Board and room
       Plant
          Rental of machines and equipment
          Scaffolding built on premises or rented
          Maintenance of machinery and equipment
          Depreciation
       Legal expense
       Insurance
          Public liability insurance
          Fire and Extended Cover insurance
          Workmen's Compensation
       Taxes
          Social Security taxes
          Federal Unemployment taxes
          State Unemployment taxes
          Sales taxes on materials
       Performance Bonds

Overhead Not Chargeable to Specific Jobs:

       Contractor's office, shop, etc.
       Rental
       Depreciation
       Heat, light and power for office, shop, etc.
       Stationery, postage, supplies
       Business machines
       Property and liability insurance

Telephone
Other
Employees
    Executives
    Clerks
    Estimators
    Draftsmen
Travel
Advertising
Donations
Legal retainers

Overhead is not a theoretical charge, but one subject to analysis. A contractor engaged in small to medium size jobs may operate out of an office in his home, and his wife may do his clerical work, answer the phone, and keep his books of account. He may store equipment and surplus materials on his premises. His general overhead would be trifling in dollar-cost contrasted with a contractor doing heavy construction work with a separate office, shop, estimators, draftsmen, clerks, etc. Yet, when the annual overhead expenses of each of these contractors is related *percentage-wise* to their income, it is surprising how, in most instances, the percentage to be charged against each job estimated, ranges from 8 percent to 10 percent.

Profit

Profit charged by a contractor varies with the size of the job, and the competition in bidding. Small jobs usually take a higher percentage rate than larger jobs where competition is strong and the percentage rate is lowered.

OSHA (Occupational Safety and Health Administration)

The U.S. Department of Labor has published safety and health regulations for the construction industry pursuant to the Williams-Steiger Occupational Safety and Health Act of 1970. While these rules or regulations are mainly applicable to heavy construction, they are enforceable as respects small contractors and builders of homes. Authorized representatives of the U.S. Labor Department have right of entry to any construction site to check on compliance or they may designate the services, personnel, or facilities of any State or Federal Agency to inspect.

A complaint of the smaller contractors and builders is that the cost of compliance significantly increases their operating overhead; some say as much as 2 percent to 5 percent, with no visible benefits. Regardless, OSHA must be considered in estimating. Federal Register, Part 2, Vol. 37, No. 243 can be obtained from the Department of Labor. This document outlines the regulations. Basically, no contractor or subcontractor shall require any laborer or mechanic to work in surroundings which are *unsanitary, hazardous,* or *dangerous to his or her health or safety.* It is the responsibility of the employer to initiate and maintain such programs necessary to comply.

The prime contractor and subcontractor(s) may agree on who shall furnish (for example) toilet facilities, first aid services, fire protection, or drinking water, but such agreement will not relieve either one of his or her legal responsibility.

OSHA's rules and regulations are undergoing substantial revision and changes to eliminate those unnecessary, burdensome and expensive to contractors.

METHODS OF PRICING ESTIMATES

In general there are three methods of pricing and setting up material and labor costs in an estimate.

1. The material is priced in detail for each item, and the total labor cost is bulked in a lump-sum amount.

2. Material and labor are individually priced for each item and shown separately.

3. A *unit cost* is developed for the combined material and labor cost and applied to the number of units.

Method No. 1: Material Priced, Labor Lumped

Many of the smaller buildings and contractors use this method, particularly on small jobs. Material is detailed and carefully priced. Labor is estimated for the overall job and set down in a lump sum. Carpentry is a good example of the use of this method.

Illustrative Example

Framing	Dimensions	FBM		
Floor joists	60- 2″ × 12″ × 16′	1,920		
Studding	120- 2″ × 4″ × 7′6″	600		
Plate and shoe	90′-2″ × 4″	60		
Girders	2- 2″ × 12″ × 16′	64		
″	2- 2″ × 12″ × 14′	56		
Rafters	24- 2″ × 6″ × 18′	432		
″	10- 2″ × 6″ × 14′	160		
		3,292	@ $200/M	$ 658.40

Roof Decking				
1,600 sq ft	¹/₂″ plywood		@ $210/M	336.00
Subflooring	1400 sq ft	⁵/₈″ plywood	@ $220/M	308.00
			Total material	$1,302.40
Carpenter labor	30 days @ $40 per day			1,200.00
			Total material and labor cost	$2,502.40

Material and Labor Priced Separately

method the material is detailed and priced separately and shown in a
column. The labor charge for each item of material and each opera-
ded to a Labor Cost column. A third column shows the total cost of
aterial.

Illustrative Example

			Material Cost	Labor Cost	Total
12- 2″ × 4″ × 10′	80 FBM				
16- 2″ × 12″ × 18′	576 FBM				
Rafters 20- 2″ × 6″ × 18′	360 FBM				
Total	1,016 FBM @ $200/M		$203.20		
Labor 30 Carpenter hours	@ $8.00			$240.00	$443.20
Sheathing					
1,500 sq ft 5/16″ plywood		@ $170/M	$255.00		
Labor 20 Carpenter hours		@ $8.00		$160.00	$415.00
			$458.20	$400.00	$858.20

Method No. 3: Unit Costs for Material and Labor Combined

Considerable estimating in the construction field is done on the *unit cost* method in which a unit cost is developed for the material and labor to install the unit of material or to perform an operation involving no material, only labor such as in repair work, removing old shingles in preparation for new ones. In the development of unit costs an example would be one for wood shingles.

A roofer knows from experience that, under given working conditions, his men can apply 24-inch wood shingles with a 7 1/2 inch exposure on a plain roof of a one-story building at the rate of 3 1/2 hours per square (100 sq ft). If he is asked to bid on a similar roof under similar working conditions, and the area of the roof is 2,400 square feet, he would estimate the job as follows:

1 Square of 24-inch cedar shingles	@ $40/Sq	$40.00
2 lbs of nails	@ .35	.70
3.5 Hours of labor	@ $9	31.50
	Unit cost per square	$72.20
	Unit cost per square foot $72.20	= $.72
	100	

2,400 sq ft of roofing @ $.72 = $1,728

This illustration does not take into consideration an underlayer of saturated felt if used, scaffolding, overhead or profit. The first item may be included but the scaffolding and the overhead and profit are best added to the total labor and material cost.

EXAMPLES OF DEVELOPING UNIT COSTS OF LABOR AND MATERIAL

Each unit cost is the combined cost of the material and labor in the unit. A few examples will illustrate:

Example 1.
Unit Cost of a Square of Slate Shingles

The cost of a square of 10″ × 20″ × $3/16$″ slate shingles delivered to the job is $60. It takes 3 lbs of copper nails for one square of shingles and they are $1 per lb. It also takes $1/2$ roll of 30 lb saturated felt roofing paper per square of shingles. The paper is $4 a roll. The roof is an uncomplicated gable roof, and the roofer estimates it will take 6 hours labor per square in an area where wages are $8 per hour. The unit cost is developed as follows:

1 square of slate shingles	@ $60 =	$60
3 lbs of copper nails	1 =	3
$1/2$ roll 30 lb saturated felt roofing paper	4 =	2
6 hours of labor	8 =	48
	Unit cost per square	$113

The unit cost per square is $113 or $1.13 per sq ft. If the roof contained 1,800 sq ft, the estimated cost for labor and material is:

$$1,800 \times \$1.13 = \$2,034$$

Example 2.
Unit Cost of a Square of Asphalt Shingles

Assume the roof in Example 1 is to have 240 lb asphalt shingles, 3-Tab strip, laid over 15 lb saturated felt roofing paper. The price of materials at the job site is $14 per sq for shingles, $3 a roll (400 sq ft) for roofing paper, and $.40 per lb for nails. The contractor estimates it will take 2 hours labor per square of shingles. Wages in the area are $10 per hour. The unit cost per square is:

1 square 240 lb asphalt shingles	@ $14.00 =	$14.00
2 lbs roofing nails	.40 =	.80
$1/4$ roll of 15 lb roofing paper	4.00 =	1.00
2 hours labor	10.00 =	20.00
	Unit cost per square	$35.80

The unit cost per square, rounded off, is $36 or $.36 per sq ft. The estimated cost for the roof is: 1,800 × .$.36 = $648.

Example 3.
Interior Painting

There are several methods for estimating interior and exterior painting. The amount of paint is determined from the gross wall area. (See Areas of Rooms With Ceiling Heights From 8' to 10'0", pages 235-237.) Gross wall area is divided by the coverage of one gallon of material. This gives the number of gallons. The hours of labor, per coat, are determined by dividing the gross area by the number of sq ft per hour a painter can paint. (See Hours of Labor Table 19.) Table 27-29D, page 235, shows that a room 17' × 19' × 8' ceiling has 899 sq ft in the walls and ceiling including the area taken up by doors and windows. The Labor Table 19 for interior painting, page 76, shows a man can paint 150 sq ft per hour on smooth plaster using a brush. If 1 gallon of paint will cover 450 sq ft per coat, and two coats are required, the material will be:

$$2 \times \frac{899}{450} = 4 \text{ gallons}$$

The hours of labor for applying 4 gallons are:

$$\frac{4 \times 450}{150} = 12 \text{ hours for 2 coats}$$

If paint is $12 per gallon and a painter is paid $8 per hour the cost to paint the room would be:

4 gallons paint	@ $12 =	$48
12 hours labor	8 =	96
		$144

Example 4.
Unit Cost of Painting

The unit cost to paint the room in Example 3 would be:

$$\frac{450}{150} = 3 \text{ hours labor}$$

1 Gallon paint	@ $12 =	$12
3 hours labor	8 =	24
Unit cost per 450 sq ft		$36
Unit cost per sq ft per coat	$= \dfrac{\$36.00}{450}$ =	$.08
Unit cost for 2 coats would be 2 × .08		$.16
Cost to paint the room 2 coats = 900 × $.16		$144

Example 5
Unit Cost for Brick Veneer

Assume that there are 11,000 4" veneer brick to be laid in the walls of a one-story ranch type dwelling. Hours of Labor Table 4 shows an average of 16 hours each for a bricklayer and a helper to lay 1,000 brick. Table 30-38C shows it will take .33 cu yds of mortar for 1,000 brick. Under Table 3 A we see that a 1:3 mortar mix takes:

> 10 sacks cement
> 1 cu yd sand
> 2 sacks hydrated lime

If cement is $2 per sack, sand is $4 a cu yd and lime is $1.50 per sack, a cubic yard of mortar would cost:

10 sacks cement	@ $2 =	$20
1 cu yd sand	4 =	4
2 sacks lime	1.50 =	3
Cost per cu yd		$27

(The mason's helper mixes and handles the mortar on the job)

If brick cost $60 per 1,000, a bricklayer's wages are $10 a day, and a helper's wages are $8 a day, the unit cost of the brick would be:

1,000 brick	@ $60 =	$60
.33 cu yds mortar	27 =	9
16 hours bricklayer	10 =	160
16 hours helper	8 =	128
Unit cost for 1,000 br.		$357

The cost for laying the 11,000 brick in the building would be:

$$11 \times \$357 = \$3,927$$

ESTIMATING ERRORS TO BE AVOIDED

Very few estimates are made that do not contain errors or faults of one kind or another made by the estimator. Most of these fall within the following sources:

1. Taking off wrong measurements and dimensions.

2. Overlooking items.

3. Allowing too much for contingencies.

4. Over-emphasizing details.

5. Duplication of subcontractor's work.

6. Improper consideration of the class or quality of workmanship.

7. Inefficient methods and equipment used.

8. Use of wrong wage rates.

9. Materials improperly priced.

10. Inadequate or excessive labor allowances.

11. Inadequate or excessive overhead charged.

12. Inadequate or excessive profit charged.

13. Arithmetical errors in computations.

Taking off Wrong Measurements and Dimensions

Any error made in taking measurements from a plan or in the field, or in recording them, will result in a corresponding error in the cost of both labor and material. When overhead and profit are added to the labor and material error, the error in cost is increased 20 percent or more.

Dimensions in *sizes* of material make a difference in their cost directly proportional to the error in measurement. For example, if a $2'' \times 8''$ joist is recorded as $2'' \times 10''$ the cost will be increased 25 percent. Accuracy in measuring and recording measurements of framing lumber, thickness of boards, plywood, flooring, insulation, glass, flashing, linoleum, roofing, doors and windows is essential to obtain the correct prices to be used in the estimate.

Overlooking Items

This source of error needs little amplification. It usually is the result of haste or carelessness.

Allowing Too Much for Contingencies

While there are conditions where an allowance for contingencies is justified, too often the fear of the unknown or unpredictable impels the estimator to balloon a figure or slip in an unwarranted contingency. If all details of an estimate have been checked and double-checked, contingencies are extremely remote.

Overemphasis of Details

Illustrative Example

A room $12' \times 16' \times 8'$ is to be painted two coats. On a gross area basis the net cost is estimated to be $.107 per square foot. This is based on painter's wages of $6.00 per hour and the cost of paint at $8.00 per gallon. The area of the room is 640 square feet. The total cost would be $640 \times \$.107$ or $68.48. A second painter estimates the cost in the following manner:

Material

4 gal paint	@ $8.00 = $32.00
1 Box detergent	.50
patching plaster	1.00
1 lb putty	.50
	$ 34.00

Labor

Remove furniture and pictures	3.50
Prepare walls	7.00
Putty holes in trim	3.50
Patch cracks in plaster	3.50
Paint wall and ceiling	30.00
Paint 2 windows and 2 doors @ $3.50	14.00
Paint baseboard	3.50
Remove and reset radiator	1.50
Paint radiator	3.50
Cleanup	7.00
	$ 77.00
	$111.00

While accuracy in estimating depends largely on a careful breakdown of material and labor for each item, over-detailing of items can result in a high figure. The reason is that too much detail produces overlapping and also slightly excessive amounts which are cumulative.

This illustration is exaggerated to emphasize what over-detailing is, and its effect on the over-all cost. It is not unusual for estimates to contain several small items to build up the cost of painting an ordinary room.

Each item in itself, though figured on a liberal basis, may not appear excessive unless carefully analyzed. Yet the effect is a cumulative error that in the aggregate makes a substantial difference. Over-detailing is readily apparent to an experienced estimator, but can be overlooked by the less experienced person unless he understands what to look for and learns to recognize the characteristics.

Duplication of Subcontractor's Work

One reason that a subcontractor's estimate should be in detail is to avoid duplications by the prime contractor or other subcontractors. There may be duplications in such items as "cutting for other trades," where both prime and subcontractor allow for cutting through studs and joists for plumbers, electricians or heating contractors; or in scaffolding, cleanup, supplying heat for plasterers, and compliance with the requirements of OSHA.

Improper Consideration of the Class or Quality of Workmanship

A contractor accustomed to building expensive high quality homes may inadvertently apply the same standards when estimating the cost of a lower grade home. Some contractors are set up to handle only work of the highest quality and their workmen are similarly constituted. Their productive rate may be lower than others, but the finished product is superb. Conversely, a contractor who routinely builds substantial homes employs workmen who may be very productive, but turn out inferior quality. Failure to give adequate thought to the quality of workmanship required in a job can lead to under- or over-estimating the cost.

Inefficient Methods and Equipment

The use of portable table saws, electrical hand saws, drills, mortising machines, movable scaffolding, pneumatic hammers, drywall equipment and other labor-saving devices has won many a contract for the enterprising contractor. The estimator should take advantage of such equipment in preparing the estimate.

Use of Wrong Wage Rates

Using either higher or lower wage rates than required for the area can lose the bid for the job or lose money for the contractor if he gets the job on the lower wage rates.

Materials Improperly Priced

The estimator in pricing materials is in the same role as the buyer in a retail store. Both, to be successful, must exhaust every means to obtain the lowest price for the kind and quality of material sought. If priced too high, the competitor will get the work. If priced too low, the contractor may get the job, but could lose money or realize a lower profit.

Inadequate or Excessive Labor Allowances, Overhead and Profit Charged

Errors from these sources speak for themselves and results will be similar to those when wrong wage rates or material prices are used.

Arithmetical Errors in Computations

This is probably one of the most common sources of error in estimates. They are generally avoided by *checking* and *double-checking* all arithmetical calculations.

HOURLY LABOR TABLES

The labor Tables in this section will serve as a guide for estimating the hours that are required to apply or install building materials or perform specific operations. They represent reasonable average rates of production for workers under what might be considered "normal" working conditions. They have been developed mainly from on-the-job time studies. It is important to give careful consideration to the 16 factors discussed under Estimating Labor, pages 52-55. These are conditions that can affect the productivity of workers in performing specific operations and it may be necessary to adjust the hours of labor accordingly.

Labor Tables for Installing and Applying Building Materials in Dwellings

1. CONCRETE FORMS

Labor To Build; Erect and Strip Wood Forms For Concrete

Kind of Form	Board Feet of Lumber Per 100 Sq Ft Surface	Hours to Build & Erect	Hours To Strip	Total
Footings	350	6	2	8
Foundations and walls	250	8	2	10
Slabs on fill	100	6	2	8
Floor slabs above grade	250	10	4	14
Columns	300	10	4	14
Beams and girders	300	12	4	16

2. CONCRETE

Labor Mixing and Placing Concrete

Kind of Work	*Hours Per Cu Yd
Hand mixing on small jobs	2
Machine mixing	1
Placing in footings and foundation walls above footings	2
Placing in walls 10″ to 18″ thick	3
Placing in slabs on fill, sidewalks, etc.	2
Placing in beams and girders, first floor	4
Add to each 25′ of wheeling over 25′	$1/2$

	*Hours Per 100 Sq Ft
Finishing slabs—wood float	2
Finishing slabs—steel troweling	3
Machine finishing	1 to 2
Cement wash on walls	3

*Hours shown represent total man-hours whether mason, helper or combination of both.

3. CONCRETE BLOCK

Labor To Lay 100 Light-weight Concrete Block

Nominal Size of Unit	Kind of Work	Mason	Helper	Blocks Layed Per Hour
8″ × 8″ × 16″	Foundations and Walls	5.5	5.5	18
8″×12″×16″	Foundations and Walls	6.5	6.5	15

4. BRICK LAYING

Labor To Lay 1,000 Brick

Kind of Work	Mason	Helper
4″ Veneer on frame or masonry	16	16
8″ Common brick walls, normal openings	12	12
8″ Common brick walls, large openings	14	14
8″ and 12″ Foundation walls	10	10
Piers and columns	14	14
Common brick chimneys	15	15
Brick fireplaces	20	20
Brick facing fireplaces	24	24
Washing down brick masonry	1	1

5. ROUGH CARPENTRY

Kind of Work			Hours Per 1,000 FBM
Sills and plates			20
Studding, 2″ × 4″ - 16″ on center			25
Joists, 2″ × 6″ and 2″ × 8″			22
″ 2″ × 10″ and 2″ × 12″			20
Girders built up from 2″ stock			20
Rafters, 2″ × 6″ and 2″ × 8″	plain gable roof		30
″ ″ ″ ″	plain hip roof		33
″ ″ ″ ″	flat roof		26
Total framing for an average house			20-30
Exterior wall sheathing,	1″ × 6″ and	1″ × 8″	16
Subflooring		1″ × 4″	18
″	1″ × 6″ and	1″ × 8″	15
Roof boards, flat roof,	1″ × 6″ and	1″ × 8″	15
″ ″ gable	″ ″	″	20
″ ″ hip, cut up	″ ″	″	22

	Thickness	Per 1,000 Sq. Ft
Plywood subflooring	5/8″	12
″ ″	3/4″	16
″ sheathing	5/16″	14
″ ″	3/8″	16
″ roof decking flat roof	1/2″	12
″ ″ ″ gable ″	5/8″	16
″ ″ ″ cut up ″	5/8″	18
Composition roof decking, insulating	1/2″	12-20
″ sheathing, ″	1 1/2″	20-30

Bridging, wood 1″ × 3″ cut on the job	1-hour per 8 sets
″ ″ ″ redi-cut	1-hour 15
″ metal	1-hour 15
″ wood, solid	1-hour 10

Furring on masonry including shimming	4-hours per 100 lin ft
″ ″ studding	3-hours

Adjust hourly labor rates for unusual and difficult working conditions.

6. STUCCO—CEMENT PLASTER

Labor To Apply 100 Square Yards

Base	Plaster Thickness In Inches	Number of Coats	Plasterer	Helper
Masonry	$1/2$	1	13	6
"	$5/8$	2	21	10
"	$3/4$	3	28	20
Wire Lath	$5/8$	2	30	20
"	$3/4$	3	40	30

7. EXTERIOR SIDING

Labor To Install 1,000 FBM of Siding

Type of Siding	Normal Size in Inches	Hours of Labor Per 1,000 FBM
Bevel siding (plus 10% for	1 × 6	38
" " Mitered corners)	1 × 8	36
" " " "	1 × 10	34
Rustic and Drop siding	1 × 6	30
" " " "	1 × 8	28
Vertical matched siding	1 × 6	36
" " "	1 × 8	32
*Batten board siding	1 × 8	22
" " "	1 × 10	20
" " "	1 × 12	20

		Hours of Labor Per 1,000 Sq. Ft
Plywood panel siding	³/₈	14
" " "	⁵/₈	14
Hardboard siding	⁷/₁₆" × 12"	25

*Add 15 hours per 1,000 FBM to apply joint strips.

8. EXTERIOR SIDING (Continued)

Kind of Siding	Hours Per Square (100 sq ft)
Wood shingles, 16" and 18"	5
" " 24"	4
Asbestos-cement shingles, one-story work	4
" " " second story work	6
Asphalt strip shingles	3
Asphalt roll brick siding	2

9. ROOFING

Kind of Roofing	Lbs of Nails	Hours to Lay one Square	
		Plain Roof	Cut Up Roof
Asphalt strip shingles	2	2	3
" individual shingles	4	4	6
Asbestos-cement rectangular	3	6	8
" " hexagonal	3	4	6
Slate shingles ³/₁₆" thick	3	6	8
Hand split shakes	2	1	2
Wood shingles	2	4	6
Corrugated aluminum on wood	2	2 ¹/₂	3 ¹/₂
" steel on wood	2	6	8

Kind of Roofing	Lbs of Nails	Hours to Lay one Square	
		Plain Roof	Cut Up Roof
3-Ply built-up gravel roof		2	
4-Ply " " " "		2 1/2	
5-Ply " " " "		3	
Roll roofing		1 1/2	2

Removing old roofing of various kinds takes an average of 1-1 1/2 hours per square.

10. WINDOWS, STORM SASH AND SCREENS

Kind of Work	Hours labor
Install single wood frames in a frame building	0.5
" " " " masonry	1.0
" double " " with mullion . . . allow additional	0.5
Fit and hang wood sash, one pair complete	1.5-2.0
" " " casement sash, per each complete	1.5
Trim, interior, window	1.0-1.5
Install window complete, factory assembled	2.0
" " " , knock-down frame and sash	4.0
" basement window complete	0.5
Window screens, wood	1.0
Storm windows, "	1.0
Shutters, wood, stationary, per pair	2.0
" " hinged	3.0
Aluminum window, install complete—double hung or sliding	2.0
" combination screens and storm sash	3.0
Weatherstripping—double hung windows	2.0

11. DOORS

Kind of Work	Hours Labor
Set interior and exterior door frames	.75-1.0
Install mortise lock set	.75
Fit and hang interior door, soft wood, light weight	1.5
" " " " " hardwood, heavy	2.0
Install stops and casings, two sides, interior doors	1.0-1.25
" frame, fit, hang and trim interior door complete	4
" " " " " " exterior	5
Garage swinging doors, 8′ × 8′, fit and hang, per pair	4
Garage overhead door, × 1³/₈″, hang complete	6
" " " 15′ × 7′ × 1 ³/₄″	8
Storm door, wood or aluminum, fit and hang complete	2
Screen " " " "	2
Weatherstrip exterior door	2
Trimmed opening, set jambs, trim two sides, 7′ × 8′	2

12. FINISHED FLOORS

Nominal Size in Inches	Hours Labor to Lay	
	100 FBM	1,000 FBM
1″ × 2″ Hardwood	4.5	45
1″ × 3″ "	3.0	30
1″ × 3″ Softwood	2.5	25
1″ × 4″ "	2.0	20
³/₈″ × 2″ Hardwood	4.5	45
³/₈″ × 3″ "	4.0	40

13. INTERIOR TRIM

Kind of Work	Hours Labor Per 100 Lin Ft
Baseboard 1-member, softwood	6
″ 2-member ″	7
″ 3-member ″	8
Baseboard, 3-member, hardwood	10
Chair rail 1-member, softwood	5
″ ″ ″ hardwood	6
Plate rail 2-member hardwood	12
″ ″ 3-member ″	16
Picture molding, softwood	5
Ceiling ″ ″	6

14. EXTERIOR TRIM

Kind of Work	Hours Labor Per 100 Lin Ft
Water table and drip cap	4
Corner board, 2-member	5
Verge board	4
2-Member closed cornice	8
3-Member boxed cornice	12
Wood gutters	10

15. DRYWALL

Kind of Finish	Hours Labor Per 100 Sq Ft
Applying $3/8''$ and $1/2''$ gypsum board on sidewalls	1.0
″ ″ ″ ″ ″ ″ ceilings	1.5-2.0
″ ″ ″ ″ ″ ″ in small areas or rooms	2.0
Taping and finishing joints (average)	1.0

16. LATHING AND PLASTERING

			Hours Labor Per 100 Sq Yds	
Plaster Base	Plaster Thickness in Inches	Number of Coats	Plasterer	Helper
Wood lath	$5/8$	2	14	10
Metal "	$5/8$	2	15	12
Gypsum lath	$1/2$	1	10	8
" "	$1/2$	2	14	10
Masonry walls	$1/2$	1	10	8
" "	$5/8$	2	12	9

White coat Finish

Lime putty	$1/16$	1	10	8
Keene's cement	$1/16$	1	13	9

17. WALLBOARD AND TILE

Kind of Work	Hours Labor Per 100 Sq. Ft
Furring on studding, 12" centers	2
" " ceiling joists, 12" centers	3
$3/8$" and $1/2$" sheetrock on studding	1
" " " " " ceiling joists	1.5-2.0
Two-ply, $3/8$" sheetrock on studding	2
Taping and finishing joints	1.5
Fiberboard-Celotex etc.	1.5-2.0
Ceiling tile, 12" × 12" on furring, stapled	5
" " " " " " flat surface, applied with adhesive	2
$1/4$" Plywood, prefinished panels, on studding	2-3
$1/2$" " " " " " , flush joint	

18. CERAMIC, METAL AND PLASTIC TILE

Kind of Work	Hours Labor Per 100 Sq Ft	
	Tile Setter	Helper
Ceramic tile, ³/₄″ or 1″ paper-backed floor tile	8	8
″ ″ 2″ square, individual floor tile	16	16
″ ″ 4 ¹/₄″ × 4 ¹/₄″ glazed wall tile	16	16
Metal and plastic tile, applied with adhesive	8	8

19. INTERIOR PAINTING

*Kind of Work	Sq Ft Per Hour Per Coat	
Washing down walls and ceilings	100-150	
Preparing and sanding woodwork	150-250	
Sizing plastered walls	300-400	
Burning paint from trim	25-40	
	Brushwork	Roller
Painting smooth plaster including dr. and wd. openings	150	—
″ ″ ″ excluding ″ ″ ″ ″	200-250	300-350
″ sand finish plaster ″ ″ ″ ″ ″	175-200	350
″ ″ ″ including ″ ″ ″	125	—
″ textured plaster, semi-gloss	100-125	350
″ ″ ″ flat paint	180	350
″ cement block and brick	150	250
″ (spray painting)		(350-400)
″ cement floors and walls	200-250	300-350
Floors, remove finish with liquid	50	
″ shellac, varnish or paint	200-300	400-500
″ wax and polish	200	
Paneling, stain or finish	250	

Windows, paint one side, 12-14 openings, one-coat, 6/6 liters,	8 hours
Doors " , " " " , flush type, 16-18 openings, one coat,	8 "
" " . " " " panel " 12-14 " " "	8 "

*Where the premises are furnished and occupied, allow time to move the furnishings and to work around people.

20. EXTERIOR PAINTING

	Sq Ft Per Hour Per Coat	
Kind of Work	Brushwork	Roller
Wood siding, including door and window openings	100-125	300-350
" " excluding " " " "	200-225	
Staining wood shingle walls	150	200
" " " roofs	200-225	250-300
Painting brick walls	125-150	200-250
" stucco and cement plastered walls	100-150	200-250
" concrete block	100-125	250-300
Floors-wood decks, etc.	200	250
" concrete	220-250	300-350

Windows, one side only, 12-14 openings per 8 hour day
Doors, flush type, one side only, 16-18 openings per 8 hour day
" panel type, " " " 12-14 " " " " "

Shutters	one coat, 4-5 units per hour
Storm sash	" " 4-5 " " "
Screens	" " 5-6 " " "

Fences, solid board	250	400
" picket	150-200	250-300
" link	125	300

Leaders and gutters, 100 lin ft per hour

21. LABOR TO HANG PAPER

A. Ceilings (residential or commercial) rolls per 8 hr. day.

		Occupied	Vacant
a.	Mica	18 to 24 rolls	26 to 30 rolls
b.	Brush-tint	16 to 18 rolls	22 to 24 rolls
c.	Lining (blank stock)	16 to 18 rolls	22 to 24 rolls

B. Sidewalls (residential or commercial) rolls per 8 hr. day.

		Occupied	Vacant
a.	Lining (blank stock)	18 to 20 rolls	22 to 24 rolls
b.	Ordinary pre-trim	16 to 18 rolls	22 to 24 rolls
c.	Hand-knifed	12 to 14 rolls	14 to 16 rolls
d.	Cork	12 to 14 rolls	14 to 16 rolls
e.	Grasscloth	14 to 16 rolls	18 to 20 rolls
f.	Flock	8 to 10 rolls	....
g.	Burlap	12 rolls	....
h.	Silk	8 to 10 rolls	....
i.	Foil	8 rolls	....
j.	Scenics	10 panels per day	
k.	Coated fabrics	14 to 16 rolls	18 to 20 rolls
l.	Lining canvas	14 to 16 rolls	18 to 20 rolls

Vinyl or Coated Fabrics (commercial) rollage & yardage per 8 hr. day:
A. Lightweight, 24″ to 27″, 18 to 22 rolls.
B. Heavyweight, 54″, 30 lineal yards average; 45-65 lin. yds. corridor & volume.

Wood Veneer, Flexwood etc. sq. ft. basis

A. 105 to 145 sq. ft. per day.

Courtesy, Painting and Decorating Contractors of America

22. INSULATION

Kind of Work	Sq Ft Per Hour
Loose fill, pouring granule insulating wool, 3″ to 5″ thick	100-125
″ ″ packing ″ ″ ″ between studs	40-60
Batt insulation stapled between wall studs	100-125
″ ″ ″ ″ joists and rafters	75-100

23. APPROXIMATE HOURS LABOR FOR ROUGHING BY A PLUMBER AND HELPER TOGETHER

Kind of Roughing	*Plumber and Helper Team—Hours
Water closet in dwelling	8 to 10
Lavatory in dwelling	6 to 8
Bath tub and shower in dwelling	8 to 10
Kitchen sink in dwelling	5 to 6
$\frac{1}{2}$ to 1-inch cast or wrought iron pipe per joint	$\frac{1}{4}$ to $\frac{1}{3}$
$1\frac{1}{4}$ to 2-inch cast or wrought iron pipe per joint	$\frac{1}{3}$ to $\frac{1}{2}$
4-Inch soil pipe per joint	$\frac{3}{4}$ to 1
Complete roughing for one-story house	50 to 60

*Add plumber and helper wage rate and multiply by hours shown.

24. APPROXIMATE HOURS LABOR FOR A PLUMBER AND HELPER TO INSTALL PLUMBING FIXTURES

Kind of Fixture	*Plumber and Helper Team—Hours
Water closet—ordinary grade	3 to 4
Lavatory—ordinary grade	3 to 4
Bath tub and shower—ordinary grade	4 to 6
Laundry tubs	4 to 6
Water heater—gas fired (45 gal)	4
Urinal—wall type	4
Urinal—floor type	6

*Add plumber and helper wage rate and multiply by hours shown.

25. APPROXIMATE HOURS TO INSTALL VARIOUS ELECTRIC WIRING AND UNITS

Type of Work		Hours
Conduit, Cable and Wire		Hours Per 100 Lin Ft
Rigid conduit-galvanized	$1/2''$ to $1''$	10-14
" " "	$1^1/4''$ to $2''$	16-20
Rigid conduit-Thin wall	$1/2''$	6-10
" " " "	$1''$	10-12
" " " "	$1^1/2''$	12-16
" " " "	$2''$	14-18
Flexible conduit (Greenfield)	$1/2''$ to $1''$	6- 8
" "	$1^1/2''$ to $2''$	10-14
Non-metalic sheathed cable	#12 and #14	3- 4
Armored cable (BX)	#10 wire	5- 6
" "	#12 and #14 wire	4- 5
Pulling wire through conduit	#10, #12 and #14	2- 4

Service Entrance Installation	
Meter	1-2 each
Main switch	$1^1/2$-2
Panel or circuit-breaker box-200 amp	2-3

Setting Outlet Boxes	
$4'' \times 3''$ and octagonal	0.5
2 gang	0.6
4 gang	1.0

Installing Switches and Receptacles	.3 to .5

ONE, ONE-AND-A-HALF AND TWO-STORY DWELLINGS

TYPICAL ONE-FAMILY DWELLINGS

One-story and basement frame dwelling with concrete block foundation, one-car garage in basement, open deck and gable roof

Two-story dwelling, part frame, part brick veneer, with attached two-car brick veneer garage. Slab portico across front, crawl space, no basement, gable roofs

82

Two-story frame dwelling with crawl space under. Hip roof, no garage

One-and-one half story frame dwelling
with basement and an open-sided carport

85

One and one-half story dwelling, frame construction, gable roof, crawl space. No basement or garage

87

One-story brick veneer dwelling with full basement containing two-car garage. Gable roof

88

One-story and basement frame dwelling with brick veneer foundation on concrete block. Two-car garage in basement, open sides deck, slab portico and gable roofs

Application of Tables and Formulas
to Dwellings

TWO-STORY DWELLING WITH A ONE-STORY
ATTACHED GARAGE

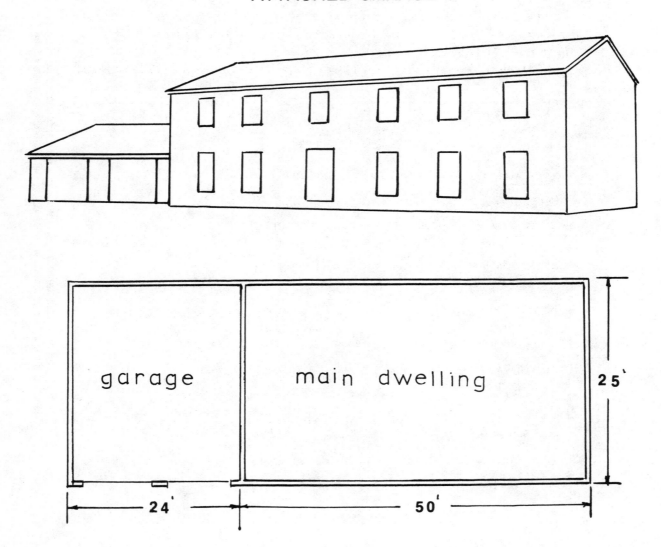

FIGURE 1

APPLICATION OF TABLES AND FORMULAS TO FIGURE 1

Two-Story Dwelling and Basement with Two-Car Attached Garage

Dwelling 25′ × 50′, Ground-Floor Area = 1,250 sq ft, Perimeter (4 sides) 150 lin ft

Length-to-Width Ratio of Dwelling = 2 : 1   Pitch of Roofs 1/4
   Garage = 1 : 1   Ground-Floor Area Garage = 600 sq ft
Perimeter of Garage = (3 sides) 2 × 24 + 25 = 73 lin ft
Construction: Brick Veneer on Frame. Specifications Follow "G", page 94.

MAIN DWELLING

*Concrete Footings, 12″ deep by 24″ wide. From Table 1   11.11 cu yds

   Alternate Method, using the formula under Table 1, page 148:

   $d'' \times w'' \times L' \times .000257$ = cu yds of concrete
   $12'' \times 24'' \times 150' \times .000257$ = ... 11.10 cu yds

Concrete Materials, Table 1A, page 151, using Mix No. 4:

For 1 cu yd:	For 11.11 cu yds:

   5 sacks cement   11.11 × 5 = 55.55 sacks cement
   .56 cu yds sand   × .56 = 6.22 cu yds sand
   .74 ″   ″ stone   × .74 = 8.22 ″   ″ stone

Concrete Materials from Table 1 B, for 11 cu yds of concrete:

                    55 sacks cement
                    6.16 cu yds sand
                    8.14 ″   ″ stone

---

*Forms not included as design, materials and labor depend on site conditions. Refer to discussion of forms, material and labor, pages 158-163.

<u>Concrete Block Foundation,</u> 8 ft high, using 12″ × 8″ × 16″ block:

From Table 3...........   1,350 block

Alternate Method No. 1, using the formula under Table 3, page 165.

L ′ × h′ × 1.125 = number of block............. 150′ × 8′ × 1.125 =   1,350 block

Alternate Method No. 2, using Table 3 B, page 169.

A wall 8′ high has 9 block per lin ft............................... 9 × 150 =   1,350 block

Mortar to Lay Concrete Block, Table 3 A

Material for 1,000-12″ × 8 ″ × 16″ block = 1.7 cu yds
Material for 1 cu yd of mortar:

10 sacks cement
1 cu yd sand
2 sacks hydrated lime

Material for 1,350 conc block, 1.7 × 1.350 = 2.295 cu yds

2.295 × 10 = 22.95 sacks cement (23 sacks)
      × 1 = 2.295 cu yds sand(2.3 cu yds sand)
      × 2 = 4.59 sacks lime   (4.6 sacks lime)

<u>Framing Lumber,</u> FBM, using Specification "G" Table 14............................   8,660 FBM

This is the total framing but excludes gable ends.

Gable framing, Table C2 shows both gables = 157 sq ft
      Table 14 A, FBM per sq ft   =× .67
                                                                    105
      Total FBM framing with gables   8,765 FBM

Alternate Method No. 1, using individual Tables.

*Exterior wall and partition studs, 16″ o.c.	Table 8	3,764 FBM
First and second floor joists, 2″ × 10″,	″ 9	3,375 ″
Second floor ceiling joists, 2″ × 4″, 24″ o.c.	″ 9	458 ″
Rafters, 2″ × 6″, 24″ o.c.	″ 12	775 ″
Bridging posts and girders	″ 10	375 ″
*Exterior studs include gables		
Total framing, alternate No. 1		8,746 ″

Alternate Method No. 2, using the simple formulas:

Exterior wall studs, 2″ × 4″, 16″ o.c. page 177
      13.4 × P = 13.4 × 150′ = ...   2,010 FBM
Partition studs, 2″ × 4″, 16″ o.c. page 177
      1.33 × A = 1.33 × 1250 = ...   1,663 ″
Add gable end framing as above..   105 ″
                                                                    3,778

		3,778 FBM

First and second floor joists, 2″ × 10″, page 184
    1.35 × A (times for 2-story) 1.35 × 2,500 =....................   3,375   ″
Second floor ceiling joists, 2″ × 4″, 24″ o.c.
    page 184, .37 × A = .37 × 1,250 = ...   463   ″
Rafters, 2″ × 6″, 24″ o.c. page 189, Table 11-12A
    .62 × A = .62 × 1,250 =.............................   775   ″
Bridging, girders etc. page 185.
    .30 × A = .30 × 1,250 = ...   375   ″
                 Total framing, alternate No. 2   8,766   ″

Nails For Framing:

    In estimating the quantity of nails required it is usually more accurate to first determine the FBM of the individual framing members and then estimate the quantity of each type of nail. But, for estimating purposes an average poundage of a mix of nails may be obtained from Table 14 B, page 205. This Table shows for 1,000 FBM of framing lumber 15 lbs of 8d, 10d, 16d and 20d are needed. The pounds of nails for framing 8,765 FBM would be: 15 × 8.765 = 131.5 lbs.

Roof Decking, 5/8″ plywood, flush cornice no overhang. Table 18   1,530 sq ft

    Alternate Method:

        Using Table 15-20 B, it shows that for a roof pitch 1/4 the surface area of a roof is 1.12 × ground-floor area.

            Area of roof = 1.12 × 1,250 = 1,400 sq ft

        Using Table 15-20 A, it shows that the sq ft of plywood decking required is 1.10 × the surface area.

            Plywood required = 1.10 × 1,400 = ...   1,540 sq ft

    Nails For Decking: Table 30-38 D shows 20 lbs per 1,000 sq ft

        Nails required = 20 × 1.540 = 31 lbs 8d

Roofing Paper, 15 lb saturated felt under asphalt shingles.   Table 24   3.9 rolls

Roofing, 240 lb 3-Tab, asphalt shingles   Table 24   1,538 sq ft
                                                                    (15.5 square)

    Alternate Method:

        Determine area of roof as above for decking,   1,400 sq ft
        Table 21-26 A shows, for this type shingle,   × 1.10
                                                             1,540 sq ft
                                                             (15.5 squares)

    Nails for roofing: Page 218, 2 lbs per square. 2 = 15.5 = 31 lbs

Exterior Sidewall Sheathing, 3/4″ Insulation Board, Gables Included:

    Method No. 1, ...Table 34,   3, 143 sq ft

Method No. 2, assuming sidewalls 18' high or use actual.

Sidewall surface area = 18 × P (perimeter) Table 30-38 B

Sidewall surface area is 18' × 150 (excluding openings)

$$18' \times 150' = \quad 2{,}700 \text{ sq ft}$$
$$\text{Add gable area as in framing} = \quad \underline{157 \text{ " "}}$$
$$\text{Total area} \quad 2{,}857 \text{ " "}$$

Table 30-38 A shows the quantity of insulation board required is 1.10 × area to be covered.

$$1.10 \times 2{,}857 = ... \qquad 3{,}143 \text{ sq ft}$$

Note: Deduct openings as required according to number and size.

Nails for insulation board, 20 lbs per 1,000 sq ft, Table 30-38C

Nails for 3,135 sq ft = 20 × 3.143 = 63 lbs

<u>4" Brick Veneer</u>, gables not included, no openings deducted.

First deduct the area where garage joins dwelling as that area will not be brick veneered.

$$\text{Main wall garage } 9' \times 25' = \quad 225 \text{ sq ft}$$
$$\text{Gable area Table C2*} \quad \underline{75 \text{ " "}}$$
$$300 \text{ " "}$$
$$\text{Number of brick/sq ft} \quad \underline{\times \ 7}$$
$$2{,}100 \text{ brick}$$
$$\text{From Table 38, total brick required} \quad 18{,}900$$
$$\text{deduct} \quad \underline{2{,}100}$$
$$\text{Brick required less less garage area.......} \quad 16{,}800 \text{ brick}$$

Alternate Method to Approximate Brick, No Openings Deducted:
Table 30-38 B, based on a 2-story wall height of 18'.
Table 30-38 B shows the number of brick as 126 × P (perimeter).

$$126 \times 150' = ... \quad 18{,}900$$
$$\text{deduct brick in area where garage joins dwelling} \quad \underline{2{,}100}$$
$$16{,}800 \text{ brick}$$

Mortar for brickwork, Table 30-38 C

Table 30-38 C shows that 1,000 brick in a 4" wall with 3/8" joints will require .33 cu yds of mortar. Therefore for 16,800 brick it will take 5.54 cu yds of mortar.

Using the same mix as for concrete block above,

$$5.54 \times 10 = 55.4 \text{ sacks cement}$$
$$\times 1 \ = 5.54 \text{ cu yds sand}$$
$$\times 2 \ = 11 \text{ sacks lime}$$

---

*Note that the gable area for the garage is based on Table C2 and a 1:1 length-to-width ratio of the garage. Also that only one half of the gable area in the Table is involved. Table C2 shows a gable area of 150 sq ft for 600 sq ft of *ground-floor* area (the garage) with a 1/4 roof pitch. This is for both gables as the Table states.

To deduct window and door openings, multiply the area of each by 7 which is the number of brick per sq ft in a 4" brick wall.

Gables of Dwelling: 1" × 10" bevel siding, 1 1/2" lap.

Under framing it was found that both gables of the dwelling contained 157 sq ft. Milling and cutting waste for 1" × 10" bevel siding is 30 percent as shown in Table 30-38 A.

Bevel siding for both gables is 157 × 1.30 = ...204 FBM

Nails for siding: Table 30-38 C shows that it requires 20 lbs of 8d nails to apply 1,000 FBM of 1" × 10" bevel siding.
For 204 FBM it will take .204 × 20 = 4 lbs of nails.

Interior Wall Finish: 1/2" Gypsum drywall, filled and taped. Table 29

Exterior sidewalls	2,400 sq ft or 267 sq yds	
Partition walls	4,000 " " " 444 " "	
Ceiling	2,500 " " " 277 " "	
Totals	8,900 " " " 988 " "	8,900 sq ft

Nails, from Table 27-29 A, 5 lbs per 1,000 sq ft, 8.9 × 5 =   44.5 lbs

Alternate Method For Figuring Interior Wall Finish:
Using Table 27-29B   A = ground-floor area   P = perimeter.

Exterior sidewalls,	16 × P = 16 × 150 ....2,400 sq ft	
Partition walls	3.2 × A = 3.2 × 1,250 = ...4,000 " "	
Ceilings	2 × A = 2 × 1,250 = ...2,500 " "	
	Total 8,900 " "	

Drywall tape and joint compound: Page 233

Five gallons of joint compound and a 500 ft roll of Perf-a-tape will take care of about 1,000 sq ft of drywall.
For 8,900 sq ft it will take:

$$8.9 × 5 = 44.5 \text{ gals compound}$$
$$× 1 = 8.9 \text{ or } 9 \text{ rolls of tape}$$

Rough Flooring, 5/8" plywood ....Table 29 ....   2,750 sq ft

Alternate Method, Table 27-29 B:

Table 27-29 B shows a formula for estimating the sq ft of plywood for under-flooring of 2.20 A for a 2-story dwelling.

$$2.20 × 1,250 = ... 2,750 \text{ sq ft}$$

Nails for underflooring, Table 27-29 A

It takes 20 lbs of 8d nails to lay 1,000 sq ft of 5/8" plywood flooring. To lay 2,750 sq ft would require

$$2.750 × 20 = 55 \text{ lbs of nails}$$

Finished Flooring, 1" × 3" matched oak .... Table 29   3,450 FBM

Alternate Method, Table 27-29 B:

Table 27-29 B shows a formula for estimating the FBM of 1″ × 3″ oak flooring of 2.76A for a 2-story dwelling.

$$2.76 \times 1{,}250 = \text{.............................} 3{,}450 \text{ FBM}$$

Nails for finished oak, 1″ × 3″ flooring: Table 27-29 A

50 lbs of 8d screw type nails will lay 1,000 FBM. To lay 3,450 FBM it will take

$$3.450 \times 50 = 173 \text{ lbs.}$$

Insulation, Walls and Ceiling:

Second floor ceiling, loose fill, 8 lbs per cu ft, 6″ deep   Table 39   118 bags
Exterior walls, 15″ × 48″ batts.. ″   43   513 batts

Concrete Floor, Basement: (23′ × 48′ = 1,104 sq ft)

3″ gravel base ....Table 4..................10.23 cu yds.
4″ concrete .... ″   4..................13.64 ″   ″

Alternate Method, using the basic formula, page 170:

Where A = area   t = thickness in inches
A × t × .0031 = cu yds of material

3″ Gravel base   1,100 × 3″ × .0031 = 10.23 cu yds.
4″ Concrete   1,100 × 4″ × .0031 = 13.64 ″   ″

Materials for concrete floor, Table 1A, page 151.

Refer to materials for footings and use same Mix No. 4.
Material for 1 cu yd:

5 sacks cement
.56 cu yds sand
.74 ″   ″   stone

*Material for 13.64 cu yds of concrete:

13.64 × 5 = 68.2 sacks cement
× .56 =   7.64 cu yds sand
× .74 = 10.09 ″   ″ stone

Reinforcing for concrete floor: page 171.

A roll of 6 × 6 − 10/10 reinforcing wire comes in sheets and in rolls 5′ × 150′. The sheets or rolls lap 6″. Enough is required to cover 1,100 sq ft (23′ × 48′) inside the basement allowing 12″ for the thickness of the walls. Two rolls should be adequate for 1,100 sq ft including the lapping.

---

*Table 1B, page 152, for 13.5 cu yds shows approximately the same quantities of materials and may be used as an alternate method for estimating.

ATTACHED GARAGE

Ground-Floor Area 24′ × 25′ = 600 sq ft Perimeter (3 sides) = 73 lin ft
Length-to-Width Ratio 1 : 1 Pitch of Roof 1/4
Construction, Brick Veneer on Frame. Specifications as Shown Below.

Concrete Footings, 8″ deep by 18″ wide ....Table 49   2.15 cu yds

Alternate Method, using the basic formula under Table 1, page 148:

d″ × w″ × L′ × .000257 = cu yds of concrete
L = Perimeter less two 8′ garage door openings
8″ × 18″ × 57′ × .000257 = 2.11 cu yds concrete

Concrete Foundation Above Footings, 10″ thick by 3′ high, Table 49..........   5.39 cu yds

Alternate Method, using basic formula under Table 2, page 154:
t″ (thickness) × h′ (height in feet) × .0031 × L′ (length) = cu yds

10″ × 3′ × .0031 × 57 = 5.30 cu yds

Concrete Materials for footing and foundation wall:

Footings   2.15 cu yds
Foundation wall   5.39 ″   ″
          Total 7.54 ″   ″

Following the procedure used under the dwelling, Table 1A:

37.7 sacks cement
4.2 cu yds sand
5.58 ″ ″   stone

Alternate Method, using Table 1B for 7.5 cu yds of Mix NO. 4:

37.5 sacks cement
4.2 cu yds sand
5.55 ″ ″   stone

Add forms and reinforcing as required. See pages 158-163.

Concrete Slab Floor in Garage.

Area = 25′ × 24′ less wall thickness

25′ − 8″ × 24′ − 8″ = 24′ − 4″ × 23′ − 4″ = 568 sq ft

Required: 5″ of gravel base and 4″ concrete.
From Table 49, using 568 sq ft:

5″ gravel base .... 8.8 cu yds
4″ concrete .... 7.0 ″   ″

Alternate Method, using basic formula under Tables 4 and 5:

A (area) × t″ (thickness) × .0031	= cu yds
Gravel base 5″, 568 × 5 × .0031	= 8.8 cu yds
Concrete 4″, 568 × 4″ × .0031	= 7.0 cu yds

Concrete Materials for 7.0 cu yds, Mix NO. 4.

Following the procedure used under the dwelling, Table 1A, page 151.

35.0   sacks cement
3.9   cu yds sand
5.18   ″   ″   stone

Alternate Method, using Table 1B for 7 cu yds:

35 sacks cement
3.92 cu yds sand
5.18   ″   ″   stone

Add forms and reinforcing as required. See pages 158-163.

Framing Lumber, FBM, per specifications shown:

Sills, plate and door header	Table 50	174 FBM
Exterior studding, 2″ × 4″, 16″ on center	″ ″	360 ″
Ceiling joists, 2″ × 4″, 24″ on center	″ ″	210 ″
Rafters, 2″ × 6″, 24″ on center	″ 54	372 ″
	Total framing	1,116 ″

Nails for framing, 1,098 FBM, Table 14B

Average per 1,000 FBM, 15 lbs 8d, 10d, 16d and 20d,

For 1,098 FBM,   1.098 × 15 =   16.47 lbs

Sheathing, 3/4″ Insulation board, gable included, Table 51.............................593 sq ft

Nails for insulation board

Average per 1,000 sq ft, 20 lbs 8d nails

For 593 sq ft,   .593 × 20 = ...11.86 lbs

Roof Decking, 5/8″ plywood,   Table 59,   738 sq ft

Nails for roof decking,

Average per 1,000 sq ft, 20 lbs 8d nails

For 738 sq ft,   .738 × 20 =   14.76 lbs

Roofing Paper, 15 lb saturated felt   Table 65   3.7 rolls

Roof Shingles, 240 lb 3-tab asphalt shingles   Table 65,   738 sq ft,   7.38 sqs

Nails for roof shingles

Average per square, 2 lbs

For 7.38 squares,   7.38 × 2 =   14.76 lbs

4″ Brick Veneer, excluding gable end,   Table 52   3,248 brick

Mortar for brick, Table 30-38C, .33 cu yds per 1,000

For 3,248 brick   .33 × 3.248 =   1.07 cu yds

Garage door openings deducted only.

Gable End, 1″ × 10″ bevel siding, 1½″ lap

Area of gable from Table C2, ½ × 150 = 75 sq ft
Milling and cutting waste, Table 30-38A, 30 percent

75 × 1.30 =   98 FBM

Nails, Table 30-38C, 20 lbs 8d per 1,000 FBM, .098 × 20 =   2 lb

ONE-STORY DWELLING AND ATTACHED TWO-CAR GARAGE

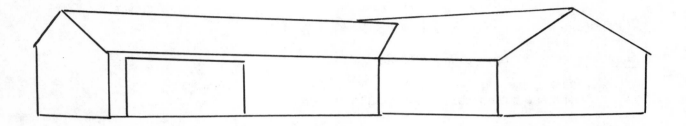

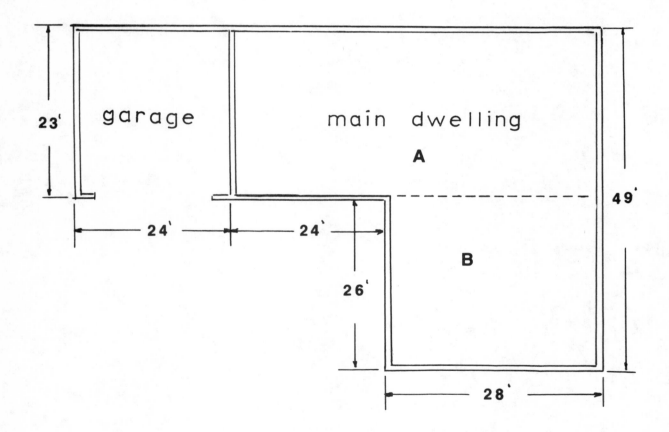

FIGURE 2

APPLICATION OF TABLES AND FORMULAS TO FIGURE 2

A One-Story-Dwelling on Slab with a Two-Car Attached Garage

Dwelling: Area = 1,924 sq ft   Garage: Area = 552 sq ft
             Perimeter = 202 lin ft   Perimeter = 71 lin ft
             L : W ratio (Table A) = 3 : 1

Assume the pitch of the roof to be 1/6 (4″ rise-per-foot-of-run) and the specifications shown below and which are Specification A, page 198. Frame construction and built on a concrete slab; 1″ × 10″ bevel siding, and a wood shingle roof. Add concrete forms and reinforcing as needed (pages 158-163).

MAIN DWELLING

<u>Concrete footings</u>, 8″ deep by 16″ wide. From Table 1, page 149, 6.14 cu yds

Adjustment for 3 : 1 length-to-width ratio, page 22:

Add 9% to Table quantity. 6.14 × 1.09 = 6.7 cu yds

Alternate Method, using the formula under Table 1, page 148:

$$d″ × w″ × L′ × .000257 = \text{cu yds of concrete}$$
$$8″ × 16″ × 202′ × .000257 = 6.6 \text{ cu yds of concrete}$$

(Note that when using formulas, there is no adjustment for L: W ratio.)

<u>Concrete Materials for footings</u>: Table 1A, page 151 using Mix No. 4

For 1 cu yd	For 6.7 cu yds
5 sacks cement	6.7 × 5 = 33.5 sacks cement
.56 cu yds sand	6.7 × .56 = 3.75 cu yds sand
.74 cu yds stone	6.7 × .74 = 4.96 cu yds stone

Alternate Method, using Table 1B for 6.5 cu yds of concrete:

32.5 sacks cement
3.64 cu yds sand
4.81 cu yds stone

<u>Foundation above Footing</u>: (Depth depends on geographic location and local Building Department ordinances)

101

Assume that 4 feet below grade is required; and 10″ thick.
Table 2 shows (interpolating) 23.09 cu yds concrete.

Adjustment for L: W ratio of 3:1, page 22, is 9%
23.09 × 1.09 = 25.17 cu yds concrete

Alternate Method No. 1, Formula page 154:

$t″ × h′ × .0031 × L$ = cu yds concrete
10″ × 4′ × .0031 × 202′ = 25.05 cu yds concrete

Alternate Method No. 2, Table 2A:

.1240 × 202′ = 25.05 cu yds concrete

Concrete Materials, Table 1A, page 151, using Mix No. 4

For 1 cu yd		For 25 cu yds
5 sacks cement	25 × 5 =	125 sacks cement
.56 cu yds sand	25 × .56 =	14 cu yds sand
.74 cu yds stone	25 × .74 =	18.5 cu yds stone

Alternate Method, using Table 1B for 25 cu yds of concrete:
(Use the quantity shown for 12.5 cu yds multiplied by 2)

125 sacks cement
14 cu yds sand
18.5 cu yds stone

Concrete Slab: 1,924 sq ft

5″ gravel base	Table 4,	29.59 cu yds
4″ concrete slab		23.86 cu yds concrete

Alternate Method, using the formula page 170:

A (area) × t″ (thickness) × .0031 = cu yds concrete
Gravel base 5″, 1,924 × 5″ × .0031 = 29.82 cu yds
Concrete slab 4″, 1.924 × 4″ × .0031 = 23.86 cu yds concrete

Concrete Materials, Table 1A, page 151, using Mix No. 4:

For 1 cu yd		For 24 cu yds
5 sacks cement	24 × 5 =	120 sacks cement
.56 cu yds sand	24 × .56 =	13.44 cu yds sand
.74 cu yds stone	24 × .74 =	17.76 cu yds stone

Alternate Method, using Table 1B for 24 cu yds:

120 sacks cement
13.44 cu yds sand
17.76 cu yds stone

Reinforcing for concrete slab. (page 171)

6 × 6 − 10/10 wire comes in sheets and in rolls.
A roll is 5′ × 150′. Sheets and rolls lap a full square (6″).
Allowing for lapping, approximately 3 rolls will be needed.

Framing Lumber, FBM, (using Specification A, Table 14, which excludes gables).

Interpolating in Table 14; ground-floor area 1,924 sq ft has total framing of 4,423 FBM.

Adjust exterior studding for L: W ratio of 1:3

Table 6, (excludes gables) exterior studs   = 1,248 FBM
Deduct exterior studs from total FBM of framing
                    4,423 − 1,248   = 3,175 FBM
Gable studs:
                gable area, Table C1 =   108 sq ft
gable area, Table C1   108 sq ft
factor for 2″ × 4″ studs, 16″ on center
                Table 14A, page 204   × .67
                                         72 FBM

Exterior studs, including gables, = 1,248 + 72 = 1,320 FBM
Adjustment for L:W ratio of 3:1, page 22, 1,320 × 1.09 = 1,439 FBM
adjusted total framing, 1,439 + 3,175 = 4,613 FBM

Note that the adjustment for L:W ratio, and for gable studs due to roof pitch being 1/6 instead of 1/4 on which the Tables are based is minor. It represents a difference of only 190 FBM or an increase over Table 14 quantity of 4.3 percent.

When it is necessary to interpolate in the Tables because the ground-floor area of a dwelling lies between the even square feet, and adjustments are necessary for roof pitches that are other than 1/4, or the L:W ratio is different from 2:1 used in the Tables, the estimator may find that the formulas supplied are easier and faster than using the Tables.

Alternate Framing Method No. 1, using individual Tables:

Exterior wall studs, 2″ × 4″, 16″ on center
        excluding gables ....Table 6.................1,248 FBM
    add gables:

                area, Table C1 page 31 =   108
                factor for 2″ × 4″, 16″ o.c.   × .67
                                            72   ″
                                         1,320 FBM
                Adjust for L:W ratio of 3:1   × 1.09
                                         1,439 FBM

			total exterior studs	1,439 FBM
Partition studs 2″ × 4″, 16″ o.c.		Table 6	1,271	″
Ceiling joists	24″	Table 9	706	″
Rafters	2″ × 6″,	Table 12	1,117	″
Bridging & catting.............................Table 10			193	″
			Total framing	4,726 FBM

Alternate Method No. 2, using formulas supplied:

Exterior wall studs, 2″ × 4″, 16″ o.c., page 176

$$6.7 \times P = 6.7 \times 202'$$ 1,353 FBM

add gable framing as in Alternate No. 1   72 ″

Partition studs, 2″ × 4″, 16″ o.c., page 176

	$.66 \times A = .66 \times 1,924$	1,270	″
Ceiling joists, page 184,	$.37A = .37 \times 1,924$	712	″
Rafters, page 189,	$.58 \times A = .58 \times 1,924$	1,116	″
Bridging, catting, page 185,	$.10 \times A = .10 \times 1,924$	192	″
	Total framing	4,715 FBM	

Nails for Framing:

Table 14B, page 205, shows it will take approximately 15 lbs of 8d, 10d, 16d, and 20d nails for 1,000 FBM of framing. Therefore to frame 4,700 FBM it will require 4.7 × 15 = 70.5 lbs of nails.

Roof decking:

$^5/_8$″ plywood, flush cornice, Table 16. Pitch $^1/_6$, interpolating 2,251 sq ft

Alternate Method:

Table 15-20B shows for a roof pitch of $^1/_6$, the surface area of this roof is 1.06 × ground-floor area. Area of roof =
1.06 × 1924 = 2,039 sq ft

Table 15-20A shows the sq ft of plywood required is 1.10 times the surface area.
1.10 × 2,039 = 2,243 sq ft

Nails for Decking:

Table 30-38D shows 20 lbs of 8d nails per 1,000 sq ft of $^5/_8$″ plywood decking. For 2,250 sq ft it would take 20 × 2.25 = 45 lbs of 8d nails.

Roofing Paper: (15 lb felt under asphalt shingles)
Using Table 22, ground-floor area of 1,924 sq ft requires 5.63 or 6 rolls.

Roofing: (240 lb, 3-tab asphalt shingle)
Table 22 shows, for roof pitch of $^1/_6$, 2,252 sq ft or 22$^1/_2$ squares.

Alternate Method:

Area of roof (see decking above)	2,039 sq ft
Table 21-26A shows for this shingle	×1.10
	2,243 sq ft or 22 ½ squares

<u>Nails for Roofing:</u>

Page 218 shows an acceptable average for this shingle is 2 lb per square.

$$2 \times 22.5 = 45 \text{ lbs}$$

Exterior Sidewall Sheathing, ¾″ Insulation Board
Method No. 1, using Table 31 (Excluding gables)............................1,844 sq ft

Add gables (roof ⅙ pitch).

Area (see Exterior Studs)...............108 sq ft		
Waste (Table 30-38A) ×1.10	119	″
	1,963	″
Adjust for L:W ratio 3:1 (page 22)	×1.09	
Total	2,140 sq ft	

Method No. 2, using formula, Table 30-38B (excludes perimeter)

Formula = 10 × P (perimeter) = 10 × 202′ =	2,020 sq ft	
Add gables as in Method No. 1	119	″ ″
Total	2,139	″ ″

Method No. 3, using actual exterior wall height.

In place of assuming that the exterior walls are 9 ft high, as in the Tables, use the actual wall height excluding the gables and mutliply by the perimeter. Add gables as determined in Methods 1 and 2.

Nails for Insulation Board. Table 30-38D, 20 lbs per 1,000 sq. ft.

$$20 \times 2.140 \text{ sq ft} = 43 \text{ lbs of 8d nails}$$

<u>4″ Brick Veneer</u>, (Gables excluded and no openings deducted)

Method No. 1, Using Table 36...11,731 brick

Deduct area where garage joins the dwelling as that area will not have brick veneer.

Main garage wall 9′ × 23′	= 207 sq ft	
Gable area is ½ that in Exterior Sheathing as only one gable involved	= 54	″
Total area	261	″
Brick per sq ft ×7	− 1,827 brick	
	9,904	″

$$9,904$$

Adjust for L:W ratio 3:1, (page 22) $\times$ 1.09

Total required   10,795 brick

Method No. 2, using table 30-38B formula and assuming wall to be 9' high:

$$63 \times P = \text{number of brick}$$
$$63 \times 202' = 12,726 \text{ brick}$$

Deduct brick where garage
joins dwelling as in Method
No. 1 $-$ 1,827   "

Total required   10,899 brick

Mortar for brickwork, Table 30-38C.

4" wall, $^3/_8$" joints, require .33 cu yds of mortar per 1,000
10,800 brick require   .33 $\times$ 10.8 = 3.56 cu yds

Material for 1 cu yd of mortar:

10 sacks cement
1 cu yd sand
2 sacks hydrated lime

3.56 cu yds of mortar will require:

35.6 sacks cement
3.56 cu yds sand
7.12 sacks hydrated lime

Note: To deduct window and door openings, multiply the area of each unit by 7, the number of brick per square foot in a 4" wall.

Gable Bevel Siding, 1" $\times$ 10", 1 $^1/_2$" lap.

There are two gable ends to be finished in bevel siding:

Garage end................23' $\times$ $^1/_2$ (3.8) =   44 sq ft
Dwelling end ....28' $\times$ $^1/_2$ (4.7) =   66   " "

Total   110   " "

Add waste from Table 30-38A   33   " "

Total   143 FBM

Note: Height of the gables is determined by multiplying the run ($^1/_2$ the span) by 4" ($^1/_6$ pitch) and dividing by 12".

Garage end $\dfrac{11.5' \times 4''}{12''}$ = 3.8'

dwelling end $\dfrac{14' \times 4''}{12''}$ = 4.7'

Nails for siding:

Table 30-38D shows it requires 20 lbs of 8d nails for 1,000 FMB of this siding.

For 143 FBM it will take .143 × 20 = 2.86 lbs

<u>Interior Wall Finish:</u> 3-Coat, 5/8″ plaster on metal lath.

Method No. 1, using Table 27

Exterior sidewalls...(1,497) sq ft	(167) sq yds
Adjusted for 3:1 L:W ratio (page 22) 1,624	182 ″
Partition walls... 3,078	341 ″
Ceiling 1,924	214 ″
Totals 6,626	737 ″

Method No. 2, using Table 27-29B where A = ground-floor-area
P = perimeter

Exterior walls, 8P = 8 × 202 =	1,616 sq ft	= 180 sq yds
Partition walls. 1.6A = 1.6 × 1,924	= 3,078	= 342 ″
Ceilings A = 1,924	= 1,924	= 214 ″
Totals	6,618 sq ft	736 sq yds

Materials for 3-coat plaster on metal lath, where plaster is 5/8″ thick including 1/16″ finish coat:

Table 27-29C shows the number of sacks of prepared gypsum plaster to cover 100 sq yds on various kinds of base. For 5/8″ thick plaster on metal lath, 35 (80 lb) sacks are required for each 100 sq yds. For the finish coat of lime putty, Table 27-29C shows 2 (100 lb) sacks of neat gypsum and 8 (50 lb) sacks of hydrated lime for 100 sq yds of finish 1/16″ thick.

For 736 sq yds: 7.35 × 35 = 257 (80 lb) sacks gypsum
7.35 × 2 = 14.7 (100 lb) ″   neat ″
7.36 × 8 = 58.8 (50 lb) ″   hydrated lime

<u>Insulation, Walls and Ceiling.</u>

Ceiling, loose fill, 8 lbs per cu ft, 6″ deep,   Table 39, 182 40-lb bags
Exterior walls, 15″ × 48″ batts   Table 43, 318 batts

ATTACHED 2-CAR GARAGE

Ground-floor area, 23′ × 24′ = 552 sq ft, Perimeter (3 sides) 71 lin ft. Length-to width ratio 1:1   Pitch of roof 1/6, Exterior walls 8′ high. Construction: Brick veneer on frame with specifications as shown.

<u>Concrete Footings,</u> 8″ deep by 18″ wide   Table 49   2 cu yds

Alternate method, using formula page 148:

$$d'' \times w'' \times L' \times .000257 = \text{cu yds concrete}$$
$$8'' \times 18'' \times 55' \times .000257 = 2 \text{ cu yds concrete}$$
(Note: L = perimeter − 16′ garage door opening.)

Concrete Block Foundation Above Footings: (24″ high)

8″ × 8″ × 16″ block.......................................Table 49   124 block

Alternate method, using Table 3B

2.25 block per lin ft of wall   2.25 × 55 =   124

Alternate method, using formula page 165:

$$L' \times h' \times 1.125 = \text{number of block}$$
$$55' \times 2' \times 1.125 = 124 \text{ block}$$

Mortar to lay block, Table 3A,   .15 cu yds per 100 block
                                      .15 × 1.24 = .186 cu yds,
                                               or 5 cu ft

Mortar materials, Table 3A

For 1 cu yd	For .186 cu yds
10 sacks cement	1.86 sacks cement
1 cu yd sand	.186 cu yds sand
2 sacks hydrated lime	.37 sacks hydrated lime

Concrete Slab Floor

Area 24′ × 23′ less one wall thickness
$$24'' - (8'') \times 23' - (8'') =$$
$$23' \, 4'' \times 22' \, 4'' \qquad = 518 \text{ sq ft}$$

Required: 5″ gravel base and 4″ concrete.

From Table 49 using 518 sq ft
5″ gravel base   8.03 cu yds
4″ concrete   6.42 cu yds

Alternate method, using formula under Tables 4 and 5, page 170

A (area) × t″ (thickness) × .0031 = cu yds
5″ gravel base   518 = 5″ × .0031 = 8.03 cu yds
4″ concrete   518 × 4″ × .0031 = 6.42 cu yds

Concrete materials for 6.75 cu yds concrete. Table 1A, page 151.

For 1 cu yd	For 6.42 cu yds
5 sacks cement	32.00 sacks cement
.56 cu yds sand	3.60 cu yds sand
.74 stone	4.75 cu yds stone

Alternate method, using Table 1 B. Same as above.

Add forms and reinforcing as required. See page 171

<u>Framing Lumber</u>, FBM, using 550 sq ft ground-floor-area.

Sills, plates, and door header	Table 50,	165 FBM
Exterior wall studding, 2″ × 4″, 16″ on center	″	340 ″
Ceiling joists,　　″　　″　″　″	″	193 ″
Rafters, 2″ × 6″, 24″ on center	Table 54	319 ″
	Total	1,017 ″

Nails for framing 1,017 FBM, Table 14 B:

Average per 1,000 FBM, 15 lbs 8d, 10d, 16d and 20d nails.
For 1,017 FBM, 1.017 × 15 = 15.25 lbs nails

<u>Sheathing</u>, $3/4$″ insulation board, gable included, Table 51,　　　　560 sq ft

Nails for insulation board, Table 30-38 D, 20 lbs per 1,000 sq ft

8d nails. For 560 sq ft,　　.560 × 20 = 11 lbs

<u>Roof Decking</u>, $5/8$″ plywood　　　　　　　Table 57　　　644 sq ft

Nails for roof decking, average per 1,000 sq ft, 20 lbs

8d nails. for 644 sq ft　　.644 × 20 = 12.88 or 13 lbs

<u>Roofing Paper</u>, 15 lb saturated felt,　　　　Table 65　　　3.22 rolls

<u>Roof Shingles</u>, 240 lb, 3-tab asphalt shingles.　　Table 63　　644 sq ft
　　　　　　　　　　　　　　　　　　　　　　　or　6.5 square

<u>4″ Brick veneer</u>, excluding gable end　　　　Table 52,　　3,080 brick

Alternate method (assume wall height of 8′)

Table 52, Exterior wall area 8′ × 55′ = 440 sq ft
　　　　　　　　　　　　brick per sq ft　× 7
　　　　　　　　　　　　　　　　　　　3,080 brick

Mortar for brick, Table 30-38 C

.33 cu yds per 1,000 brick
For 3,080 brick,　　　　　　.33 × 3.080 = 1 cu yd

ONE-STORY DWELLING AND CARPORT AND OPEN PORCH
WITH ROOF OVER

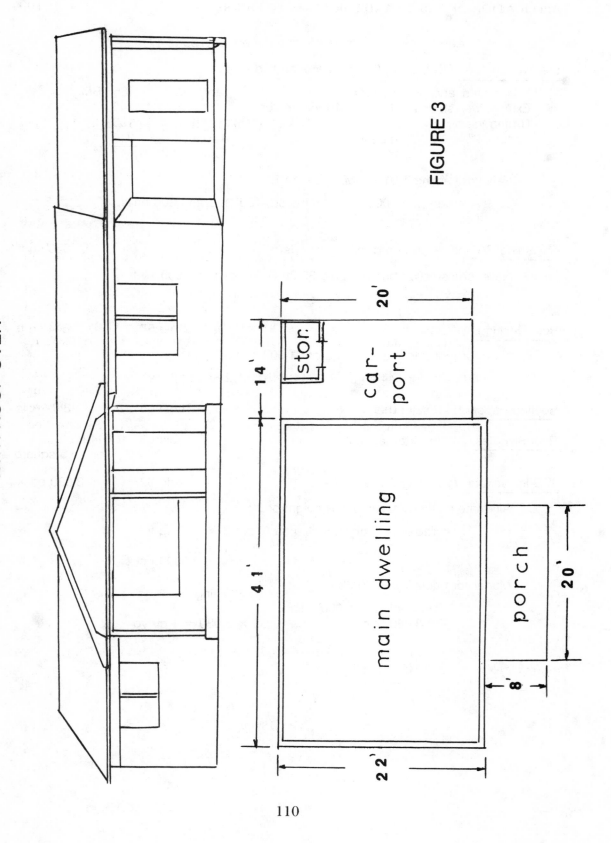

FIGURE 3

APPLICATION OF TABLES AND FORMULAS TO FIGURE 3

The quantities of construction materials for the main dwelling should be estimated as in figure No. 2.

Estimate the roof structure and materials as though the intersecting roof does not exist. As stated under General Instructions, the roof framing, decking and roofing of the area taken up by the dormer in the main roof are approximately equivalent to that in dormer roof. With the exception of any overhang and sidewall materials the dormer may be ignored.

The same thing is true with respect to an intersecting roof. The portion of the intersecting roof from the eave-line in to the main roof may also be ignored for all practical purposes in estimating as the materials in that portion are approximately the same as the materials that would be in the main roof if there were no intersecting roof.

So, in the case of the roof over the open porch in Figure 3, treat the porch roof separately beginning at the eave-line of the main roof. In the following illustration it will be assumed that the porch roof has a horizontal overhang at the eaves and at the gable. Add concrete forms (pages 158-163) and reinforcing as needed.

PORCH

Area = 8′ × 20′ = 160 sq ft   Perimeter of slab = 36 lin ft (3 sides)

Roof area, 24′ long including overhang; 10′ wide including overhang
$$10′ × 24′ = 240 \text{ sq ft}$$

Assume roof pitch of 1/6

Concrete Footings, (3 sides) 8′ + 8′ + 20′ = 36 lin ft footing 10″ × 16″

Using the formula under Table 1, page 148:
d″ × w″ × L′ × .000257 = cu yds 10″ × 16″ × 36′ × .000257 =   1.48 cu yds
Corners may be taken out to be precise. In this case it would reduce L to 33′ and reduce the cu yds to 1.36

Concrete Foundation Wall Above Footing, 36 lin ft

Assume foundation to be 8″ wide × 3′ 6″ high and 36′ long
Using the formula under Table 2, page 154:
t″ × h′ × .0031 × L′ = cu yds   8″ × 3.5′ × .0031 × 36′ =   3.12 cu yds

Concrete materials for footings and foundation 4.6 cu yds

For 1 cu yd	For 4.6 cu yds
5 sacks cement	4.6 × 5 = 23 sacks cement
.56 cu yds sand	4.6 × .56 = 2.58 cu yds sand
.74 ″ ″ stone	4.6 × .74 = 3.40 ″ ″ stone

Roof Structure (overhang 24″ horizontally) Roof pitch ¹/₆

Horizontal or ground-floor area, 10′ × 24′ = 240 sq ft
Perimeter 10′ + 10′ + 24′ =44 lin ft
Framing:

Girder-plate 4″ × 12″ × 44′ =		176 FBM
Ceiling joists 2″ × 4″ − 24″ o.c.	Table 9,	88 ″
Rafters 2″ × 6″, 24″ o.c.	Table 12	139 ″
		403 FBM

Roof Decking, ⁵/₈″ plywood   (¹/₆ pitch)   Table 16   281 sq ft

Nails, Table 30-38 D, 20 lbs 8d nails per 1,000 sq ft
For 281 sq ft   .281 × 20 =   5.62 lbs

Roofing Paper, 15 lb saturated felt, Table 22   .71 rolls

Roof Shingles, 240 lb 3-tab asphalt shingles, Table 22   2.81 sq ft

Nails, average 2 lbs per sq (page 218)   2.81 × 2 =   5.62 lbs

Gable End of Porch

The roof pitch is ¹/₆ and *ground-floor* area is 8′ × 20′ = 160 sq ft.

The L:W ratio is $\frac{20}{8}$ = 2.5:1

The formula, page 28, shows a factor of .067 for a 2.5:1 L:W ratio and roof pitch of ¹/₆. Since the gable is on the long side the factor must be multiplied by 6.25, page 29.*

Area of both gables = 6.25 × .067 × 160 = 67 sq ft
Area of one gable = $\frac{67}{2}$ = 33.5 or 34 sq ft

Alternate method is to treat the gable as a triangle with base of 20′ and height of 3′ − 4″ (6″ rise per foot of run).

¹/₂ × 20′ × 3.33′ = 34 sq ft.

---

*See Estimating Gable Studs, Table 14, page 200.

Framing 2″ × 4″ studs 16″ on center Table 14 A, .67 × 34 = 23 FBM

Sheathing, ¾″ composition board, Table 30-38 A, 1.10 × 34 = 38 sq ft

Bevel siding, 1″ × 8″ × 1 ¼″ lap, Table 30-38 A. 34 × 1.35 = 46 FBM

Add nails.

CARPORT

Area of slab 14′ × 20′ = 280 sq ft   Perimeter, 2 × 14′ + 20′ = 48 lin ft
There is a 2′ horizontal overhang at the eaves and the gable of the roof.
Roof pitch is 1/6. The horizontal or ground-floor area of the roof is
16′ × 24′ = 384 sq ft.

Construction Details:

Concrete foundation, 3 sides, 8″ wide and 4′-0″ deep
Concrete slab 4″ thick over 8″ of gravel base
Frame roof on 4″ × 12″ girder-plate, 2″ × 6″ rafters 24″ on center, and 2″ ×
4″ ceiling joists 24″ on center; 3-4″ × 6″ posts and 2-4″ × 4″ posts.
Roof decking 5/8″ plywood
Roofing, 240 lb, 3-tab asphalt shingles over 15 lb saturated felt paper.
Bevel siding at gable end over 3/4″ composition sheathing.
Storage area may be estimated according to size and construction.

Concrete foundation, 8″ × 4′ × 48′

Table 2A shows a factor for a 4′ wall of .0992   48 × .0992 = 4.76 cu yds

Alternate method using the formula on page 154

t″ × h′ × L′ × .0031 = cu yds 8″ × 4′ × 48′ × .0031 = 4.76 cu yds

Concrete materials for 4.76 cu yds of concrete, Table 1A page 151, using
Mix No. 4

For 1 cu yd	For 4.76 cu yds
5 sacks cement	4.76 × 5 = 23.8 sacks cement
.56 cu yds sand	4.76 × .56 = 2.67 cu yds sand
.74 cu yds stone	4.76 × .76 = 3.62 cu yds stone

Concrete Floor Slab, 14′ × 20′ = 280 sq ft

From Table 49, interpolating between 250 and 300 sq ft

5″ gravel base	4.34 cu yds
4″ concrete over	3.47 ″ ″

Alternate method using the formula under Tables 4 and 5

$$A \times t'' \times .0031 = \text{cu yds of material}$$

5″ gravel base	$280 \times 5'' \times .0031 = 4.34$ cu yds
4″ concrete	$280 \times 4'' \times .0031 = 3.47$ ″ ″

Concrete materials for 3.47 cu yds concrete, Table 1A, Mix No. 4

For 1 cu yd	For 3.47 cu yds
5 sacks cement	$3.47 \times 5 = 17.35$ sacks cement
.56 cu yds sand	$3.47 \times .56 = 1.94$ cu yds sand
.74 cu yds stone	$3.47 \times .74 = 2.57$ cu yds stone

Forms are not included. See pages 158-163 for a discussion of forms Add reinforcing as required. See page 171.

Framing:

Posts, 3 − 4″ × 6″ × 8′ posts at dwelling		48.0 FBM
2 − 4″ × 4″ × 8′	20′ side	21.3 ″
Girder-plate 48′ − 4″ × 12″		192.0 ″
Ceiling joists 2″ × 4″ − 24″ on center, Table 9		154.0 ″
Rafters 2″ × 6″ − 24″ on center		223.0 ″
		638.3 FBM

Nails for framing 638.3 FBM, Table 14B

Average per 1,000 FBM 20 lbs 8d, 10d, 16d, and 20d

$$.6383 \times 20 = \qquad 12.76 \text{ lbs}$$

Roof Decking, ⅝″ plywood, using 384 sq ft and ⅙ roof pitch
    Interpolating in Table 57   439 sq ft

Nails, Table 30-38D, page 261, 20 lbs 8d nails per 1,000 sq ft

$$.439 \times 20 = \qquad 8.78 \text{ lbs}$$

Roofing Paper, 15 lb saturated felt, Table 63   1.12 rolls

Roofing, 240 lb 3-tab asphalt shingles, Table 63   439 sq ft

Nails for roofing, page 218, 2 lbs per square $4.38 \times 2 = \qquad$ 8.78 lbs

Gable End of Carport

The roof pitch is ⅙ and ground-floor area is 14′ × 20′ = 280 sq ft. The L:W ratio is $\frac{20}{14} = 1.43$. Use 1.5, the nearest in the formula, page 28, for Gable areas.

The formula shows a factor of .111 for a 1.5:1 L:W ratio and roof pitch of ⅙.

Since the gable is on the long side of the porch, this factor must be multiplied by 2.25, page 29.*

Area of both gables = 2.25 × .111 × 280 = 70 sq ft
Area of one gable = $\frac{70}{2}$ = 35 sq ft

Alternate method is to treat the gable as a triangle with base of 20′ and height of 3′ - 4″ (6″ rise per foot of run). $^{1}/_{2}$ × 20′ × 3.33′ = 34 sq ft

Framing, 2″ × 4″ studs 16″ on center Table 14A .67 × 34 = 23 FBM

Sheathing, $^{3}/_{4}$″ composition board, Table 30-38A, 1.10 × 34 = 38 sq ft

Bevel siding, 1″ × 8″ × 1-$^{1}/_{4}$″ lap, Table 30-38A, 34 × 1.35 = 46 FBM

Add nails

---

*See estimating Gable Studs, Table 14, page 200.

A ONE-STORY DWELLING WITH CARPORT
ADJOINING ONE SIDE
AND A ROOFED-OVER TERRACE
ADJOINING THE OTHER SIDE

(This is an example of the main roof area extending over areas
outside of the perimeter of the main dwelling.)

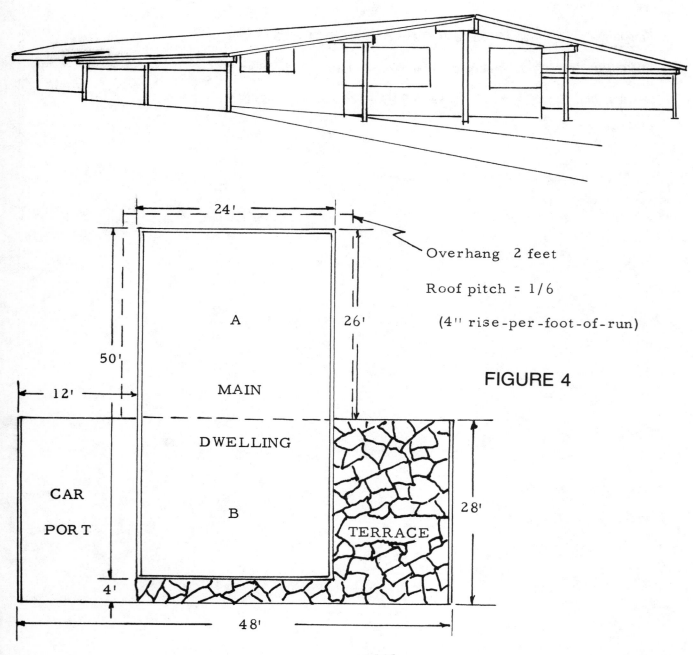

Overhang 2 feet

Roof pitch = 1/6

(4'' rise-per-foot-of-run)

FIGURE 4

APPLICATION OF TABLES TO FIGURE 4

(An example of a roof extending beyond the main dwelling to include garage and carport.) In this example, section "A" is assumed to have a horizontal overhang on the sides and at the gable end, of 2 feet. Roof framing over the dwelling portion, "A" and "B," consists of prefabricated trusses with 2" × 6" rafters and 2" × 4" cords. The roof over the terrace and carport has 2" × 6" rafters which, for our purposes, are an extension of the rafter trusses, with the exception of the 4 ft projection in the front. This projection is framed with 2" × 6" rafters on 4" × 8" girders supported on 6" × 6" posts. Rafters over carport and terrace, rest on 4" × 8" girders which are also supported on 6" × 6" posts.

The purpose of this example is basically to illustrate how the framing, decking, and roofing are estimated.

Roof Framing:

    Main dwelling "A" and "B," 26 trusses.
      (horizontal area, 28' × 50' = 1,400 sq ft) Table 13   1,736 FBM

    Carport and terrace, Rafters 2" × 6" — 24" on center
      (horizontal area, 2 × 12' × 28' + 4' × 24' = 768 sq ft)
                                Table 12   445   "

    Gable look-out rafters, 2" × 6"
      (Pitch = 1/6, run = 14' including 2' overhang)
          From Table 11-12B, 14' × 1.06 = 14.84
          2 — 16' rafters required   32 "

    Girders and posts.

2 — 4" × 8" × 26' girders	139 FBM		
3 — " × 6' "	48 "		
1 — 6" × 6" × 16' posts	48 "		
2 " × 10' "	60 "		
6 " × 8' "	144 "	439 "	

                                         Total framing 2,652 FBM

Decking, 5/8" plywood. Horizontal area,   2,168 sq ft, Table 16   2,537 sq ft

Roofing, asphalt shingles.   "   "   2,168 "   Table 22   2,537 "
                                                        (25 squares)

APPLICATION OF TABLES AND FORMULAS TO FIGURE 5

Open Porch 12′ × 24′ With Roof Over ....Roof Pitch ¼

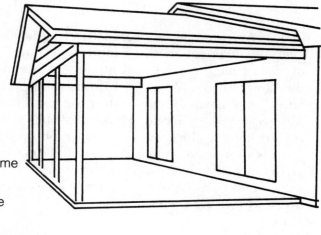

Slab area 12′ × 24′ = 288 sq ft

Perimeter (3 sides)
   12′ + 12′ + 24′ = 48 lin ft

Horizontal area covered by
      the roof including 24″ over-
      hang at eaves and gable:
         14′ × 28′ = 392 sq ft

Construction Details: Concrete slab, frame
roof over.

Concrete footings, 10″ deep × 18″ wide

Foundation on top of footings (3 sides)
      Two courses of 8″ × 8″ × 16″ concrete block

Concrete slab on gravel base. 4″ concrete
                          5″ gravel base

Posts, 4″ × 4″ × 8′

Girder-plate 4″ × 10″

Ceiling beams 2″ × 4″ − 16″ on center

Rafters 2″ × 6″ − 24″ on center

Roof decking ⁵/₈″ plywood

Roofing, asphalt strip shingles

Bevel siding at gable end over insultation board

Finished ceiling, ³/₈″ plywood

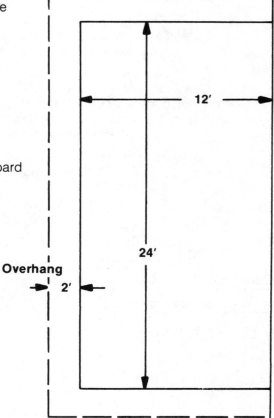

FIGURE 5

<u>Concrete Footings</u>, 10″ deep × 18″ wide, Using formula under Table 1, page 148:

$$d'' \times w'' \times L' \times .000257 = \text{cubic yards}$$
$$10'' \times 18'' \times 48' \times .000257 = 2.22 \text{ cu yds concrete}$$

Concrete Materials, Table 1A, page 151, Using Mix No. 4

For 1 cu yd	For 2.22 cu yds
5 sacks cement	11.1 sacks cement
.56 cu yds sand	1.24 cu yds sand
.74 cu yds stone	1.64 cu yds stone

<u>Foundation Above Footings</u>, 2 courses 8″ × 8″ × 16″ concrete block

From Table 3B, page 169, there is 1.5 block per lin ft

$$1.5 \times 48 = \qquad \qquad 72 \text{ conc. block}$$

Mortar required, Table 3A, page 167, 4 cu ft per 100 block

$$4 \times .72 = \qquad \qquad 2.88 \text{ cu ft}$$

Mortar material:

$$\frac{3}{27} \times 10 \text{ sacks cement} \qquad = 1.11 \text{ sacks cement}$$

$$\frac{3}{27} \times 1 \text{ cu yd sand} \qquad = .11 \text{ cu yds sand}$$

$$\frac{3}{27} \times 2 \text{ sacks hydrated lime} \quad = .22 \text{ sacks hydrated lime}$$

<u>Concrete slab</u>, area 12′ × 24′ = 288 sq ft

Gravel base, 5″ thick, Table 5 (interpolating)	4.46 cu yds
Concrete, 4″ thick, Table 5 ″	3.57 ″ ″

Alternate Method, using formula under Tables 4 and 5

$$A \times t'' \times .0031 = .0031 = \text{cu yds of material}$$
$$288 \times 5'' \times .0031 = 4.46 \text{ cu yds gravel base}$$
$$288 \times 4'' \times .0031 = 3.57 \text{ cu yds concrete}$$

Concrete materials for 3.57 cu yds, Table 1A, Mix No. 4

$$3.57 \times 5 \text{ sacks cement} \quad = 17.85 \text{ sacks of cement}$$
$$3.57 \times .56 \text{ cu yds sand} \quad = 2.0 \text{ cu yds sand}$$
$$3.57 \times .74 \text{ cu yds stone} \quad = 2.6 \text{ ″ ″ stone}$$

<u>Forms</u> for the slab are not included. See page 158-163 for discussion of forms.

Reinforcing is not included. See page 171.

Framing Lumber, FBM using an area of 400 sq ft.

Posts	4-4″ × 4″ × 8′		43 FBM
Girder-plate	48′-4″ × 12″		192 ″
Rafters (pitch ¼)	2″ × 6″-24″ o.c. Table 12		248 ″
Ceiling joists:			

           Use area of slab, 228 sq ft (interpolate)

                    2″ × 4″-16″ o.c. Table 9   158 ″

        (or Table 9A, .55 × 288 = 158)

                                                    _____   641 FBM

        Nails for framing, Table 14B, average per 1,000 FBM

        15 lbs 8d, 10d, 16d, and 20d nails.   .641 × 15 = 9.6 or 10 lbs

Roof Decking, pitch ¼, ⅝″ plywood. Use horizontal area covered by the roof,
            14′ × 28′ rounded out to 400 sq ft

                                  From Table 15   492 sq ft

        Nails for roof decking, Table 30-38E, page 261.

        Average per 1,000 sq ft, 20 lbs 8d nails.   .492 × 20 = 9.84 lbs

Roofing Paper, 15 lb saturated felt, using a horizontal area of 400 sq ft

                                  From Table 24   1.24 rolls

Roof Shingles, 240 lb 3 tab asphalt shingles, Table 24, 492 sq ft or   5 square

        Nails for roofing, average per sq 2 lbs (page 218) 5 × 2 = 10 lbs

Gable End: Area from Table C2 using horizontal or ground floor area of the slab 12′ × 24′ = 288 sq ft and a L:W ratio of 2:1

    Note that Tables C1 and C2, also the formula on page 28 are applicable when the gable is on the narrow side of the building. If the gable is on the long side, the quantities in Tables C1 and C2 must be multiplied by 4 in the case of a L:W ratio of 2:1 and by 9 in the case of a L:W ratio of 3:1. This adjustment will seldom be encountered but should be kept in mind.

    The formula for both gable areas, on page 28, is .125 for a L:W ratio of 2:1.

                288 × .125 = 36 sq ft
                  4 × 36   = 144 sq ft

This is for both gable ends. One gable end area is $\dfrac{144}{2}$ = 72 sq ft

<u>Gable Studs</u>, 2″ × 4″ − 16″ o.c. The FBM of studding per square ft of wall including cutting and fitting, plates etc. is .67 FBM (see page 204).

$$72 \times .67 = 48 \text{ FBM}$$

<u>Insulation sheathing</u>, Table 30-38A $72 \times 1.10 = 79$ sq ft

<u>Bevel siding</u>, 1″ × 10″, 1 ¹/₂″ lap, table

30-38A $72 \times 1.30 = 94$ FBM

<u>Finished ceiling</u>, ³/₈″ plywood.

Table 30-38A $288 \times 1.10 = 317$ sq ft

APPLICATION OF TABLES AND FORMULAS
TO FIGURE 6

An Open Breezeway 10′ × 20′, and Attached Two-Car Garage 24′ × 25′

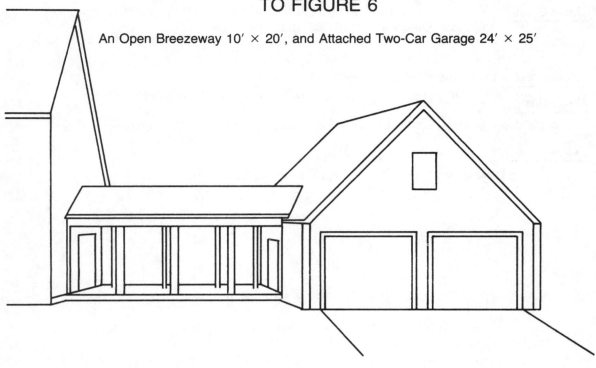

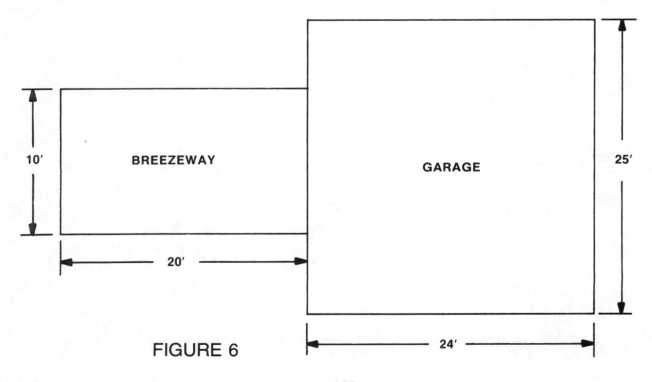

FIGURE 6

BREEZEWAY, 10′ × 20′   1/8 Roof Pitch

Construction: Details: Concrete slab, frame roof over.
Concrete footings, 8″ × 12″ on sandy soil
Foundation on top of footings, (2 sides), two courses concrete block 8″ × 8″ × 16″
Concrete slab on gravel base. Gravel base 5″ thick, slab 4″ thick.
Framing:

4″ × 4″ × 8′ posts	2″ × 4″ ceiling joists
4″ × 10″ girder-plates	2″ × 6″ rafters

Roof decking 5/8″ plywood;
Roofing, 3-tab asphalt shingles
Flush cornice, no overhang

GARAGE 24′ × 25′ (Perimeter 82′)*

Construction Details: Frame on concrete slab, roof pitch 1/4
Concrete footings, 8″ × 18″ on sandy soil
Foundation on top of footings, two courses 8″ × 8″ × 16″ concrete block
Concrete slab 4″ thick on 5″ gravel base
Exterior walls 2″ × 4″ studs, 16″ on center; insulation board and bevel siding
Rafters 2″ × 6″ - 24″ on center
Plywood decking, 5/8″
Roofing paper, 15 lb saturated felt
Roofing, asphalt shingles
Garage doors, 2- 8′ × 7′

BREEZEWAY

Concrete Footings, 8″ × 12″, using the formula under Table 1, page 148:

d″ × w″ × L′ × .000257 = cu yds   8″ × 12″ × 40′ × .000275 = 1 cu yd

Concrete materials, Table 1A, Mix No. 4

5 sacks cement
.56 cu yds sand
.74 ″ ″ stone

Foundation Above Footings, 2 courses of 8″ × 8″ × 16″ concrete block

---

*Note: Garage perimeters exlude the width of the door or doors if there are two. Single garage doors are figured at 8′ wide; double doors are 16′ wide.

From Table 3B, page 169, 1.5 block per lin ft   1.5 × 40 =   60 conc. block

Mortar required, from Table 3A, 4 cu ft mortar per 100 block

$$4 \times .60 = \text{2.4 cu ft}$$

Converting quantities in Table 3A to cu ft

$\dfrac{2.4}{27} \times$ 10 sacks cement   = .90 sacks cement

$\dfrac{2.4}{27} \times$ 1 cu yd sand   = .09 cu yds sand

$\dfrac{2.4}{27} \times$ 2 sacks hydrated lime = .18 sacks hydrated lime

Concrete Slab, 10′ × 20′ = 200 sq ft

Gravel base 5″ thick, Table 5	=	3.10 cu yds
Concrete over, 4″ thick ″ ″	=	2.48 ″ ″

Alternate Method, using formula page 170

A × t″ × .0031 = cu yds of material
Gravel base 200 × 5″ × .0031 = 3.1 cu yds
Concrete over 200 × 4″ × .0031 = 2.48 cu yds

Concrete materials for 2.48 cu yds of concrete, Mix No. 4, Table 1A

2.48 × 5 sacks cement   = 12.4 sacks cement
2.48 × .56 cu yds sand   = 1.39 cu yds sand
2.48 × .74 cu yds stone   = 1.84 ″   ″   stone

Forms are not included, see pages 158-163 for discussion
Reinforcing not included, see page 171.

Framing For Roof, ⅛ pitch, flush cornice, ground-floor area of slab,   200 sq ft

Posts	6-4″ × 4″ × 8″		64 FBM
Girder-plate	2-4″ × 10″ × 20′		133 ″
Ceiling joists	2″ × 4″ - 16″ o.c. Table 9		110 ″
Rafters	2″ × 6″ - 24″ o.c.	12	114 ″
		Total	421 FBM

Nails for framing 421 FBM, Table 14B

Average per 1,000 FBM, 15 lbs of 8d, 10d, 16d, and 20d
.421 × 15 =   6.3 lbs

Roof Decking, ⅝″ plywood, ⅛ pitch Table 15   226 sq ft

Nails for 226 sq ft of plywood, table 30-38D,
Average, 20 lb 8d nails per 1,000 sq ft   .226 × 20 =   4.5 lbs

Roofing Paper, 15 lb saturated felt, Table 21   .57 rolls

Roof Shingles, 240 lb asphalt strip shingles, Table 21   226 sq ft

Nails for shingles, average 2 lbs per square, page 218, 2.26 × 2 =4.5 lbs

<u>Finished Ceiling,</u> 1″ × 6″ tongue and groove boards,   Table 27   242 FBM

Nails for 242 FBM 1″ × 6″ tongue and groove boards

Table 30-38D, 25-30 lbs per 1,000 FBM   30 × .242 =   7.26 lbs

GARAGE

<u>Concrete Footings,</u> 8″ × 18″ on sandy soil, Table 45 (perimeter 82′)   3.03 cu yds

Alternate Method, using formula page 148:

d″ × w″ × L′ × .000257 = cu yds concrete
8″ × 18″ × 82′ × .000257 = 3.03 cu yds

Concrete materials for 3.03 cu yds concrete, Table 1A, page 151

For 1 cu yd	For 3.03 cu yds
5 sacks cement	15.15 sacks cement
.56 cu yds sand	1.70 cu yds sand
.74 ″ ″ stone	2.24 ″ ″ stone

<u>Foundation Above Footings,</u> 2 courses 8″ × 8″ × 16″ concrete block

From Table 3B, page 169, 1.5 block per lin ft,   1.5 × 82′ =   123 conc block

Mortar required, from Table 3A, 4 cu ft per 100 concrete block
4 × 1.23 = 4.92 or 5 cu ft

Mortar material:

$\frac{5}{27}$ × 10 sacks cement   = 1.85 sacks cement

$\frac{5}{27}$ × 1 cu yd sand   = 0.185 cu yds sand

$\frac{5}{27}$ × 2 sacks hydrated lime = 0.37 sacks hydrated lime

<u>Concrete Slab,</u> area 24′ × 25′ = 600 sq ft

Gravel base, 5″ thick,	Table 4		9.30 cu yds
Concrete, 4″ thick,	Table 4		7.44 ″ ″

Alternate method using the formula, page 170

A × t″ × .0031 = cu yds of material
Gravel base 600 × 5″ × .0031 = 9.30 cu yds
Concrete   600 × 4″ × .0031 = 7.44 cu yds

Concrete materials for 7.44 cu yds. Mix No. 4, Table 1A

For 1 cu yd	For 7.44 cu yds
5 sacks cement	7.44 × 5 = 37.2 sacks cement
.56 cu yds sand	7.44 × .56 = 4.17 cu yds sand
.74 " " stone	7.44 × .74 = 5.51 cu yds stone

Forms for concrete are not included. See page 158-163 for discussion of forms. Reinforcing is not included. See page 171.

Framing

Sill, plate and door header,	Table 46,	221 FBM
Studding for exterior wall, 2″ × 4″ - 16″ o.c.		537 "
Ceiling joists, 2″ × 4″ - 24″ o.c.		210 "
Rafters, 2″ × 6″ - 24″ o.c.	" 54	372 "
	Total	1,340 FBM

Nails for 1,340 FBM of framing

From Table 14B, average per 1,000 FBM, 15 lbs 8d, 10d, 16d, 20d

1.340 × 15 =   20 lbs

Roof Decking, 5/8″ plywood, Table 59,   738 sq ft

Nails for decking, Table 30-38D, average per 1,000 sq ft 20 lbs 8d

.738 × 20 =   14.76 lbs

Roofing Paper, 15 lb saturated felt, Table 62   1.85 rolls

Roof Shingles, 240 lb 3-tab asphalt shingles, Table 62   738 sq ft or   7.38 sqs

Nails for shingles, average per sq (page 218) 2 lbs, 7.38 × 2   14.76 lbs

Exterior Sidewalls Including Gables

3/4″ Insulation board sheathing   Table 47   887 sq ft

Nails, Table 30-38D, 20 lbs per 1,000 sq ft

.887 × 20 =   17.74 lbs

Bevel siding, 1″ × 10″, 1 1/2″ lap   Table 47   1,048 FBM

Nails, Table 30-38D, 20 lbs per 1,000 FBM

1.048 × 20 =   21 lbs

Typical One- and Two-Car Attached and Detached Garages

Photographs of six one-car and two-car attached and detached garages follow. See page 276 for details on using Tables 45-67 which apply to one- and two-car garages.

Detached one-car brick garage with hip roof

Detached frame two-car garage with single
door. Slab floor, gable roof

Detached two-door frame garage with loft over.
Dirt floor, gable roof

130

Detached two-car frame garage. Slab floor, single overhead door, gable roof

131

Attached two-car carport with slab floor, gable roof and storage area in rear

132

Detached two-car frame garage with double door and gable roof

Application of Tables and Formulas
To Small Commercial Buildings

Tables 1 through 45 in which quantities are related to the *ground-floor* area of the building may be used for areas up to 3,000 square feet and only when the specifications conform to those prescribed for the particular Table. Otherwise the simple formulas are recommended. For example, a one-story commercial building 36′ wide and 72′ long, occupied as a public garage or warehouse, has a *ground-floor* area of 36′ × 72′ = 2,592 square feet. It would be in order to use the Tables, using 2,600 sq ft, to estimate *footings, foundations, exterior walls* (adjusting for wall height), *joisted floor* or *concrete slab, rafters, roof decking* and *roofing*. Where it is more convenient the formulas should be used.

On pages 138-146 are shown several pictures of typical, small commercial-type buildings to which the Tables and formulas apply.

Footings

The formula $(d'' \times w'') \times L' \times .000257 = $ cu yds (page 148), will apply to any structure. Tables 1A and 1B for concrete materials per cubic yard may also be used.

Concrete Foundation Walls

The formula $t'' \times h' \times .0031 \times L' = $ cu yds (page 154), applies to any structure for computing the cubic yards of concrete in walls.

Table 2A may also be used to determine the cubic yards of concrete in any wall. For heights greater than 12′ use multiples of the quantities shown in the Table. For example, a wall 15 feet high will have three times the cubic yards of concrete shown for a wall 5 feet high. Window and door openings would be deducted as explained on page 154.

Tables 1A and 1B are for estimating concrete materials per cubic yard of concrete.

Concrete Block Foundation Walls

The formula $L' \times h' \times 1.125 =$ number of $8'' \times 16''$ concrete block, applies to any structure. Table 3B may be used also. When the wall is higher than 10 feet, use multiples of the number of block per lineal foot in the Table. For example, if a wall is 16-feet high use twice the factor shown for a wall 8-feet high.

Deduct window and door openings as discussed on page 165.

Mortar and mortar materials for laying concrete block are provided in Table 3A.

Concrete Floors on Gravel Base

For concrete floors, patios, sidewalks and driveways Tables 4 and 5 may be used for areas up to 3,000 square feet. For larger areas use the simple formula (page 170), $A \times t'' \times .0031 =$ cubic yards of gravel base or concrete.

Concrete materials can be estimated from Tables 1A and 1B.

Forms for Concrete

Refer to Table 2B and the discussion on forms pages 158-163.

Exterior Wall Framing

Tables 6, 7 and 8 may be used for exterior walls 9-, 15-and 18-feet high respectively up to 3,000 square feet *ground-floor* area. Adjustments will need to be made for other wall heights and for a L:W ratio other than 2:1 (see Tables A and B)

An easier method is to use Table 6-8A or Table 14A to estimate the FBM of exterior wall framing. Table 14B shows the nails required for framing.

Deduct openings required.

Floor and Ceiling Joists

Table 9 should be used for areas up to 3,000 square feet. For larger floor areas use Table 9A. Nail quantities are shown in Table 14B.

Rafters

Tables 11 and 12 may be used for areas up to 3,000 square feet, otherwise use the formula in Table 11-12A. Nail quantities are shown in Table 14B.

Prefab W—Trusses

The FBM of truss framing is obtained by multiplying the appropriate factor in Table 13A by the horizontal area covered under the truss roof. Gussets, metal connectors and nails should be added.

Roof Decking

Tables 15 through 20 should be used for *ground-floor* areas up to 3,000 square feet adding any overhang.

For larger *ground-floor* areas use Table 15-20B to compute the *surface* area of the roof and Table 15-20A to obtain the quantity of the specified decking.

Nail requirements are shown on page 261.

Roofing

Tables 21 through 26 should be used for *ground-floor* areas up to 3,000 square feet, adding any overhang.

For larger *ground-floor* areas use Table 21B to compute the surface area of the roof. Use Table 21A to compute the quantity of the specified roofing.

Nail requirements are shown on page 218.

Interior Surface Materials

These materials include, but are not limited to, drywall, lath and plaster, paneling, cement plaster on masonry, painting, rough and finished flooring.

Vertical side wall areas are obtained by multiplying the perimeter by the height. *Partition wall areas* are obtained by multiplying the lineal feet of a partition by its height and doubling that if both sides are being estimated. Deductions for window and door openings are at the custom and practice of the estimator. (See page 227.)

Floor and ceiling areas are obtained by computing the number of square feet involved.

If walls and ceiling are to be finished in *drywall*, materials may be estimated from page 233, adding any trim accessories such as corner reinforcements, casing beads, and decorating moldings. If walls and ceilings are finished in *lath and plaster*, Table 27-29C shows the quantity of materials. If *Cement-plaster* is the wall finish Table 30-38D shows quantities on masonry base or wire lath.

Subflooring is estimated by computing the area to be covered and multiplying by the amount of milling and cutting waste, Table 30-38A, for the specified material. Nail requirements are shown in Table 30-38E.

Finish floors are also estimated by multiplying the area to be covered by the amount of milling and cutting waste shown on page 228. Nails for finish flooring are shown in Table 27-29A.

Painting materials and methods of estimating are discussed on pages 238 to 243 using Table 27-29E for quantities.

Exterior Sidewall Materials

These materials include, but are not limited to, various types of sheathing, bevel and drop siding, 4″, 8″ and 12″ brick, concrete block, stucco (cement plaster) and painting.

The exterior square foot surface area is computed by multiplying the perimeter by the wall height.

Specified materials are then estimated by multiplying the surface area by the applicable waste shown in Table 30-38A

Mortar for masonry is shown in Table 30-38C. Stucco and cement plaster are shown in Table 30-38D. Nail requirements are shown in Table 30-38E. Painting (same as above, Interior Surface Materials).

Insulation

Wall and ceiling insulation can be estimated from Table 39A.

Estimating Labor and Material

The discussion on Estimating Labor and Material, pages 50-66, and the 25 labor Tables (pages 67-80), apply to these commercial buildings as well as dwellings.

TYPICAL ONE- AND TWO-STORY COMMERCIAL TYPE BUILDINGS

Two-story and basement stores with loft over. Concrete block foundation, 12″ and 8″ exterior walls, frame floors and roof

Two-story and basement stores with loft over. Brick foundation, 12" and 8" exterior walls. Frame floors and roof structure.

One-story with partial basement. 12″ and 8″ concrete block walls, framed gable roof with storage area attic and basement.

140

Two-story brick. Concrete slab first floor,
frame second floor and roof structure

141

One-story on slab with concrete block
walls and shed roof

142

One-story brick veneer on slab. Hip roof

143

One story on slab, trussed gable roof, brick front, sides and rear walls 12' concrete block

144

One-story Long John Silver's seafood shop under construction. Slab floor, part gable, part flat, roof

145

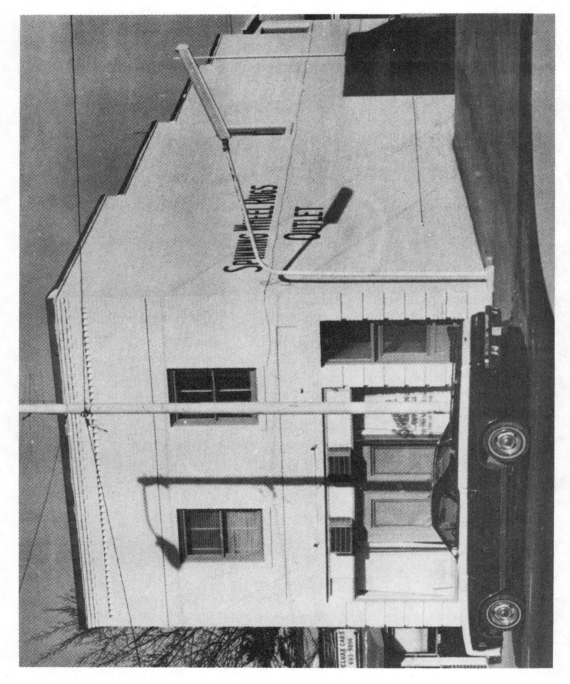

Two-story and basement. Loft over store, 12" brick foundation and first floor, 8" brick second. Flat roof, concrete slab basement; first, second floors and roof framed

146

TABLE 1

Concrete Footings

This Table shows the cubic yards of concrete for footings of various sizes for all dwellings that have ground-floor areas of 200 to 3,000 square feet.

HOW TO USE THIS TABLE

1. Determine the *ground-floor* area of your dwelling following the method outlined under Computation of Areas in the General Instructions, page 17.

2. Determine the perimeter of your dwelling following the method outlined under Perimeter Measurement in the General Instructions, page 18.

3. Using Table A, check the *ground-floor* area and the lineal feet of perimeter to obtain the length-to-width ratio of your dwelling.

4. This Table is based on dwellings with a length-to-width ratio of two to one (2:1). If the length-to-width ratio of your dwelling is significantly different adjust the quantity in the Table upward or downward by the percentages under Table A, page 25.

Illustrative Example

A dwelling 90′ long and 30′ wide has a L:W ratio of 3:1 and a *ground floor* area of 2,700 square feet. Table 1 shows that when the *ground-floor* area is 2,700 it will require 10.9 cu yds of concrete for a footing 8″ deep and 24″ wide. This is based on a L:W ratio of 2:1. For a L:W ratio of 3:1 page 22 shows an adjustment of 9% more, or 10.9 × 1.09 = 11.88 cu yds.

BASIC FORMULA FOR FOOTINGS

A short method for estimating the cubic yards of concrete in any footing is to multiply its cross-section *in square inches* by .000257. This gives the cu yds per lineal foot. Multiply that result by the number of lineal feet of footing.

Illustrative Example

A footing 7″ deep and 22″ wide is 160′ long. Determine the cu yds of concrete required.

Where:

d = depth in inches
w = width in inches
L = lineal feet of footing

$(d″ \times w″) \times L′ \times .000257$ = cu yds of concrete
$(7″ \times 22″) \times 160′ \times .000257$ = 6.33 cu yds of concrete

Note: The material for any forms must be added to the estimate. The shape and use of forms vary as does the material. See Forms For Concrete, page 160. Also, any reinforcing specified must be added.

TABLE 1—CONCRETE FOOTINGS 149

TABLE 1

CONCRETE FOOTINGS FOR ALL DWELLINGS

| Ground Floor Area | CUBIC YARDS OF CONCRETE NEEDED FOR SIZE OF FOOTING SHOWN | | | | | | | | | |
| | 6 Inches Deep By: | | | | | 8 Inches Deep By: | | | | |
	12"	16"	18"	20"	24"	12"	16"	18"	20"	24"
200	1.11	1.48	1.67	1.85	2.22	1.48	1.97	2.22	2.47	2.96
300	1.37	1.83	2.06	2.28	2.74	1.83	2.44	2.74	3.04	3.65
400	1.57	2.10	2.36	2.62	3.15	2.10	2.80	3.15	3.49	4.19
500	1.76	2.35	2.64	2.93	3.52	2.35	3.13	3.52	3.90	4.68
600	1.92	2.57	2.89	3.20	3.85	2.57	3.43	3.85	4.27	5.13
700	2.07	2.77	3.11	3.45	4.14	2.77	3.69	4.14	4.60	5.52
800	2.22	2.96	3.34	3.70	4.44	2.96	3.96	4.44	4.93	5.92
900	2.35	3.14	3.53	3.91	4.70	3.14	4.19	4.70	5.22	6.26
1000	2.48	3.31	3.73	4.13	4.96	3.31	4.42	4.96	5.51	6.61
1100	2.61	3.48	3.92	4.34	5.22	3.48	4.65	5.22	5.80	6.95
1200	2.72	3.63	4.09	4.53	5.44	3.63	4.85	5.44	6.04	7.25
1300	2.83	3.78	4.25	4.71	5.66	3.78	5.05	5.66	6.29	7.54
1400	2.94	3.93	4.42	4.90	5.88	3.93	5.25	5.88	6.53	7.84
1500	3.03	4.05	4.56	5.05	6.07	4.05	5.41	6.08	6.74	8.09
1600	3.15	4.20	4.73	5.24	6.29	4.20	5.61	6.29	6.99	8.38
1700	3.24	4.32	4.87	5.39	6.48	4.32	5.77	6.48	7.19	8.63
1800	3.33	4.45	5.00	5.54	6.66	4.45	5.94	6.66	7.40	8.87
1900	3.42	4.57	5.14	5.70	6.85	4.57	6.10	6.85	7.60	9.12
2000	3.52	4.69	5.28	5.85	7.03	4.69	6.27	7.03	7.81	9.37
2100	3.59	4.79	5.39	5.98	7.18	4.79	6.40	7.18	7.97	9.56
2200	3.68	4.92	5.53	6.13	7.36	4.92	6.57	7.36	8.18	9.81
2300	3.76	5.01	5.64	6.25	7.51	5.01	6.70	7.51	8.34	10.01
2400	3.85	5.14	5.78	6.41	7.70	5.14	6.86	7.70	8.55	10.25
2500	3.92	5.24	5.89	6.53	7.84	5.24	6.99	7.84	8.71	10.45
2600	4.00	5.34	6.00	6.65	7.99	5.34	7.13	7.99	8.88	10.65
2700	4.07	5.43	6.12	6.78	8.14	5.43	7.26	8.14	9.04	10.85
2800	4.14	5.53	6.23	6.90	8.29	5.53	7.39	8.29	9.21	11.04
2900	4.22	5.63	6.34	7.02	8.44	5.63	7.52	8.44	9.37	11.24
3000	4.31	5.76	6.48	7.18	8.62	5.76	7.69	8.62	9.58	11.49

TABLE 1
(Continued)

CONCRETE FOOTINGS FOR ALL DWELLINGS

Ground Floor Area	CUBIC YARDS OF CONCRETE NEEDED FOR SIZE OF FOOTING SHOWN									
	10 Inches Deep By:					12 Inches Deep By:				
	12″	16″	18″	20″	24″	12″	16″	18″	20″	24″
200	1.85	2.47	2.78	3.08	3.70	2.22	2.96	3.33	3.70	4.44
300	2.28	3.04	3.43	3.80	4.57	2.74	3.65	4.11	4.57	5.48
400	2.62	3.49	3.94	4.37	5.24	3.15	4.19	4.72	5.24	6.29
500	2.93	3.90	4.40	4.88	5.86	3.52	4.68	5.27	5.86	7.03
600	3.20	4.27	4.82	5.35	6.42	3.85	5.13	5.77	6.42	7.70
700	3.45	4.60	5.19	5.76	6.91	4.14	5.52	6.22	6.91	8.29
800	3.70	4.93	5.56	6.17	7.40	4.44	5.92	6.66	7.40	8.88
900	3.91	5.22	5.88	6.53	7.84	4.70	6.26	7.05	7.84	9.40
1000	4.13	5.51	6.20	6.89	8.27	4.96	6.61	7.44	8.27	9.92
1100	4.34	5.80	6.53	7.25	8.70	5.22	6.95	7.83	8.70	10.43
1200	4.53	6.04	6.81	7.56	9.07	5.44	7.25	8.16	9.07	10.89
1300	4.71	6.29	7.08	7.86	9.44	5.66	7.54	8.49	9.44	11.32
1400	4.90	6.53	7.36	8.17	9.81	5.88	7.84	8.82	9.81	11.77
1500	5.05	6.74	7.59	8.43	10.12	6.08	8.09	9.10	10.12	12.14
1600	5.24	6.99	7.87	8.74	10.49	6.29	8.38	9.44	10.49	12.58
1700	5.39	7.19	8.10	9.00	10.80	6.48	8.63	9.71	10.80	12.95
1800	5.54	7.40	8.33	9.25	11.11	6.66	8.87	9.99	11.11	13.32
1900	5.70	7.60	8.57	9.51	11.41	6.85	9.12	10.27	11.41	13.69
2000	5.85	7.81	8.80	9.77	11.72	7.03	9.37	10.55	11.72	14.06
2100	5.98	7.97	8.98	9.97	11.97	7.18	9.56	10.77	11.97	14.36
2200	6.13	8.18	9.21	10.23	12.28	7.36	9.81	11.04	12.28	14.73
2300	6.25	8.34	9.40	10.43	12.53	7.51	10.01	11.27	12.53	15.02
2400	6.41	8.55	9.63	10.69	12.83	7.70	10.25	11.54	12.83	15.39
2500	6.53	8.71	9.82	10.90	13.08	7.84	10.45	11.77	13.08	15.69
2600	6.65	8.88	10.00	11.10	13.33	7.99	10.65	11.99	13.33	15.98
2700	6.78	9.04	10.19	11.31	13.57	8.14	10.85	12.21	13.57	16.28
2800	6.90	9.21	10.37	11.51	13.82	8.29	11.04	12.43	13.82	16.58
2900	7.02	9.37	10.56	11.72	14.07	8.44	11.24	12.65	14.07	16.87
3000	7.18	9.58	10.79	11.98	14.38	8.62	11.49	12.93	14.38	17.24

TABLE 1—CONCRETE FOOTINGS   151

TABLE 1A

QUANTITIES OF CEMENT, SAND AND STONE REQUIRED
FOR 1 CUBIC YARD CONCRETE

Materials Per Cu Yd of Concrete					
No. *	Mix	Sacks of Cement	Cu Yds Sand	Cu Yds Stone	Max. Size Aggregate
1	1:1:1 $3/4$	10	.37	.63	$3/8''$
2	1:2:2 $1/4$	7 $3/4$	.56	.65	$3/4''$
3	1:2 $1/4$:3	6 $1/4$	.52	.70	$1''$
4	1:3:4	5	.56	.74	1 $1/2''$

* Mix No. 1 . . . Concrete for heavy wearing surface

Mix No. 2 . . . Concrete exposed to weak acid or alkali solutions

Mix No. 3 . . . Concrete for watertight floors, foundations, swimming pools, septic tanks and for structural reinforced concrete, beams, slabs, residence floors, etc.

Mix No. 4 . . . Concrete for foundations and walls not subjected to weather or water pressure.

A mix of 1:3:4 means the proportions are:

> 1 cu ft cement
> 3 cu ft sand
> 4 cu ft stone

In terms of a cu yd of concrete, using Mix No. 4 above, the materials required would be: (A sack of cement contains 1 cu ft.)

> 5 Sacks of cement (5 cu ft)
> 15 cu ft sand (.56 cu yds)
> 20 cu ft stone (.74 cu yds)

While the total cu ft is 40, when mixed together into a solid mass it is 1 cu yd of concrete, which is 27 cu ft.

TABLE 1B

QUANTITIES OF CEMENT, SAND AND STONE FOR ONE CUBIC YARD OF VARIOUS CONCRETE MIXES

Cu Yds Concrete	MIX 1 1:1:1 ¾ AGGREGATE			MIX 2 1:2:2 ¼ AGGREGATE			MIX 3 1:2.25:3 AGGREGATE			MIX 4 1:3:4 AGGREGATE		
	Sacks Cement	Yards Sand	Yards Stone	Sacks Cement	Yards Sand	Yards Stone	Sacks Cement	Yards Sand	Yards Stone	Sacks Cement	Yards Sand	Yards Stone
1	10	.37	.63	7.75	.56	.65	6.25	.52	.70	5.0	.56	.74
2	20	.74	1.26	15.50	1.12	1.30	12.50	1.04	1.40	10.0	1.12	1.48
3	30	1.11	1.89	23.25	1.68	1.95	18.75	1.56	2.10	15.0	1.68	2.22
4	40	1.48	2.52	31.00	2.24	2.60	25.00	2.08	2.80	20.0	2.24	2.96
5	50	1.85	3.15	38.75	2.80	3.25	31.25	2.60	3.50	25.0	2.80	3.70
6	60	2.22	3.78	46.50	3.36	3.90	37.50	3.12	4.20	30.0	3.36	4.44
7	70	2.59	4.41	54.25	3.92	4.55	43.75	3.64	4.90	35.0	3.92	5.18
8	80	2.96	5.04	62.00	4.48	5.20	50.00	4.16	5.60	40.0	4.48	5.92
9	90	3.33	5.67	69.75	5.04	5.85	56.25	4.68	6.30	45.0	5.04	6.66
10	100	3.70	6.30	77.50	5.60	6.50	62.50	5.20	7.00	50.0	5.60	7.40
11	110	4.07	6.93	85.25	6.16	7.15	68.75	5.72	7.70	55.0	6.16	8.14
12	120	4.44	7.56	93.00	6.72	7.80	75.00	6.24	8.40	60.0	6.72	8.88
13	130	4.82	8.20	100.76	7.28	8.46	81.26	6.76	9.10	65.0	7.28	9.62
14	140	5.18	8.82	108.50	7.84	9.10	87.50	7.28	9.80	70.0	7.84	10.36
15	150	5.56	9.46	116.26	8.40	9.76	93.76	7.80	10.50	75.0	8.40	11.10
16	160	5.92	10.08	124.00	8.96	10.40	100.00	8.32	11.20	80.0	8.96	11.84
17	170	6.30	10.72	131.76	9.52	11.06	106.26	8.84	11.90	85.0	9.52	12.58
18	180	6.66	11.34	139.50	10.08	11.70	112.50	9.36	12.60	90.0	10.08	13.32
19	190	7.04	11.98	147.26	10.64	12.36	118.76	9.84	13.30	95.0	10.64	14.06
20	200	7.40	12.60	155.00	11.20	13.00	125.00	10.40	14.00	100.0	11.20	14.80
21	210	7.77	13.23	162.75	11.76	13.65	131.25	10.92	14.70	105.0	11.76	15.54
22	220	8.14	13.86	170.05	12.32	14.30	137.50	11.44	15.40	110.0	12.32	16.28
23	230	8.51	14.49	178.25	12.88	14.95	143.75	11.96	16.10	115.0	12.88	17.02
24	240	8.88	15.12	186.00	13.44	15.60	150.00	12.48	16.80	120.0	13.44	17.76
25	250	9.25	15.75	193.75	14.00	16.25	156.25	13.00	17.50	125.0	14.00	18.50
26	260	9.64	16.40	201.52	14.56	16.92	162.52	13.52	18.20	130.0	14.56	19.24
27	270	10.00	17.00	209.26	15.12	17.56	168.76	14.04	18.90	135.0	15.02	20.00
28	280	10.36	17.64	217.00	15.68	18.20	175.00	14.56	19.60	140.0	15.68	20.72
29	290	10.74	18.28	224.76	16.24	18.86	181.26	15.08	20.30	145.0	16.24	21.46

TABLE 2

Foundation Walls . . . Concrete

Table 2 shows the cu yds of concrete in foundation walls above the footings. It includes wall thicknesses of 8″, 9″, 10″, and 12″. It includes wall heights 1′, 2′, 4′, 6′ and 8′. Other wall height (3′, 5′, 10′ etc) are multiples of these.

HOW TO USE THIS TABLE

1. Determine the *ground-floor* area of your dwelling following the method outlined under Computation of Areas in the General Instructions, page 17.

2. Determine the perimeter of your dwelling following the method outlined under Perimeter Measurement in the General Instructions, page 18.

3. Using Table A check the *ground-floor* area and the lineal feet of perimeter to obtain the length-to-width ratio of your dwelling.

4. This Table is based on dwellings with a length-to-width ratio of two to one (2:1). If the length-to-width ratio of your dwelling is significantly different, adjust the quantity in the Table upward or downward by the percentages shown under Table A, page 22.

Illustrative Example

A dwelling 40′ long and 40′ wide has a L:W ratio of 1:1 and a *ground floor* area of 1,600 sq ft. Table 2 shows that a foundation wall 10″ thick and 7′ high requires 42.16 cu yds of concrete. This quantity is based on dwellings with a L:W ratio of 2:1. Table A shows that the Table quantity should be reduced 5% for a L:W ratio of 1:1 or 42.16 × .95 = 40.05 cu yds.

153

BASIC FORMULA FOR FOUNDATION WALLS

A short method for estimating the cu yds of concrete in any foundation wall is to multiply the *thickness in inches* by the *height in feet*. Multiply that result by .0031. This will give the cu yds per lineal foot.

Illustrative Example

A foundation wall is 10″ thick, 7′ high and 160′ long. Determine the cu yds of concrete required.

Where:

$\quad$ t = thickness in inches
$\quad$ h = height in feet
$\quad$ L = lineal feet of wall
$\qquad$ t″ × h′ × .0031 × L′ = cu yds of concrete in wall
$\qquad$ (10″ × 7′) × .0031 × 160′ = 34.72 cu yds of concrete

Note: The material for any forms must be added to the estimate. The shape and use of forms vary as does the material. Also, any reinforcing specified must be added. See pages 158-163.

Window and Door Openings

No deduction is made in the Table for window or door openings. The size and number vary. If a garage door, side door or windows are in the foundation wall, use the following formula to estimate the cu yds of concrete to be deducted.

Where:

$\quad$ A = total sq ft area of openings
$\quad$ t = thickness of foundation wall *in inches*
$\quad$ A × t″ × .0031 = cu yds of concrete to be deducted

Quantity of Materials Required for a Cu Yd of Concrete

The materials needed for one cu yd of concrete of various mixes is shown in Table 1A, page 151.

TABLE 2—FOUNDATION WALLS...CONCRETE 155

TABLE 2

CONCRETE FOUNDATION WALLS ABOVE FOOTINGS
(NO DEDUCTION HAS BEEN MADE FOR OPENINGS)
Interpolate for intermediate heights of wall

Ground Floor Area	CUBIC YARDS OF CONCRETE NEEDED FOR SIZE FOUNDATION WALL SHOWN									
	8 Inch Wall By Height Of:					9 Inch Wall By Height Of:				
	1'	2'	4'	6'	8'	1'	2'	4'	6'	8'
200	1.49	2.98	5.95	8.93	11.90	1.67	3.25	6.70	10.04	13.39
300	1.83	3.67	7.34	11.01	14.68	2.06	4.13	8.26	12.39	16.52
400	2.11	4.22	8.43	12.65	16.86	2.37	4.74	9.49	14.23	18.97
500	2.36	4.72	9.42	14.14	18.85	2.65	5.30	10.60	15.90	21.20
600	2.58	5.16	10.32	15.48	20.63	2.90	5.80	11.61	17.41	23.21
700	2.78	5.56	11.11	16.67	22.22	3.13	6.25	12.50	18.75	25.00
800	2.97	5.95	11.90	17.86	23.81	3.35	6.70	13.39	20.09	26.78
900	3.15	6.30	12.60	18.90	25.20	3.54	7.09	14.17	21.26	28.35
1000	3.33	6.65	13.29	19.94	26.59	3.74	7.48	14.95	22.43	29.91
1100	3.50	6.99	13.99	20.98	27.97	3.93	7.87	15.74	23.60	31.47
1200	3.64	7.29	14.58	21.87	29.16	4.10	8.20	16.41	24.61	32.81
1300	3.79	7.59	15.18	22.77	30.36	4.27	8.54	17.07	25.61	34.15
1400	3.95	7.89	15.77	23.66	31.55	4.44	8.87	17.74	26.62	35.49
1500	4.06	8.13	16.27	24.40	32.54	4.56	9.15	18.30	27.45	36.60
1600	4.22	8.43	16.86	25.30	33.73	4.75	9.49	18.97	28.46	37.94
1700	4.34	8.68	17.39	26.04	34.72	4.89	9.77	19.53	29.30	39.06
1800	4.47	8.93	17.86	26.78	35.71	5.02	10.04	20.09	30.13	40.18
1900	4.59	9.18	18.35	27.53	36.70	5.16	10.32	20.65	30.97	41.29
2000	4.71	9.42	18.85	28.27	37.70	5.30	10.60	21.20	31.81	42.41
2100	4.81	9.62	19.24	28.87	38.49	5.42	10.83	21.65	32.48	43.30
2200	4.93	9.87	19.74	29.61	39.48	5.55	11.10	22.21	33.31	44.42
2300	5.03	10.07	20.14	30.21	40.28	5.67	11.33	22.65	33.98	45.31
2400	5.16	10.32	20.63	30.95	41.27	5.81	11.61	23.21	34.82	46.43
2500	5.26	10.52	21.03	31.55	42.06	5.92	11.83	23.66	35.49	47.32
2600	5.35	10.71	21.43	32.14	42.85	6.02	12.05	24.11	36.16	48.21
2700	5.45	10.91	21.82	32.74	43.65	6.14	12.28	24.55	36.83	49.10
2800	5.56	11.11	22.22	33.33	44.44	6.25	12.50	25.00	37.50	50.00
2900	5.66	11.31	22.62	33.93	45.24	6.36	12.72	25.44	38.17	50.89
3000	5.78	11.56	23.11	34.67	46.23	6.50	13.00	26.00	39.00	52.00

TABLE 2
(Continued)

CONCRETE FOUNDATION WALLS ABOVE FOOTINGS
(NO DEDUCTION HAS BEEN MADE FOR OPENINGS)
Interpolate for intermediate heights of wall

Ground Floor Area	CUBIC YARDS OF CONCRETE NEEDED FOR SIZE FOUNDATION WALL SHOWN									
	10 Inch Wall By Height Of:					12 Inch Wall By Height Of:				
	1'	2'	4'	6'	8'	1'	2'	4'	6'	8'
200	1.86	3.72	7.44	11.16	14.88	2.23	4.46	8.93	13.39	17.86
300	2.30	4.59	9.18	13.76	18.35	2.75	5.51	11.01	16.52	22.08
400	2.63	5.27	10.54	15.81	21.08	3.16	6.32	12.65	18.97	25.30
500	2.94	5.89	11.78	17.67	23.56	3.53	7.07	14.14	21.20	28.27
600	3.23	6.45	12.90	19.34	25.79	3.87	7.74	15.48	23.21	30.95
700	3.47	6.94	13.89	20.83	27.78	4.16	8.33	16.67	25.00	33.33
800	3.72	7.44	14.88	22.32	29.76	4.46	8.93	17.86	26.78	35.71
900	3.93	7.87	15.75	23.62	31.50	4.73	9.45	18.90	28.35	37.80
1000	4.15	8.31	16.62	24.92	33.23	4.99	9.97	19.94	29.91	39.88
1100	4.37	8.74	17.48	26.23	34.97	5.25	10.49	20.98	31.47	41.96
1200	4.56	9.11	18.23	27.34	36.46	5.47	10.94	21.87	32.81	43.75
1300	4.74	9.49	18.97	28.46	37.94	5.69	11.38	22.77	34.15	45.53
1400	4.93	9.86	19.72	29.57	39.43	5.92	11.83	23.66	35.49	47.32
1500	5.09	10.17	20.34	30.50	40.67	6.10	12.20	24.40	36.60	48.81
1600	5.27	10.54	21.08	31.62	42.16	6.33	12.65	25.30	37.94	50.59
1700	5.43	10.85	21.70	32.55	43.40	6.51	13.02	26.04	39.06	52.08
1800	5.53	11.16	22.32	33.48	44.64	6.70	13.39	26.78	40.18	53.57
1900	5.70	11.47	22.94	34.41	45.88	6.88	13.76	27.53	41.29	55.06
2000	5.89	11.78	23.56	35.34	47.12	7.07	14.14	28.27	42.41	56.54
2100	6.01	12.03	24.06	36.08	48.11	7.22	14.43	28.87	43.30	57.73
2200	6.17	12.34	24.68	37.01	49.35	7.40	14.81	29.61	44.42	59.22
2300	6.30	12.59	25.17	37.76	50.34	7.55	15.10	30.21	45.31	60.41
2400	6.45	12.90	25.79	38.69	51.58	7.74	15.48	30.95	46.43	61.90
2500	6.57	13.14	26.29	39.43	52.58	7.89	15.77	31.55	47.32	63.09
2600	6.70	13.39	26.78	40.18	53.57	8.04	16.07	32.14	48.21	64.28
2700	6.82	13.64	27.28	40.92	54.56	8.19	16.37	32.74	49.10	65.47
2800	6.95	13.89	27.78	41.66	55.55	8.33	16.67	33.33	50.00	66.66
2900	7.07	14.14	28.27	42.41	56.54	8.48	16.96	33.93	50.89	67.85
3000	7.22	14.45	28.89	43.34	57.78	8.67	17.34	34.67	52.00	69.34

TABLE 2A

Cubic Yards of Concrete Per Lineal Foot
of Foundation Wall

When the thickness and height of a concrete wall are known, Table 2A provides factors that represent the cubic yards of concrete per lineal foot. Some estimators may prefer this method to either Table 2 or to using the basic formula.

To illustrate the application of all three methods, assume a dwelling 30′ × 60′ has an 8′ concrete foundation wall 10″ thick. The *ground-floor* area is 1800 sq ft and the wall is equal to the perimeter, 180 feet.

Method I

Table 2 shows that for a dwelling with a *ground-floor* area of 1800 sq ft, a foundation wall 8′ high and 10″ thick contains 44.64 cu yds of concrete.

Method II

Using the basic formula, $t'' × h' × .0031 × L'$:

$$10'' × 8' × .0031 × 180' = 44.64 \text{ cu yds}$$

Method III

Table 2A shows that a wall 8′ high and 10″ thick contains .2480 cu yds per lineal foot. The wall is 180′ long.

$$180'' × .2480 = 44.64 \text{ cu yds}$$

The advantage of using Methods II or III is that Table 2 is based on a length-to-width ratio of 2:1. When the length-to-width ratio of a dwelling is other than 2:1, an adjustment to quantities in Table 2 is required.

157

TABLE 2A

CUBIC YARDS OF CONCRETE PER LINEAL FOOT OF
FOUNDATION WALL

Wall Height In Feet	Thickness of Wall in Inches						
	6″	7″	8″	9″	10″	11″	12″
1	.0185	.0217	.0248	.0279	.0310	.0341	.0372
2	.0360	.0434	.0496	.0558	.0620	.0682	.0744
3	.0556	.0651	.0744	.0837	.0930	.1023	.1116
4	.0741	.0868	.0992	.1116	.1240	.1364	.1488
5	.0926	.1085	.1240	.1395	.1550	.1705	.1860
6	.1111	.1302	.1488	.1674	.1860	.2046	.2232
7	.1296	.1519	.1736	.1953	.2170	.2387	.2606
8	.1482	.1736	.1984	.2232	.2480	.2728	.2976
9	.1667	.1953	.2232	.2511	.2790	.3069	.3348
10	.1852	.2170	.2480	.2790	.3100	.3410	.3720
11	.2046	.2387	.2728	.3069	.3410	.3751	.4092
12	.2232	.2604	.2976	.3348	.3720	.4092	.4464

For intermediate wall heights and thicknesses, interpolate between factors in the Table above.

To obtain the number of cubic feet of concrete, multiply the factors above by 27, or multiply the cubic yards determined by 27.

Window and door openings may be deducted by using the formula shown on page 154.

FORMS

The unit of measurement of forms should be the actual square feet of concrete *in contact with the forms*. A foundation wall 20 feet long, 8 feet high and 12 inches thick would require 8′ × 20′ = 160 square feet of forms for each side or a total of 320 square feet excluding the ends. Wood forms are conventionally constructed of 2 by 4-inch studs and sheathing or plywood with necessary bracing. The

TABLE 2—FOUNDATION WALLS...CONCRETE 159

studding is spaced from 12 inches to 24 inches on center depending on the height of the form. Where the wall height is 3 or 4 feet, spacing of 24 inches is adequate. For higher walls the studs are placed closer together to withstand the outward pressure exerted by the plastic mass of wet concrete.

ESTIMATING MATERIALS AND LABOR

For average estimating purposes the quantity of lumber (studding, sheathing and bracing) required *per square foot of concrete surface* is between 2 1/2 to 3 board feet. Using this basis, the board feet of lumber needed for the forms for a wall 8 feet high and 20 feet long, assuming 2 1/2 FBM per square foot of surface, would be:

$$2(8' \times 20') = \begin{array}{ll} 320 & \text{sq ft} \\ \times\ 2\frac{1}{2} & \text{FBM} \\ \hline 800 & \text{FBM} \end{array}$$

In pricing the lumber, unless quantities in excess of two or three thousand board feet are involved, an average price between the cost of sheathing boards and the studding may be used. If sheathing, for example is $150 per 1,000 FBM, and 2″ × 4″ studding is $200 per 1,000 FBM, an average price of $175 may be used.

Wood forms are usually built and erected on the job by carpenters. In some localities, carpenter helpers, or common laborers assist in the work. Laborers generally strip the forms. The number of hours required to build, erect, and strip concrete forms varies with the type of structure for which the form is being made.

Figures 1 and 2 show several common types of forms, and the method of estimating the board feet of lumber for each type, when an accurate quantity of form material is desired.

Labor Table 1 shows the approximate board feet of lumber *and* the average hours of labor required to build, erect, and strip 100 square feet of forms of various types.

Forms for Slabs on Fill

Forms for concrete slabs that are placed directly on the surface of the ground such as sidewalks, garage or basement floors, or the floors of one-story dwellings without basements, will require a minimum of form work.

Table 2B

APPROXIMATE BOARD FEET OF LUMBER AND HOURS OF LABOR REQUIRED TO BUILD, ERECT, AND STRIP 100 SQUARE FEET OF WOODEN FORMS

Type of Form	FBM Lumber Per 100 Sq Ft Surface	Hours Labor Per 100 Sq Ft Surface		
		Build and Erect	Strip	Total Hours
Footings	350	6	2	8
Foundations and walls	250	8	2	10
Floor slabs above grade	250	10	4	14
Columns	300	10	4	14
Beams and girders	300	12	4	14
Stairs and steps	300	12	2	16

After the area has been prepared, stakes are driven and side pieces to contain the concrete are put in place using braced boards, 2 × 4's, 2 × 6's or other stock of suitable dimensions. These curbing pieces are usually placed so that the upper edges are even with the top of the finished concrete slab. In this way they serve as leveling guides. When estimating the amount of material, and the labor to set forms of this kind, each job should be figured according to its individual circumstances and requirements.

A rule of thumb for determining the number of board feet of form lumber for slabs on fill is to use the same number of lineal feet of side curbing as the distance around the slab and add 25 percent for stakes and braces.

Illustrative Example

Determine the board feet of lumber for a walk 4 inches thick, 3 feet wide by 30 feet long.

```
Perimeter = 2(30' + 3') = 66 lin ft
66 lin ft 2" × 4" =      44 FBM
Plus 25% Braces
and Stakes              11 FBM
        Total           55 FBM
```

TABLE 2—FOUNDATION WALLS...CONCRETE   161

A carpenter can place, level, drive the stakes and brace ground slab forms at the average rate of 20 lineal feet per hour. The number of hours of labor to install the forms in the above example would be

$$\frac{55}{20} = 2^3/_4 \text{ hours}$$

Estimating Forms By Unit Costs

Because the unit of measurement for concrete forms is the square feet of surface area in contact with the concrete, the unit cost of the forms is readily obtained using Table 2B for the number of board feet of lumber and hours of labor per 100 square feet of form. In the following examples, nails and wire are not included. If large quantities of forms are involved an allowance of 30 lbs of nails per 1,000 FBM of lumber may be added, and 40 feet of No. 8 form wire per 100 square feet of form. Add also reinforcing as specified. In the following examples, assume the average price of form lumber to be $200 per 1,000 FBM; wages for a carpenter are $9 per hour and a helper, $5 per hour.

Footing Forms:

350 FBM form lumber	@ $200.00 =	$ 70.00
6 carpenter hours to build	9.00 =	54.00
2 helper hours to strip	5.00 =	10.00
Unit cost per 100 sq ft		$134.00
Unit cost per sq ft	$134 =	$1.34
	100	

Foundation and Wall Forms:

250 FBM form lumber	@ $200.00 =	$ 50.00
8 carpenter hours, build and erect	9.00 =	72.00
2 helper hours to strip	5.00 =	10.00
Unit cost per 100 sq ft		$132.00
Unit cost per sq ft	$132 =	$1.32
	100	

Floor Slab Above Ground:

250 FBM form lumber	@ $200.00 =	$ 50.00
10 carpenter hours, build and erect	9.00 =	90.00
4 helper hours to strip	5.00 =	20.00
Unit cost per 100 sq ft		$160.00
Unit cost per sq ft	$160.00 =	$1.60
	100	

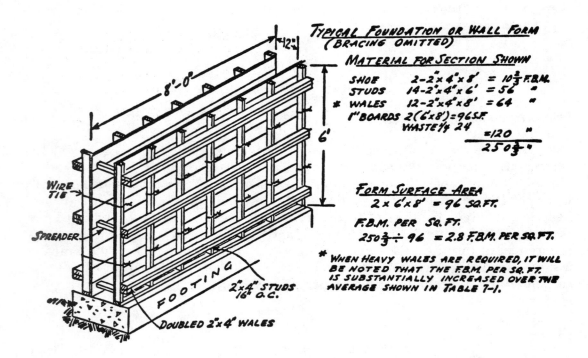

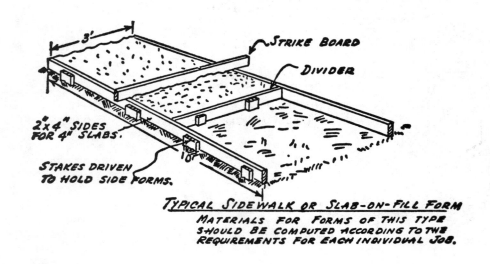

FIGURE 1

CONCRETE FORMS

TABLE 2—FOUNDATION WALLS...CONCRETE   163

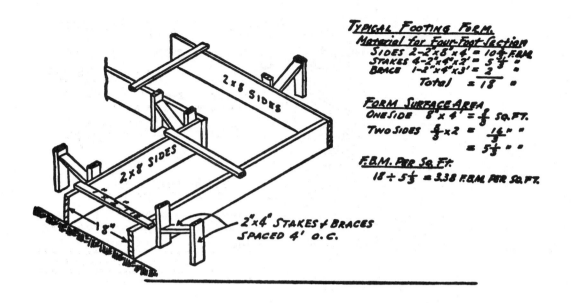

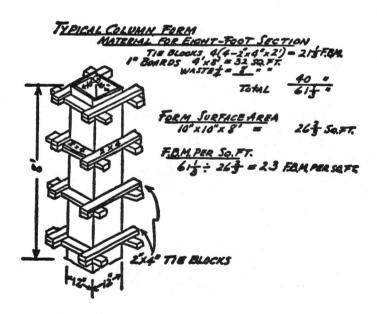

FIGURE 2

CONCRETE FORMS (footing and column)

TABLE 3

Foundation Walls . . . Concrete Block

This Table shows the number of 8″ × 16″ concrete blocks in foundation walls that are 2′ to 8′ high.

HOW TO USE THIS TABLE

1. Determine the *ground-floor* area of your dwelling following the method outlined under Computation of Areas in the General Instructions, page 17.

2. Determine the perimeter of your dwelling following the method outlined under Perimeter Measurement in the General Instructions, page 18.

3. Using Table A check the *ground-floor* area and lineal feet of perimeter to obtain the length-to-width ratio of your dwelling.

4. This Table is based on dwellings with a length-to-width ratio of two to one (2:1). If the length-to-width ratio of your dwelling is significantly different, adjust the quantity in the Table upward or downward by the percentages shown under Table A, page 22.

Illustrative Example

A dwelling 30′ × 90′ has a *ground-floor* area of 2,700 square feet. Determine the number of 8″ × 16″ concrete blocks in the foundation wall which is 6′ high. Disregard window and door openings.

Table 3 shows that 1,485 blocks are required for a dwelling of 2,700 square feet. This quantity is based on a length-to-width ratio of 2:1 whereas the subject dwelling is 3:1. Table A shows an adjustment percentage of 9 percent must be added to the Table 3 quantity, or 1,485 × 1.09 = 1,619 concrete blocks are required.

TABLE 3—FOUNDATION WALLS...CONCRETE BLOCK   165

BASIC FORMULA FOR ESTIMATING CONCRETE BLOCK

To estimate the number of concrete blocks, 8″ × 16″, in any wall use the following formula where:

$$L = \text{length of wall in feet}$$
$$h = \text{height of wall in feet}$$
$$L' \times h' \times 1.125 = \text{number of blocks in wall}$$

Illustrative Example

A foundation wall is 6′ high and 60′ long. Determine the number of concrete blocks required if there are no window or door openings.

$$60' \times 6' \times 1.125 = 405 \text{ concrete blocks}$$

Window and Door Openings

No deduction has been made in Table 3 for window and door openings. When openings such as windows, doors or garage doors are to be deducted, multiply the total square foot area of such openings by 1.125 to determine the number of blocks to be deducted.

Illustrative Example

A dwelling 30′ × 60′ has a *ground-floor area* of 1,800 square feet. The foundation wall is 8′ high. There are three 30″ × 24″ window openings and a garage door opening 8′ × 9′. Determine the number of blocks needed.

Table 3 shows a total of 1,620 blocks, no openings deducted.

3 windows 2′6″ × 2′	= 15 sq ft	
1 garage door 8′ × 9′	= 72 ″ ″	
	87 ″ ″	
	× 1.125 ″ ″	
	98 concrete blocks to be deducted	

1,620 - 98 = 1,522 concrete blocks required

Note: Include reinforcing or bond beams where specified.

TABLE 3

FOUNDATION WALLS . . . CONCRETE BLOCK
FOR ALL DWELLINGS
(NO DEDUCTION HAS BEEN MADE FOR OPENINGS)

Ground Floor Area	NUMBER OF 8″ × 16″ BLOCKS NEEDED FOR HEIGHT OF WALL SHOWN									
	2'-0″	2'-8″	3'-4″	4'-0″	4'-8″	5'-4″	6'-0″	6'-8″	7'-4″	8'-0″
200	135	180	225	270	315	360	405	450	495	540
300	167	222	278	333	389	444	500	555	611	666
400	191	255	319	383	446	510	574	638	701	765
500	214	285	356	428	499	570	641	713	784	855
600	234	312	390	468	546	624	702	780	858	936
700	252	336	420	504	588	672	756	840	924	1008
800	270	360	450	540	630	720	810	900	990	1080
900	286	381	476	572	667	762	857	953	1048	1143
1000	302	402	503	604	704	804	905	1005	1106	1206
1100	317	423	529	634	740	846	952	1058	1163	1269
1200	331	441	551	662	772	882	992	1103	1213	1323
1300	344	459	574	689	803	918	1033	1148	1262	1377
1400	358	477	596	716	835	954	1073	1193	1312	1431
1500	369	492	615	738	861	984	1107	1230	1353	1476
1600	383	510	638	765	893	1020	1148	1275	1403	1530
1700	394	525	636	788	919	1050	1181	1313	1444	1575
1800	405	540	675	810	945	1080	1215	1350	1485	1620
1900	416	555	694	833	971	1110	1249	1388	1526	1665
2000	428	570	713	855	998	1140	1283	1425	1568	1710
2100	437	582	728	873	1019	1164	1310	1455	1601	1746
2200	448	597	746	896	1045	1194	1343	1493	1642	1791
2300	457	609	761	914	1066	1218	1370	1523	1675	1827
2400	468	624	780	936	1092	1248	1404	1560	1716	1872
2500	477	636	795	954	1113	1272	1431	1590	1749	1908
2600	486	648	810	972	1134	1296	1458	1620	1782	1944
2700	495	660	825	990	1155	1320	1485	1650	1815	1980
2800	504	672	840	1008	1176	1344	1512	1680	1848	2016
2900	513	684	855	1026	1197	1368	1539	1710	1881	2052
3000	524	699	874	1049	1223	1398	1573	1748	1922	2097

TABLE 3—FOUNDATION WALLS...CONCRETE BLOCK   167

MORTAR FOR CONCRETE BLOCK

The quantity of mortar to lay up concrete block will vary with the thickness of the block (that is 6″, 8″, 10″, or 12″) and the thickness of the mortar joint. The quantities shown below may be considered for general estimating purposes. If the cells of the blocks are to be filled with mortar the quantities should be increased to take care of that mortar.

A nominal block 8″ × 8″ × 16″ actually measures 7 5/8″ × 7 5/8″ × 15 5/8″ which allows for a 3/8″ mortar joint. Where precise estimating is indicated, consideration must be given to including whatever special shapes of blocks are needed such as corners, sash block, beam block etc.

TABLE 3A

NOMINAL SIZE OF BLOCK (³/₈″ Mortar Joint)	CU YDS MORTAR		CU FT MORTAR	
	Per 1000 Units	Per 100 Units	Per 1000 Units	Per 100 Units
8″ × 8″ × 16″	1.5	.15	40	4.0
12″ × 8″ × 16″	1.7	.17	46	4.6

Materials for a *cubic yard* of mortar based on an ordinary service mix of (1:3) 1 part cement, 1/4 part hydrated lime and 3 parts of sand would be:

Cement...........................10 sacks
Sand .... 1 cu yd
Hydrated lime .... 2 sacks

Materials for a cubic foot of mortar of this mix would be as follows, assuming (Portland) cement weighs 94 lbs per sack, sand 2,500 lbs per cu yd and lime 40 lbs per sack.

Cement......................0.37 sacks...........................35 lbs
Sand ....0.037 cu yds......................94 ″
Lime ....0.074 sacks........................ 3 ″

TABLE 3B

Number of 8″ × 16″ Concrete Blocks
Per Lineal Foot of Foundation Wall

When the height of a concrete block foundation wall is known, Table 3B provides factors that represent the number of 8″ × 16″ concrete blocks per lineal foot of wall. Some estimators prefer this method to either Table 3, or the basic formula, page 165.

To illustrate the application of all three methods, assume a dwelling 25′ × 50′ with a concrete block wall 7′-4″ high. (This would be 11 blocks high). The *ground-floor* area is 1,250 sq ft and the perimeter is 150′, which we will assume is the length of the wall.

Method 1.

Table 3 shows that the *ground-floor* area lies in between 1200 and 1300 sq ft. From Table 3:

1,300 sq ft contains	1,262 blocks
1,200	1,213 ″
Difference	49 ″

1,250 sq ft contains 1,213 + 25 = 1,238 blocks

Method 2.

Using the basic formula L × h × 1.125 = number of blocks

150′ × 7.33 × 1.125 = 1,237 blocks

Method 3.

Table 3B shows that a wall 7′-4″ high contains 8.246 concrete blocks per lineal foot of wall.

150′ × 8.246 = 1,237 blocks

168

TABLE 3—FOUNDATION WALLS...CONCRETE BLOCK   169

   While all of the methods produce the same number of blocks in this wall, Methods 2 and 3 have an advantage, i.e., it is not necessary to adjust the **Table 3** quantities if the dwelling has a length-to-width ratio other than 2:1.

TABLE 3B

NUMBER OF 8″ × 16″ CONCRETE BLOCKS PER LINEAL FOOT OF FOUNDATION WALL

Wall Height In Inches	Wall Height In Feet		Number of Blocks Per Lineal Foot of Foundation
8	.67	(0′-8″)	.754
16	1.33	(1′-4″)	1.500
24	2.00	(2′-0″)	2.250
32	2.67	(2′-8″)	3.004
40	3.33	(3′-4″)	3.746
48	4.00	(4′-0″)	4.500
56	4.67	(4′-8″)	5.254
64	5.33	(5′-4″	6.000
72	6.00	(6′-0″)	6.750
80	6.67	(6′-8″)	7.504
88	7.33	(7′-4″)	8.246
96	8.00	(8′-0″)	9.000
104	8.67	(8′-8″)	9.754
112	9.93	(9′-4″)	10.500
120	10.00	(10′-0″)	11.250

   Window and door openings may be deducted by multiplying the **surface** area of such openings by 1.125 to determine the number of blocks to be deducted.

TABLES 4 and 5

Concrete Slabs, Walks, Patios, Driveways, etc.

Table No. 4 Applies to Areas from 200 to 3000 Square Feet

Table No. 5 Applies to Areas from 10 to 500 Square Feet

These Tables show the number of cubic yards of gravel base, concrete, and cement topping for floor slabs, patios, porches, walks and driveways.

HOW TO USE THESE TABLES

Determine the *ground-floor* area of your dwelling following the method outlined under Computation of Areas in the General Instructions; page 17. No perimeter measurement is needed and no adjustment is necessary for the length-to-width ratio. The tables are based on square foot areas only.

BASIC FORMULA FOR CONCRETE SLABS

A short method for estimating the number of cubic yards of gravel base, concrete and cement topping in slabs in as follows:

Where:

A = Area of surface in square feet
t = Thickness in inches
$A \times t'' \times .0031^* =$ cubic yards of material

---

*Actually 1 sq ft, 1″ thick = .08333 divided by 27 = .0030864

Illustrative Example

A concrete slab has 1650 sq ft. The gravel base is 5″ thick, and the concrete over the base is 3½″ thick. Determine the material required.

Gravel base	1650 x 5″ x .0031	= 25.6 cu yds
Concrete slab	1650 x 3½″ x .0031	= 17.9 cu yds

Forms and Reinforcing

Any forms or reinforcing should be added to the estimate. Wire mesh reinforcing or welded steel fabric reinforcing is customarily used in slabs, driveways and walks. It comes in rolls 5 feet wide and 150 feet long. The most popular size mesh in residential work is 6 × 6 − 10/10 which means the 10 gauge wires form 6 inch squares. When laid, the mesh laps a full square.

Note: Materials required for a cubic yard of concrete are shown on page 151.

TABLE 4

CONCRETE SLABS, WALKS, PATIOS, DRIVEWAYS, ETC.
FOR LARGE AREAS INCLUDING GRAVEL BASE
& CEMENT TOPPING FOR FINISH
(To Obtain Cubic Feet, Multiply By 27)

Ground Floor Area	CUBIC YARDS OF GRAVEL BASE; CONCRETE OR TOPPING FOR THICKNESS SHOWN											
	1"	2"	3"	4"	5"	6"	7"	8"	9"	10"	11"	12"
200	0.62	1.24	1.86	2.48	3.10	3.72	4.34	4.96	5.58	6.20	6.82	7.44
300	0.93	1.86	2.79	3.72	4.65	5.58	6.51	7.44	8.37	9.30	10.23	11.16
400	1.24	2.48	3.72	4.96	6.20	7.44	8.68	9.92	11.16	12.40	13.64	14.88
500	1.55	3.10	4.65	6.30	7.75	9.30	10.85	12.40	13.95	15.50	17.05	18.60
600	1.86	3.72	5.58	7.44	9.30	11.16	13.02	14.88	16.74	18.60	20.46	22.32
700	2.17	4.34	6.51	8.68	10.85	13.02	15.19	17.36	19.53	21.70	23.87	26.04
800	2.48	4.96	7.44	9.92	12.40	14.88	17.36	19.84	22.32	24.80	27.28	29.76
900	2.79	5.58	8.37	11.16	13.95	16.74	19.53	22.32	25.11	27.90	30.69	33.48
1000	3.10	6.20	9.30	12.40	15.50	18.60	21.70	24.80	27.90	31.00	34.10	37.20
1100	3.41	6.82	10.23	13.64	17.05	20.46	23.87	27.28	30.69	34.10	37.51	40.92
1200	3.72	7.44	11.16	14.88	18.60	22.32	26.04	29.76	33.48	37.20	40.92	44.64
1300	4.03	8.06	12.09	16.12	20.15	24.18	28.21	32.24	36.27	40.30	44.33	48.36
1400	4.34	8.68	13.02	17.36	21.70	26.04	30.38	34.72	39.06	43.40	47.74	52.08
1500	4.65	9.30	13.95	18.60	23.25	27.90	32.55	37.20	41.85	46.50	51.15	55.80
1600	4.96	9.92	14.88	19.84	24.80	29.76	34.72	39.68	44.64	49.60	54.56	59.52
1700	5.27	10.54	15.81	21.08	26.35	31.62	36.89	42.16	47.43	52.70	57.97	63.24
1800	5.58	11.16	16.74	22.32	27.90	33.88	39.06	44.64	50.22	55.80	61.38	66.96
1900	5.89	11.78	17.67	23.56	29.45	35.34	41.23	47.12	53.01	58.90	64.79	70.68
2000	6.20	12.40	18.60	24.80	31.00	37.20	43.40	49.60	55.80	62.00	68.20	74.40
2100	6.51	13.02	19.53	26.04	32.55	39.06	45.57	52.08	58.59	65.10	71.61	78.12
2200	6.82	13.64	20.46	27.28	34.10	40.92	47.74	54.56	61.38	68.20	75.02	81.84
2300	7.13	14.26	21.39	28.52	35.65	42.78	49.91	57.04	64.17	71.30	78.43	85.56
2400	7.44	14.88	22.32	29.76	37.20	44.64	52.08	59.52	66.96	74.40	81.84	89.28
2500	7.75	15.50	23.25	31.00	38.75	46.50	54.26	62.00	69.75	77.50	85.25	93.00
2600	8.06	16.12	24.18	32.24	40.30	48.36	56.42	64.48	72.54	80.60	88.66	96.72
2700	8.37	16.74	25.11	33.48	41.85	50.22	58.59	66.96	75.33	83.70	92.07	100.44
2800	8.68	17.36	26.04	34.72	43.40	52.08	60.76	69.44	78.12	86.80	95.48	104.16
2900	8.99	17.98	26.97	35.96	44.95	53.94	62.93	71.92	80.91	89.90	98.89	107.88
3000	9.30	18.60	27.90	37.20	46.50	55.80	65.10	74.40	83.70	93.00	102.30	111.60

TABLE 5

CONCRETE SLABS, WALKS, PATIOS, DRIVEWAYS, ETC.
FOR SMALL AREAS INCLUDING GRAVEL BASE
& CEMENT TOPPING FOR FINISH
(To Obtain Cubic Feet, Multiply By 27)

Ground Floor Area	CUBIC YARDS OF GRAVEL BASE; CONCRETE OR TOPPING FOR THICKNESS SHOWN											
	1″	2″	3″	4″	5″	6″	7″	8″	9″	10″	11″	12″
20	.06	.12	.19	.25	.31	.37	.43	.50	.56	.62	.68	.74
30	.09	.18	.28	.37	.47	.56	.65	.75	.84	.93	1.02	1.12
40	.12	.24	.37	.50	.62	.74	.87	.99	1.12	1.24	1.36	1.49
50	.16	.32	.47	.62	.78	.93	1.09	1.24	1.40	1.55	1.71	1.86
60	.19	.38	.56	.74	.93	1.12	1.30	1.49	1.67	1.86	2.05	2.23
70	.22	.43	.65	.87	1.09	1.30	1.52	1.74	1.95	2.17	2.39	2.60
80	.25	.50	.74	.99	1.24	1.49	1.74	1.98	2.23	2.48	2.73	2.98
90	.28	.56	.84	1.12	1.40	1.67	1.95	2.23	2.51	2.79	3.07	3.35
100	.31	.62	.93	1.24	1.55	1.86	2.17	2.48	2.79	3.10	3.41	3.72
120	.37	.74	1.12	1.49	1.86	2.23	2.60	2.98	3.35	3.72	4.09	4.46
140	.43	.87	1.30	1.74	2.17	2.60	3.04	3.47	3.91	4.34	4.77	5.21
160	.49	.99	1.49	1.98	2.48	2.98	3.47	3.97	4.46	4.96	5.46	5.95
180	.56	1.12	1.67	2.23	2.79	3.35	3.91	4.46	5.02	5.58	6.14	6.70
200	.62	1.24	1.86	2.48	3.10	3.72	4.34	4.96	5.58	6.20	6.82	7.44
220	.68	1.36	2.05	2.73	3.41	4.09	4.77	5.46	6.14	6.82	7.50	8.18
240	.74	1.49	2.23	2.98	3.72	4.46	5.21	5.95	6.70	7.44	8.18	8.93
260	.81	1.61	2.42	3.22	4.03	4.84	5.64	6.45	7.25	8.06	8.87	9.67
280	.87	1.74	2.60	3.47	4.34	5.21	6.08	6.94	7.81	8.68	9.55	10.42
300	.93	1.86	2.79	3.72	4.65	5.58	6.51	7.44	8.37	9.30	10.23	11.16
320	.99	1.98	2.98	3.97	4.96	5.95	6.94	7.94	8.93	9.92	10.91	11.90
340	1.05	2.11	3.16	4.22	5.27	6.32	7.38	8.43	9.49	10.54	11.59	12.65
360	1.12	2.23	3.35	4.46	5.58	6.70	7.81	8.93	10.04	11.16	12.28	13.39
380	1.18	2.36	3.53	4.71	5.89	7.07	8.25	9.42	10.60	11.78	12.96	14.14
400	1.24	2.48	3.72	4.96	6.20	7.44	8.68	9.92	11.16	12.40	13.64	14.88
420	1.30	2.60	3.91	5.21	6.51	7.81	9.11	10.42	11.72	13.02	14.32	15.62
440	1.36	2.73	4.09	5.46	6.82	8.18	9.55	10.91	12.28	13.64	15.00	16.37
460	1.43	2.85	4.28	5.70	7.13	8.56	9.98	11.41	12.83	14.26	15.69	17.11
480	1.45	2.98	4.46	5.95	7.44	8.93	10.42	11.90	13.39	14.48	16.37	17.86
500	1.55	3.10	4.65	6.20	7.75	9.30	10.85	12.40	13.95	15.50	17.05	18.60

TABLES 6, 7, and 8

Exterior Wall Studs and Partition Studs

Table No. 6 Applies to 1-Story Dwellings

Table No. 7 Applies to 1¹/₂ Story Dwellings

Table No. 8 Applies to 2-Story Dwellings

These three Tables show the number of board feet (FBM) of framing lumber for exterior walls and partition walls. Such framing consists of 2″ × 4″ studding 16″ on center and on 24″ centers; shoes and plates, plus an adequate amount to take care of framing at corners, doors and windows.

HOW TO USE THESE TABLES

1. Determine the *ground-floor* area of your dwelling following the method outlined under Computation of Areas in the General Instructions, page 17.

2. Determine the perimeter of your dwelling following the method outlined under Perimeter Measurement in the General Instructions, page 18.

3. Using Table A check the *ground-floor* area and the lineal feet of perimeter to obtain the length-to-width ratio of your dwelling.

4. These Tables are based on dwellings with a length-to-width ratio of two to one (2:1). If the length-to-width ratio of your dwelling is significantly different, adjust the quantity in the Tables upward or downward by the percentages shown under Table A, page 22.

Illustrative Example

A two-story dwelling 40′ long and 40′ wide has a *ground-floor* area of 1,600 square feet and a length-to-width ratio of 1:1. The pitch of the gable roof is ¼ (6″ rise-per-foot-of-run). Studs are all on 16″ centers.

This is a two-story dwelling to which Table 8 applies. For a ground-floor area of 1,600 sq ft Table 8 shows:

Exterior wall studs including gables ....2,413 FBM
Partition studs including shoe and plate   2,112 ″
                                    Total 4,525 ″

Table quantities are based on a length-to-width ratio of 2:1. The adjustment percentage shown on page 22, when the length-to-width ratio is 1:1 as in this illustration, is a 5% deduction from the Table quantities.

This is for exterior studs only.

The adjustment to Table 8 exterior studs therefor is:

Exterior wall studs 2,413 × .95   = 2,292 FBM
Partition studs (no change)   = 2,112 ″
                          Total 4,404 ″

GABLE FRAMING ADJUSTMENT WHEN ROOF PITCH IS OTHER THAN 1/4

When the roof pitch is other than ¼, on which these Tables are based, it may be desirable to make an adjustment to the gable framing. If so, proceed as follows:

1. Select from the appropriate Table (6, 7 or 8) the framing quantity under the column "No Gables".

2. From Table C1 or C2 determine the square foot area of the gables in your dwelling. These Tables show the area for both gables.

3. Multiply the gable area determined in Step 2 by the factor (footnote) Table 14A:
   .67 for 2″ × 4″ studding 16″ on center
   .50 ″   ″   ″   ″   24″ ″   ″
This will give the board feet (FBM) of studding in your gables and allows for cutting and fitting waste.

4. Add the board feet developed in Step 3 to that in Step 1 to obtain the total board feet of exterior wall framing for your dwelling.

Add to this the board feet of partition framing shown in the appropriate Table 6, 7 or 8.

Illustrative Example

Assume a 2-story dwelling 30' x 60', with a roof pitch of ⅓ and 2" x 4" studding 16" on center. The ground-floor area is 1800 sq ft.

1. Table 8 shows 2412 FBM of exterior studding under the "No Gables" column.
2. Table C2 shows that a dwelling with a roof pitch of ⅓, a length-to-width ratio of 2:1, and a ground-floor area of 1800 sq ft will have 300 sq ft of gable area.
3. From Step 3 above, 2" x 4" studs 16" on center will have .67 board feet per sq ft. Therefor 300 x .67 = 201 FBM of gable framing.
4. The total FBM of framing for exterior walls including gables is 2,412 + 201 or 2,613 FBM. Add to this the partition framing shown in Table 8 for a dwelling with 1,800 sq ft of **ground-floor** area.

Exterior wall framing	=	2,613 FBM
Partition framing	=	2,376 FBM
Total		4,989 FBM

NAILS

For estimating the quantity of nails required for framing see page 205. Table 14B.

BASIC FORMULAS FOR ESTIMATING FBM EXTERIOR WALL AND PARTITION STUDS

These formulas include shoe, plate, normal door, window, and corner framing. No provision is made for gable framing. The FBM of gable framing is readily determined by obtaining the sq ft in the gables from Table C1 and C2, then multiply that area by .67 if the studs are on 16" centers or by .50 if the studs are on 24" centers. This will allow for cutting and fitting waste.

1-Story Dwellings:

Exterior wall studs.......................16" on center.....................		6.7P
" " " ....24"		5.0P
Partition studs............................16"		.66A
" " ....24"		.44A

1¹/₂-Story Dwellings:

Exterior wall studs	16″ on center	11.67P
″ ″ ″	24″	8.75P
Partition studs	16″	1.17A
″ ″	24″	.77A

2-Story dwellings:

Exterior wall studs	16″ on center	13.4P
″ ″ ″	24″	10.0P
Partition studs	16″	1.33A
″ ″	24″	.88A

Note: P is the perimeter
A is the *ground-floor* area

TABLE 6

EXTERIOR WALL AND PARTITION FRAMING
FOR 1-STORY DWELLINGS.
NUMBER OF BOARD FEET INCLUDING
SHOE AND PLATE.

| Ground Floor Area | 2″ × 4″ EXTERIOR WALL STUDS | | | | 2″ × 4″ PARTITION STUDS | | TOTAL FBM WALL & PARTITION STUDS, 16″ O.C. | |
| | SPACED 16″ O.C. | | SPACED 24″ O.C. | | SPACING ON CENTER | | | |
	Gables Included	No Gables	Gables Included	No Gables	16″	24″	Gables Included	No Gables
200	419	402	313	300	132	88	551	534
300	521	496	389	370	198	132	719	694
400	603	570	450	425	264	176	867	834
500	678	637	506	475	330	220	1008	967
600	747	697	558	520	396	264	1143	1093
700	809	750	604	560	462	308	1271	1212
800	871	804	650	600	528	352	1400	1332
900	925	850	691	635	594	396	1520	1444
1000	981	898	732	670	660	440	1641	1558
1100	1037	945	774	705	726	484	1763	1671
1200	1085	985	810	735	792	528	1877	1777
1300	1134	1025	847	765	858	572	1992	1883
1400	1182	1065	883	795	924	616	2106	1990
1500	1225	1100	914	820	990	660	2215	2090
1600	1273	1140	950	850	1056	704	2329	2196
1700	1314	1173	981	875	1122	748	2436	2295
1800	1356	1206	1013	900	1188	792	2544	2394
1900	1400	1240	1044	925	1254	836	2654	2494
2000	1440	1273	1075	950	1320	880	2760	2593
2100	1475	1300	1100	970	1386	924	2861	2686
2200	1516	1333	1133	995	1452	968	2968	2785
2300	1550	1360	1158	1015	1518	1012	3068	2878
2400	1594	1394	1190	1040	1584	1056	3178	2978
2500	1628	1420	1216	1060	1650	1100	3278	3070
2600	1664	1447	1242	1080	1716	1144	3380	3163
2700	1700	1474	1269	1100	1782	1188	3482	3256
2800	1733	1500	1295	1120	1848	1232	3581	3348
2900	1768	1528	1320	1140	1914	1276	3682	3442
3000	1811	1561	1353	1165	1980	1320	3791	3541

TABLE 7

EXTERIOR WALL AND PARTITION FRAMING FOR 1 ½ STORY DWELLINGS
NUMBER OF BOARD FEET INCLUDING SHOE AND PLATE

| Ground Floor Area | 2″ × 4″ EXTERIOR WALL STUDS | | | | 2″ × 4″ PARTITION STUDS SPACING ON CENTER | | TOTAL FBM WALL & PARTITION STUDS, 16″ O.C. | |
| | SPACED 16″ O.C. | | SPACED 24″ O.C. | | | | | |
	Gables Included	No Gables	Gables Included	No Gables	16″	24″	Gables Included	No Gables
200	713	696	541	528	234	154	947	930
300	883	858	670	651	351	231	1234	1209
400	1019	986	773	748	468	308	1487	1454
500	1143	1102	867	836	585	385	1728	1687
600	1256	1206	953	915	702	462	1958	1908
700	1360	1300	1053	986	819	539	2178	2119
800	1459	1392	1106	1056	936	616	2395	2328
900	1550	1475	1174	1118	1053	693	2603	2528
1000	1638	1555	1241	1179	1170	770	2808	2725
1100	1728	1636	1310	1241	1287	847	3015	2923
1200	1806	1706	1369	1294	1404	924	3210	3110
1300	1884	1775	1428	1346	1521	1000	3405	3296
1400	1961	1844	1488	1400	1638	1078	3600	3482
1500	2027	1902	1537	1443	1755	1155	3782	3657
1600	2105	1972	1596	1496	1872	1232	3977	3844
1700	2171	2030	1646	1540	1990	1310	4161	4020
1800	2238	2088	1697	1584	2106	1386	4344	4194
1900	2305	2146	1744	1628	2223	1463	4528	4369
2000	2371	2204	1797	1672	2340	1540	4711	4544
2100	2425	2250	1838	1707	2457	1617	4882	4707
2200	2492	2309	1890	1751	2574	1694	5066	4883
2300	2545	2355	1930	1786	2691	1771	5236	5046
2400	2613	2413	1980	1830	2808	1848	5421	5221
2500	2668	2460	2022	1866	2925	1925	5593	5385
2600	2723	2506	2062	1900	3042	2000	5765	5548
2700	2777	2552	2105	1936	3159	2080	5936	5711
2800	2831	2598	2146	1971	3276	2156	6107	5874
2900	2885	2645	2186	2006	3393	2233	6278	6038
3000	2953	2703	2238	2050	3510	2310	6463	6213

TABLE 8

EXTERIOR WALL AND PARTITION FRAMING FOR 2-STORY DWELLINGS
NUMBER OF BOARD FEET INCLUDING SHOE AND PLATE

| Ground Floor Area | 2″ × 4″ EXTERIOR WALL STUDS | | | | 2″ × 4″ PARTITION STUDS | | TOTAL FBM WALL & PARTITION STUDS, 16″ O.C. | |
| | SPACED 16″ O.C. | | SPACED 24″ O.C. | | SPACING ON CENTER | | | |
	Gables Included	No Gables	Gables Included	No Gables	16″	24″	Gables Included	No Gables
200	821	804	613	600	264	176	1085	1068
300	1017	992	759	740	396	264	1413	1388
400	1172	1140	875	850	528	352	1700	1668
500	1315	1274	981	950	660	440	1975	1934
600	1444	1394	1078	1040	972	528	2236	2186
700	1559	1500	1164	1120	924	616	2483	2424
800	1675	1608	1250	1200	1056	704	2731	2664
900	1775	1700	1326	1270	1188	792	2963	2888
1000	1879	1796	1402	1340	1320	880	3200	3116
1100	1982	1890	1479	1410	1452	968	3434	3342
1200	2070	1970	1545	1470	1584	1056	3654	3554
1300	2159	2050	1612	1530	1716	1144	3875	3766
1400	2247	2130	1678	1590	1848	1232	4095	3980
1500	2325	2200	1734	1640	1980	1320	4305	4180
1600	2413	2280	1800	1700	2112	1408	4525	4392
1700	2487	2346	1856	1750	2244	1496	4731	4590
1800	2562	2412	1913	1800	2376	1584	4938	4788
1900	2639	2480	1969	1850	2508	1672	5147	4988
2000	2713	2546	2025	1900	2640	1760	5353	5186
2100	2775	2600	2071	1940	2772	1848	5547	5372
2200	2849	2666	2128	1990	2904	1936	5753	5570
2300	2910	2720	2173	2030	3036	2024	5946	5756
2400	2988	2788	2230	2080	3168	2112	6156	5956
2500	3048	2840	2276	2121	3300	2200	6348	6140
2600	3111	2894	2322	2160	3432	2288	6543	6326
2700	3173	2948	2369	2200	3564	2376	6737	6512
2800	3233	3000	2415	2240	3696	2464	6929	6696
2900	3296	3056	2460	2280	3828	2552	7124	6884
3000	3372	3122	2518	2330	3960	2640	7332	7082

TABLE 6-8A

FBM OF EXTERIOR WALL AND PARTITION FRAMING PER LIN FT FOR THE HEIGHT OF WALL SHOWN

Height of Wall in Feet	FBM Per Lineal Foot	
	16″ Centers	24″ Centers
7	4.67	3.11
8	5.33	3.55
9	6.00	4.00
10	6.67	4.45
11	7.33	4.89
12	8.00	5.33
13	8.67	5.78
14	9.33	6.22
15	10.00	6.67

This Table is based on an allowance of one 2″ × 4″ for each lineal foot of wall which will allow for framing around openings, doubling at corners and bracing. No allowance has been made for either plate or shoe. If it is desired to estimate the exact FBM per lineal foot for height of wall shown, take 75% of the figures in the Table. In other words, for a wall 8 ft high with studs 16″ on center, the exact number of FBM per lineal foot of wall will be .75 × 5.33 = 4 FBM. Thus a wall 40 ft long and 8 ft high will have 160 FBM considering only the 2″ × 4″ studs allowing for nothing else. (See also Table 14A).

If one 2″ × 4″ per lineal foot is to be used, as many estimators do, read the FBM directly from the Table. Interpolate for walls of heights in between those shown. For example, a wall 8′-6″ high would have $\frac{5.33 + 6.00}{2} = 5.67$ FBM per lineal foot of wall.

TABLE 9

Floor and Ceiling Joists Per Floor

This Table shows the number of board feet (FBM) of lumber for floor joists and ceiling joists in dwellings. Framing members are 2″ × 4″, 2″ × 6″, 2″ × 8″, 2″ × 10″ and 2″ × 12″, on centers of 16″, 20″ and 24″.

HOW TO USE THIS TABLE

Determine the *ground-floor* area of your dwelling as outlined under Computation of Areas in the General Instructions, page 17. It is not necessary to measure the perimeter as Table quantities are based only on the square foot area. Also, no adjustment is to be made for the length-to-width ratio. Quantities in the Table can be read directly according to the *ground-floor* area of a particular dwelling.

FLOOR OPENINGS

No deduction has been made for floor openings. For practical purposes the board feet of lumber that would occupy openings such as stairwells is used in framing around these openings.

NAILS

For estimating purposes, an acceptable average quantity of nails is as follows:

```
2″ ×   4″ Joists, 10 lbs 16d per 1000 FBM
2″ ×   6″    "     9  "   "   "    "    "
2″ ×   8″    "     8  "   "   "    "    "
2″ × 10″     "     7  "   "   "    "    "
2″ × 12″     "     6  "   "   "    "    "
```

TABLE 9

FLOOR AND CEILING JOISTS, PER FLOOR, FOR ALL DWELLINGS.
NUMBER OF BOARD FEET FOR SIZE OF JOIST AND SPACING SHOWN.

Ground Floor Area	2″ × 4″ On Center			2″ × 6″ On Center			2″ × 8″ On Center			2″ × 10″ On Center			2″ × 12″ On Center		
	16″	20″	24″	16″	20″	24″	16″	20″	24″	16″	20″	24″	16″	20″	24″
200	110	88	73	170	136	114	220	176	147	270	216	180	330	264	220
300	165	132	110	255	204	170	330	264	220	405	324	270	495	396	330
400	220	176	147	340	272	227	440	352	293	540	432	360	660	528	440
500	275	220	183	425	340	283	550	440	367	695	540	450	825	660	550
600	330	264	220	510	408	340	660	528	440	810	648	540	990	792	660
700	385	308	257	595	476	397	770	616	514	945	756	630	1155	924	770
800	440	352	293	680	544	454	880	704	587	1080	864	720	1320	1056	880
900	495	396	330	765	612	510	990	792	660	1215	972	810	1485	1188	990
1000	550	440	367	850	680	567	1100	880	734	1350	1080	900	1650	1320	1100
1100	605	484	404	935	748	624	1210	968	807	1485	1188	990	1815	1415	1210
1200	660	528	440	1020	816	680	1320	1056	880	1620	1296	1080	1980	1584	1320
1300	715	572	477	1105	884	737	1430	1144	954	1755	1404	1170	2145	1716	1430
1400	770	616	514	1190	952	794	1540	1232	1027	1890	1512	1260	2310	1848	1540
1500	825	660	550	1275	1020	850	1650	1320	1100	2025	1620	1350	2475	1980	1650
1600	880	704	587	1360	1088	907	1760	1408	1177	2160	1728	1440	2640	2112	1760
1700	935	748	624	1445	1156	964	1870	1496	1247	2295	1836	1530	2805	2244	1870
1800	990	792	660	1530	1224	1021	1980	1584	1320	2430	1944	1620	2970	2376	1980
1900	1045	836	697	1615	1292	1077	2090	1672	1394	2565	2052	1710	3135	2508	2090
2000	1100	880	734	1700	1360	1134	2200	1760	1467	2700	2160	1800	3300	2640	2200
2100	1155	924	770	1785	1428	1190	2310	1848	1540	2835	2268	1890	3465	2772	2310
2200	1210	968	807	1870	1496	1247	2420	1936	1614	2970	2376	1980	3630	2904	2420
2300	1265	1012	844	1955	1564	1304	2530	2024	1688	3105	2484	2070	3795	3036	2530
2400	1320	1056	880	2040	1632	1360	2640	2112	1760	3240	2592	2160	3960	3168	2640
2500	1375	1100	917	2125	1700	1417	2750	2200	1834	3375	2700	2250	4125	3300	2750
2600	1430	1144	953	2210	1768	1474	2860	2288	1908	3510	2808	2340	4290	3432	2860
2700	1485	1188	990	2295	1836	1530	2970	2376	1980	3645	2916	2430	4455	3564	2970
2800	1540	1232	1027	2380	1904	1587	3080	2464	2054	3780	3024	2520	4620	3696	3080
2900	1595	1276	1064	2465	1972	1644	3190	2552	2128	3915	3132	2610	4785	3828	3190
3000	1650	1320	1100	2550	2040	1700	3300	2640	2200	4050	3240	2700	4950	3960	3300

TABLE 9A

FORMULAS FOR THE FBM OF FLOOR OR CEILING JOISTS PER FLOOR

(A = Area of The Floor or The Ground-floor Area of the Dwelling)
Quantities include 10% allowance for an end joist and cutting
and fitting waste.

Size of Joist	Inches Center to Center	Formula
2″ × 4″	16 20 24	.55A .44A .37A
2″ × 6″	16 20 24	.85A .68A .56A
2″ × 8″	16 20 24	1.10A .88A .73A
2″ × 10″	16 20 24	1.35A 1.08A .90A
2″ × 12″	16 20 24	1.65A 1.32A 1.10A

Illustrative Example

A 2-story dwelling, 32′ × 70′, has a *ground-floor* area of 2,240 sq ft. The first floor joists are 2″ × 12″, the second floor are 2″ × 10″, and the second floor ceiling joists are 2″ × 6″. All are on 16″ centers.

First floor joists,	2″ × 12″ ....2,240 × 1.65	=3,696 FBM
Second ″	2″ × 10″ ....2,240 × 1.35	=3,024 ″
Ceiling joists,	2″ × 6″ ....2,240 × .85	=1,904 ″
	Total	8,624 ″

TABLE 10

Wood Bridging, Catting, Posts and Girders

This Table shows the approximate number of board feet (FBM) of wood bridging, catting, blocking, wood posts and girders in dwellings with ground-floor areas from 200 to 3,000 square feet.

HOW TO USE THIS TABLE

Determine the *ground-floor* area of the dwelling. Read off the approximate board feet directly from the Table.

EMPIRICAL FORMULA USED

The empirical formula used in developing this Table is:

        One-story dwellings, posts and girders, 1/10 × area
             "   "   "   bridging and catting, 1/10 × area
        One and a half and two-story dwellings,
          "   "   "   "   "   posts and girders, 1/10 × area
          "   "   "   "   "   bridging and catting, 1/5 × area

NAILS

For the quantity of nails needed, refer to Table 14B, page 205.

TABLE 10

WOOD BRIDGING, CATTING, POSTS & GIRDERS FOR ALL DWELLINGS
NUMBER OF BOARD FEET REQUIRED

Ground Floor Area	1-Story Dwellings		1 ½ & 2-Story Dwellings		
	Bridging Catting etc.	Posts & Girders	Bridging Catting etc.	Posts & Girders	
200	20	20	40	20	
300	30	30	60	30	
400	40	40	80	40	
500	50	50	100	50	
600	60	60	120	60	
700	70	70	140	70	
800	80	80	160	80	
900	90	90	180	90	
1000	100	100	200	100	
1100	110	110	220	110	
1200	120	120	240	120	
1300	130	130	260	130	
1400	140	140	280	140	
1500	150	150	300	150	
1600	160	160	320	160	
1700	170	170	340	170	
1800	180	180	360	180	
1900	190	190	380	190	
2000	200	200	400	200	
2100	210	210	420	210	
2200	220	220	440	220	
2300	230	230	460	230	
2400	240	240	480	240	
2500	250	250	500	250	
2600	260	260	520	260	
2700	270	270	540	270	
2800	280	280	560	280	
2900	290	290	580	290	
3000	300	300	600	300	

TABLES 11 and 12

Rafters

Tables 11 and 12 show the number of board feet of lumber for 2″ × 4″ and 2″ × 6″ rafters, 16″ and 24″ on center for dwellings. The Tables include roof pitches of:

1/8 or 3″ rise-per-foot-of-run	1/4 or 6″ rise-per-foot-of-run
1/6 or 4″ ″ ″ ″ ″ ″	1/3 or 8″ ″ ″ ″ ″ ″
5/24 or 5″ ″ ″ ″ ″ ″	1/2 or 12″ ″ ″ ″ ″ ″

HOW TO USE THESE TABLES

Determine the *ground-floor* area of your dwelling as outlined under "Computation of Areas", page 17. Read the number of board feet directly from the Tables. No adjustment for length-to-width radio is necessary.

Special Note:

An alternate area computation for roof framing, decking, and roofing is shown and explained on page 17, where the horizontal area covered by a roof includes carports, breezeways, driveways, decks and porches and other areas beyond the perimeter of the main dwelling.

When using this alternate area computation, the horizontal square foot area is substituted in the Tables for the *ground-floor* area in column one.

Overhang

The quantities shown in these Tables do not include any overhang at the eaves or at gable ends. For each 12″ of horizontal overhang at the eaves add 5% the quantities in the Tables.

Dormer Framing

The board feet (FBM) of framing for dormers, in most cases, will be only slightly more than the board feet of rafters that are eliminated from the main roof by installing the dormers.

Hip and Gable Roofs

The surface area of a hip roof is identical to the surface area of a gable roof of the same pitch and covering the same horizontal area.

In other words, a dwelling 30' × 60' with a *ground-floor* area of 1,800 square feet, and having a roof pitch of 1/4 (6" rise-per-foot-of-run), will have the same *roof surface area* whether it is a hip roof or a gable roof.

The board feet of rafters in the hip roof will be approximately the same as in the gable roof except for a minor increase due to slightly larger members in the four corner hips.

Nails

For estimating purposes, an acceptable average quantity of nails is as follows: (Refer to Table 14B for nails for other framing members)

2" × 4" Rafters..................10 lbs 16d per 1,000 FBM

2" × 6"   "   ....9 "   "   "   "   "

Trusses

For Pre-fab trusses, see Table No. 13, page 194.

BASIC FORMULAS FOR RAFTERS

The following formulas may be used to estimate the number of board feet (FBM) of rafters, excluding any overhang, for all dwellings. These formulas may be used in place of Tables 11 and 12 to determine the board feet needed to frame a roof of any dimension, whether gable or hip roof. Simply mutliply the appropriate factor by the ground-floor area of the dwelling. Add 5% to the quantity developed for each 12" of horizontal overhang.

A = *ground-floor* area in square feet.

TABLE 11-12A

Size of Rafter	Pitch of Roof					
and Centers	$^1/_8$	$^1/_6$	$^5/_{24}$	$^1/_4$	$^1/_3$	$^1/_2$
2″ × 4″ - 16″ on center	.57 × A	.58 × A	.60 × A	.62 × A	.66 × A	.78 × A
″ - 24″ ″ ″	.39 × A	.40 × A	.41 × A	.43 × A	.46 × A	.54 × A
2″ × 6″ - 16″ ″ ″	.82 × A	.85 × A	.87 × A	.90 × A	.96 × A	1.14 × A
″ -24″ ″ ″	.57 × A	.58 × A	.60 × A	.62 × A	.66 × A	.78 × A

Illustrative Example No. 1

A dwelling 40′ × 50′ has a *ground-floor* area of 2,000 sq ft. The roof pitch is $^1/_3$ and the roof has 2″ × 6″ rafters, 24″ on center. The total FBM for the rafters is:

2,000 × .66 = 1,320 FBM

If the rafters were 16″ on center, the answer would be:

2,000 × .96 = 1,920 FBM

Where the roof extends over areas outside the perimeter of the dwelling, such as over a carport, breezeway, open porch or other non-dwelling area, use the horizontal area covered by the roof in place of the *ground-floor* area of the dwelling. See page 17 for the explanation of this method.

Illustrative Example No. 2

A dwelling 36′ × 72′ has a roof pitch of $^1/_2$ (12″ rise-per-foot-of-run). The ground-floor area is 36′ × 72′ = 2,592 sq ft. The rafters are 2″ × 6″-24″ on center and there is a horizontal overhang of 12″ at the eaves and gable, or only at the eaves if it is a hip roof. This adds 2′ to both the width and the length. The area of the horizontal plane covered by the roof is 38′ × 74′ = 2,812 sq ft.

Method 1.

From Table 11-12A for 2″ × 6″ rafters 24″ on center in a roof with a $^1/_2$ pitch is .78 × A.

.78 × 2,592 = 2,022 FBM

For each 12″ of horizontal overhang the approximate factor to multiply the FBM by is 5 percent.

1.05 × 2,022 = 2,123 FBM

Method 2.

Using a *ground-floor* area of 2,812 sq ft which includes the 12″ overhang, Table 12 shows there are 2,194 FBM of rafters. This is by interpolating. Table 11-12B gives the factor by which the run is multiplied to get the rafter length when the pitch (rise-per-foot-of-run) is known. For example, a roof with a span of 36' has a pitch of 1/4 and a run of 18'. The rafter length would be 18' × 1.12 = 20.16 feet.

Table 11-12C shows the length of rafters when the height of the roof and width of the building are known. Using the previous example, the height of the roof is 9' and the width is 36'. Table 11-12C shows rafter lengths of 20'-2".

TABLE 11-12B

FACTOR BY WHICH RUN IS MULTIPLIED TO OBTAIN RAFTER LENGTH WHEN RISE-PER-FOOT-OF-RUN IS KNOWN

No. Inches Rise-per-foot-of-run	*Pitch	Rafter length in inches per foot of run	To get rafter length multiply run in ft by
3.0	1/8	12.37 ÷ 12 =	1.030
3.5			1.045
4.0	1/6	12.65	1.060
4.5			1.075
5.0	5/24	13.00	1.090
5.5			1.105
6.0	1/4	13.42	1.120
6.5			1.140
7.0	7/24	13.89	1.160
7.5			1.185
8.0	1/3	14.42	1.201
8.5			1.230
9.0	3/8	15.00	1.250
9.5			1.280
10.0	5/12	15.62	1.301
10.5			1.335
11.0	11/24	16.28	1.360
11.5			1.390
12.0	1/2	16.97	1.420

*Pitch is determined by dividing the inches rise-per-foot-of-run by 24. (Most roofs of dwellings are constructed with a pitch of 1/8, 1/6, 1/4, 1/3 or 1/2.)

TABLE 11-12C

TABLE OF RAFTER LENGTHS

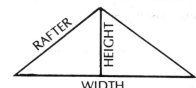

Height (Feet & Inches)

Height	Width of Building in Feet									
	18	20	22	24	26	28	30	32	34	36
	Length of Rafters in Feet and Inches									
4 6	10 2	10 11	11 9	12 10	13 9	14 9	15 8	16 8	17 7	18 7
5 0	10 4	11 3	12 1	13 0	13 11	14 11	15 10	16 9	17 9	18 8
5 6	10 6	11 5	12 4	13 3	14 2	15 1	16 0	16 11	17 11	18 10
6 0	10 9	11 8	12 6	13 5	14 4	15 3	16 2	17 1	18 1	19 0
6 6	11 0	11 11	12 9	13 8	14 6	15 5	16 4	17 3	18 3	19 2
7 0	11 4	12 3	13 0	13 11	14 8	15 8	16 7	17 5	18 5	19 4
7 6	11 8	12 6	13 4	14 2	15 0	15 11	16 9	17 8	18 7	19 6
8 0	12 0	12 10	13 8	14 5	15 3	16 2	17 0	17 10	18 9	19 8
8 6	12 4	13 2	13 11	14 8	15 6	16 5	17 3	18 2	18 11	19 11
9 0	12 9	13 5	14 3	15 0	15 10	16 8	17 6	18 5	19 3	20 2
9 6	13 2	13 10	14 6	15 4	16 1	16 11	17 9	18 8	19 6	20 5
10 0	13 6	14 2	14 10	15 8	16 5	17 3	18 1	18 11	19 9	20 7
10 6	13 10	14 6	15 3	15 11	16 9	17 6	18 4	19 3	20 0	20 10
11 0	14 3	14 10	15 7	16 4	17 0	17 10	18 8	19 6	20 3	21 1
11 6	14 7	15 3	15 11	16 8	17 4	18 2	18 11	19 9	20 6	21 4
12 0	15 0	15 8	16 4	17 0	17 9	18 5	19 3	20 0	20 10	21 8
12 6	15 5	16 0	16 8	17 4	18 0	18 9	19 7	20 4	21 1	21 11
13 0	15 10	16 5	17 0	17 8	18 5	19 2	19 10	20 8	21 5	22 2
13 6	16 3	16 10	17 5	18 0	18 9	19 6	20 3	20 11	21 9	22 6
14 0	16 8	17 3	17 10	18 5	19 2	19 10	20 7	21 3	22 0	22 10
14 6	17 1	17 8	18 3	18 10	19 6	20 2	20 10	21 7	22 4	23 2
15 0	17 6	18 0	18 8	19 3	19 11	20 7	21 3	21 11	22 8	23 6
15 6	17 11	18 5	19 0	19 8	20 3	20 11	21 7	22 4	23 0	23 10
16 0	18 4	18 10	19 5	20 0	20 8	21 4	21 11	22 8	23 4	24 1
16 6	18 10	19 4	19 10	20 5	21 0	21 8	22 4	23 0	23 8	24 5
17 0	19 3	19 9	20 3	20 11	21 5	22 1	22 8	23 4	24 1	24 9
17 6	19 9	20 2	20 8	21 3	21 10	22 5	23 0	23 8	24 5	25 1
18 0	20 1	20 7	21 0	21 8	22 3	22 10	23 5	24 1	24 9	25 6
18 6	20 7	21 0	21 6	22 0	22 8	23 3	23 10	24 5	25 2	25 10
19 0	21 0	21 5	22 0	22 6	23 1	23 8	24 3	24 10	25 6	26 2
19 6	21 5	21 11	22 5	22 11	23 5	24 0	24 8	25 3	25 10	26 7
20 0	21 11	22 4	22 10	23 4	23 10	24 5	25 0	25 8	26 3	26 11
20 6	22 5	22 10	23 3	23 9	24 4	24 10	25 5	26 0	26 8	27 4

TABLE 11

2″ × 4″ RAFTERS INCLUDING RIDGE POLE . . . BOARD FEET
REQUIRED FOR ROOF PITCH SHOWN. 16″ and 24″ CENTERS

Ground Floor Area	16″ CENTER TO CENTER							24″ CENTER TO CENTER					
	ROOF PITCH							ROOF PITCH					
	1/8	1/6	5/24	1/4	1/3	1/2		1/8	1/6	5/24	1/4	1/3	1/2
200	114	116	120	124	132	156		78	80	82	86	92	108
300	171	174	180	186	198	234		117	120	123	129	138	162
400	228	232	240	248	264	312		156	160	164	172	184	216
500	285	290	300	310	330	390		195	200	205	215	230	270
600	342	348	360	372	396	468		234	240	246	258	276	324
700	399	406	420	434	462	546		273	280	287	301	322	378
800	456	464	480	496	528	624		312	320	328	344	368	432
900	513	522	540	558	594	702		351	360	369	387	414	486
1000	570	580	600	620	660	780		390	400	410	430	460	540
1100	627	638	660	682	726	858		429	440	451	473	506	594
1200	684	696	720	744	792	936		468	480	492	516	552	648
1300	741	754	780	806	858	1014		507	520	533	559	598	702
1400	798	812	840	868	924	1092		546	560	574	602	644	756
1500	855	870	900	930	990	1170		585	600	615	645	690	810
1600	912	928	960	992	1056	1248		624	640	656	688	736	864
1700	969	986	1020	1054	1122	1326		663	680	697	731	782	918
1800	1026	1044	1080	1116	1188	1404		702	720	738	774	828	972
1900	1083	1102	1140	1178	1254	1482		741	760	779	817	874	1026
2000	1140	1160	1200	1240	1320	1560		780	800	820	860	920	1080
2100	1197	1218	1260	1302	1386	1638		819	840	861	903	966	1134
2200	1254	1276	1320	1363	1452	1716		858	880	902	946	1012	1188
2300	1311	1334	1380	1426	1518	1794		897	920	943	989	1058	1242
2400	1368	1392	1440	1488	1584	1872		936	960	984	1032	1104	1296
2500	1425	1450	1500	1550	1650	1950		975	1000	1025	1075	1150	1350
2600	1482	1508	1560	1612	1716	2028		1014	1040	1066	1118	1196	1404
2700	1539	1566	1620	1674	1782	2106		1053	1080	1107	1161	1242	1458
2800	1596	1624	1680	1736	1848	2184		1092	1120	1148	1204	1288	1512
2900	1653	1682	1740	1798	1914	2262		1131	1160	1189	1247	1334	1566
3000	1710	1740	1800	1860	1980	2340		1170	1200	1230	1290	1380	1620

TABLE 12

2″ × 6″ RAFTERS INCLUDING RIDGE POLE
BOARD FEET REQUIRED FOR PITCH SHOWN

Ground Floor Area	16″ CENTER TO CENTER							24″ CENTER TO CENTER					
	ROOF PITCH							ROOF PITCH					
	1/8	1/6	5/24	1/4	1/3	1/2		1/8	1/6	5/24	1/4	1/3	1/2
200	164	170	174	180	192	228		114	116	120	124	132	156
300	246	255	261	270	288	342		171	174	180	186	198	234
400	328	340	348	360	384	456		228	232	240	248	264	312
500	410	425	435	450	480	570		285	290	300	310	330	390
600	492	510	522	540	576	684		342	348	360	372	396	468
700	574	595	609	630	672	798		399	406	420	434	462	546
800	656	680	696	720	768	912		456	464	480	496	528	624
900	739	765	783	810	864	1026		513	522	540	558	594	702
1000	820	850	870	900	960	1140		570	580	600	620	660	780
1100	902	935	957	990	1056	1254		627	638	660	682	726	858
1200	984	1020	1044	1080	1152	1368		684	696	720	744	792	936
1300	1066	1105	1131	1170	1248	1482		741	754	780	806	858	1014
1400	1148	1190	1218	1260	1344	1596		798	812	840	868	924	1092
1500	1230	1274	1305	1350	1440	1710		855	870	900	930	990	1170
1600	1312	1360	1392	1440	1536	1824		912	928	960	992	1056	1248
1700	1394	1445	1479	1530	1632	1938		969	986	1020	1054	1122	1326
1800	1476	1530	1566	1620	1728	2052		1026	1044	1080	1116	1188	1404
1900	1558	1615	1653	1710	1824	2166		1083	1102	1140	1178	1254	1482
2000	1640	1700	1740	1800	1920	2280		1140	1160	1200	1240	1320	1560
2100	1722	1785	1827	1890	2016	2394		1197	1218	1260	1302	1386	1638
2200	1804	1870	1914	1980	2112	2508		1254	1276	1320	1364	1452	1716
2300	1886	1955	2001	2070	2208	2622		1311	1334	1380	1426	1518	1794
2400	1968	2040	2088	2160	2304	2736		1368	1392	1440	1488	1584	1872
2500	2050	2125	2175	2250	2400	2850		1425	1450	1500	1550	1650	1950
2600	2132	2210	2262	2340	2496	2964		1482	1508	1560	1612	1716	2028
2700	2214	2295	2349	2430	2592	3078		1539	1566	1620	1674	1782	2106
2800	2296	2380	2436	2520	2688	3192		1596	1624	1680	1736	1848	2184
2900	2378	2465	2523	2610	2784	3306		1653	1682	1740	1798	1914	2262
3000	2460	2550	2610	2700	2880	3420		1710	1740	1800	1860	1980	2340

TABLE 13

Prefabricated Roof Trusses

Table 13 shows the number of board feet (FBM) of lumber for roof trusses with 2″ × 4″ and 2″ × 6″ rafters and 2″ × 4″ cords, spaced 24″ on center. The Table includes roof pitches of:

1/8 or 3″ rise-per-foot-of-run	1/4 or 6″ rise-per-foot-of-run
1/6 or 4″ ″ ″ ″ ″ ″	1/3 or 8″ ″ ″ ″ ″ ″
5/24 or 5″ ″ ″ ″ ″ ″	1/2 or 12″ ″ ″ ″ ″ ″

HOW TO USE THIS TABLE

Determine the *ground-floor* area of your dwelling as outlined under Computation of Areas, page 17. Read the number of board feet directly from the Table. No adjustment for length-to-width ratio is necessary.

Special Note:

An alternate area computation for roof framing, decking and roofing is shown and explained on page 17, where the horizontal area covered by a roof includes carports, breezeways, driveways, decks and porches and other areas beyond the perimeter of the main dwelling.

When using this alternate area computation, the horizontal square foot area is to be substituted in the Table for the *ground-floor* area in column one.

Overhang

The quantities shown in Table No. 13 do not include any overhang at the eaves or at the gable ends. For each 12″ of horizontal overhang add 3% to the quantity in the Table.

TABLE 13—PREFABRICATED ROOF TRUSSES   195

Dormer Framing

The Board feet (FBM) of framing for dormers will be only slightly more in most cases, than the board feet of rafters that are eliminated from the main roof by installing the dormers. The additional framing is due to any overhang on the dormer.

Hip and Gable Roofs

The surface area of a hip roof is identical to the surface area of a gable roof of the same pitch and covering the same horizontal area. In other words, a dwelling 30′ × 60′ with a *ground-floor* area of 1,800 square feet, and having a roof pitch of 1/4 or 6″ rise-per-foot-of-run will have the same *roof surface area* whether it is a hip roof or a gable roof.

The board feet of rafter material in the hip roof will be approximately the same as in the gable roof except for minor increase due to slightly larger framing members at the four corner hips.

Gussets, Metal Connectors, and Nails

Table No. 13 does not include gussets, metal connectors or nails. These items should be added in estimating the total material necessary to complete the trusses.

Struts and Braces

All 2″ × 4″ struts and braces are included in the quantities shown.

TABLE 13

ROOF TRUSSES . . . 24″ ON CENTER . . . INCLUDING BRACES AND STRUTS
BOARD FEET REQUIRED FOR RAFTER SIZE AND ROOF PITCH SHOWN
(W-TYPE TRUSSES)

Ground Floor Area	2″ × 4″ RAFTER AND CORD							2″ × 6″ RAFTER . . . 2″ × 4″ CORD					
	ROOF PITCH							ROOF PITCH					
	1/8	1/6	5/24	1/4	1/3	1/2		1/8	1/6	5/24	1/4	1/3	1/2
200	210	212	214	218	224	240		246	248	252	256	264	288
300	315	318	321	327	336	360		369	372	378	384	396	432
400	420	424	428	436	448	480		492	496	504	512	528	576
500	525	530	535	545	560	600		615	620	630	640	660	720
600	630	636	642	654	672	720		738	744	756	768	792	864
700	735	742	749	763	784	840		861	868	882	896	924	1008
800	840	848	856	872	896	960		984	992	1008	1024	1056	1152
900	945	954	963	981	1008	1080		1107	1116	1134	1152	1188	1296
1000	1050	1060	1070	1090	1120	1200		1230	1240	1260	1280	1320	1440
1100	1155	1166	1177	1199	1232	1320		1353	1364	1386	1408	1452	1584
1200	1260	1272	1284	1308	1344	1440		1476	1488	1512	1536	1584	1728
1300	1365	1378	1391	1417	1456	1560		1599	1612	1638	1664	1716	1872
1400	1470	1484	1498	1526	1568	1680		1722	1736	1764	1792	1848	2016
1500	1575	1590	1605	1635	1680	1800		1845	1860	1890	1920	1980	2160
1600	1680	1696	1712	1744	1792	1920		1968	1984	2016	2048	2112	2304
1700	1785	1802	1819	1853	1904	2040		2091	2108	2142	2176	2244	2448
1800	1890	1908	1926	1962	2016	2160		2214	2232	2268	2304	2376	2592
1900	1995	2014	2033	2071	2128	2280		2337	2356	2394	2432	2508	2736
2000	2100	2120	2140	2180	2240	2400		2460	2480	2520	2560	2640	2880
2100	2205	2226	2247	2289	2352	2520		2583	2604	2646	2688	2772	3024
2200	2310	2332	2354	2398	2464	2640		2706	2728	2772	2816	2904	3168
2300	2415	2438	2461	2507	2576	2760		2829	2852	2898	2944	3036	3312
2400	2520	2544	2568	2616	2688	2880		2952	2976	3024	3072	3168	3456
2500	2625	2650	2675	2725	2800	3000		3075	3100	3150	3200	3300	3600
2600	2730	2756	2782	2834	2912	3120		3198	3224	3276	3328	3432	3744
2700	2835	2862	2889	2943	3024	3240		3321	3348	3402	3456	3564	3888
2800	2940	2968	2996	3052	3136	3360		3444	3472	3528	3584	3696	4032
2900	3045	3074	3103	3161	3248	3480		3567	3596	3654	3712	3828	4176
3000	3150	3180	3210	3270	3360	3600		3690	3720	3780	3840	3960	4320

TABLE 13—PREFABRICATED ROOF TRUSSES 197

BASIC FORMULA FOR ROOF TRUSSES

The following formula may be used to estimate the board feet of material in roof trusses for any dwelling with roof pitches shown. Two types of truss are shown. One with 2″ × 4″ rafters and cords: the other with 2″ × 6″ rafters and 2″ × 4″ cords, and struts and braces are included for each type. Multiply the factor shown by the ground-floor area of your dwelling.

TABLE 13A

PITCH OF ROOF

Rafter Size 24″ Center To Center	1/8	1/6	5/24	1/4	1/3	1/2
2″ × 4″	1.05	1.06	1.07	1.09	1.12	1.20
2″ × 6″	1.23	1.24	1.26	1.28	1.32	1.44

Illustrative Example

A dwelling 35′ × 80′ has a *ground-floor* area of 2,800 square feet. The roof pitch is 1/3 and the rafters are 2″ × 6″ with no overhang. The above formula shows a factor of 1.32 by which the area is to be multiplied to obtain the board feet of truss material.

1.32 × 2,800 = 3,696 FBM

For each 12″ of horizontal overhang add 3% to the above figure.

TABLE 14

Total Board Feet (FBM) of
Framing Lumber Required in
Dwellings for the Specifications Shown

This Table shows the total board feet (FBM) of framing in dwellings for which various specifications are stated below. These specifications include frame, brick veneer and solid masonry walls; dwellings with and without basements.

The specifications apply to dwellings that have a roof pitch of 1/4 which is 6″ rise-per-foot-of-run. The length-to-width ratio is 2:1. Simple adjustments are illustrated for roof pitches and length-to-width ratios other than those used in the Table.

The framing for gables is not included. Where there are gables, the framing is readily estimated as shown in the illustrated example on page 200.

SPECIFICATIONS

Specification A: One Story on a Slab, Frame or Brick Veneer Construction.

2″ × 4″ exterior wall and partition studding, 16″ on center
2″ × 6″ rafters, 24″ on center
2″ × 4″ ceiling joists, 24″ on center (equal to light trusses).

Specification B: One Story on a Slab, Solid Masonry Wall Construction

Same as Specification A but omits exterior wall studding.

Specification C: One Story and Basement or Crawl Space, Frame or Brick Veneer Construction.

Same as Specification A, plus 2″ × 10″ floor joists, 16″ on center
Bridging, catting, posts and girders.

198

TABLE 14—TOTAL BOARD FEET (FBM) FOR DWELLINGS   199

Specification D: One Story and Basement or Crawl Space, Solid Masonry Wall Construction.

Same as Specification C but omits exterior wall studding.

Specification E: One and a Half Story and Basement or Crawl Space, Frame or Brick Veneer Construction.

2″ × 4″ exterior wall and partition studding, 16 ″ on center
2″ × 10″ first and second floor joists, 16″ on center
2″ × 4″ ceiling joists (second floor) 24″ on center
2″ × 6″ rafters, 24″ on center,
wood posts, girders, bridging, blocking and catting.

Specification F: One and a Half Story and Basement or Crawl Space, Solid Masonry Wall Construction.

Same as Specification E but omits exterior wall studding.

Specification G: Two Story and Basement or Crawl Space, Frame or Brick Veneer Construction.

Same as Specification E.

Specification H: Two Story and Basement or Crawl Space. Solid Masonry Wall Construction.

Same as Specification F.

HOW TO USE THIS TABLE

1. Determine the *ground-floor* area of your dwelling following the method outlined under Computation of Areas in the General Instructions, page 17.

2. Determine the lineal feet perimeter of your dwelling following the method outlined under Perimeter Measurement in General Instructions, page 18.

3. Using Table A, check the *ground-floor* area and lineal feet of perimeter of your dwelling to obtain the length-to-width ratio.

4. Under the appropriate specifications for your dwelling and its *ground-floor* area, read the quantity of framing from Table 14.

LENGTH-TO-WIDTH ADJUSTMENT

Table 14 is based on a length-to-width ratio of 2:1. If the length-to-width ratio of your dwelling is significantly different, adjust the quantity in Table 14 upward or downward by the percentages under Table A, page 22.

Illustrative Example

Under Specification A, Table 14, a one-story dwelling on a slab, 26′ × 77′, has a *ground-floor* area of 2,002 sq ft and a total of board feet of framing of 4,573 FBM exclusive of gable framing.

The length-to-width ratio is 3:1 rather than the 2:1 used in the Table. The only length-to-width radio adjustment necessary is for exterior wall studding.

Referring to Table 6 we find that there is 1,273 FBM of exterior wall studding in a dwelling of 2,000 sq ft *ground-floor* area. On page 22, Table A, it shows that 9% is to be added where the length-to-width ratio is 3:1. Therefore, the amount to be added is 9% of 1,273 or 115 FBM.

4,573 + 115 = 4,688 FBM total framing

ROOF PITCH ADJUSTMENT

Table 14 is based on a roof pitch of 1/4. If the roof pitch of your dwelling is other than 1/4, refer to the rafter Tables 11 and 12 to adjust the quantity in Table 14 upward or downward as the case may be.

Illustrative Example

Assume the roof pitch in the preceding Illustrative Example is 1/3. Refer to Table 12 and read across the *ground-floor* area to roof pitch 1/3 and roof pitch 1/4. The difference in FBM is 80 (1,320-1,240 = 80). This 80 FBM is to be added to the board feet of framing in the dwelling.

ESTIMATING THE GABLE STUDS

Table 14 does not include gable framing. Determine the sq ft area of both gables from Table C1 or C2 and multiply that area by .67 if the studs are 16″ on center or .50 if they are on 24″ centers. This allows for cutting and fitting the gable studs. Add the FBM so determined to the total board feet in the dwelling.

Illustrative Example

Assume the same roof pitch of 1/3 as in the previous Illustrative Example and the same dwelling . . . a 1-story 26′ × 77′ on a concrete slab.

Table C2 shows that there are 224 sq ft in the both gables where the *ground-floor* area is 2,000 sq ft and the roof pitch is 1/3. Since the studding is 16″ on center the amount to be added (see Table 14A) is 224 × .67 = 150 FBM.

TABLE 14—TOTAL BOARD FEET (FBM) FOR DWELLINGS 201

SUMMARY OF ADJUSTMENTS

Table 14......................................Framing 4,573 FBM
Length-to-width adjustment..................... 115 "
Gable studding .... 150 "
Total framing adjusted 4,838 "

BASIC FORMULAS FOR TOTAL FBM FRAMING IN DWELLINGS

The basic formulas on which Table 14 is based are shown below. Where the perimeter and *ground-floor* are known, the estimator may wish to compute the total FBM of framing from the basic formulas, where P = perimeter and A = ground-floor area.

Specification	Formula
A	6.7P + 1.65A
B	1.65A
C	6.7P + 3.2A
D	3.2A
E	11.6P + 5.16A
F	5.16A
G	13.4P + 5.32A
H	5.32A

Illustrative Example

A two-story and basement dwelling, 28′ × 56′, has a *ground-floor* area of 1,568 sq ft. It is brick veneer, roof pitch is ¼, and specifications are those stated for "G." Total FBM of framing from basic formula for specification "G" is 13.4P + 5.32A.

$$P = 2 (28 + 56) = 168 \text{ lin ft}$$
$$A = 28' \times 56' = 1{,}568 \text{ sq ft}$$
$$13.4 \times 168 + 5.32 \times 1{,}568 = 10{,}593 \text{ FBM}$$

This does not include the framing for the gable if this is a gable roof. Assume a roof pitch of ⅓ in place of the pitch of ¼ contemplated in the basic formulas.

Adjustment for Roof Pitch for Rafters

The basic formula for rafters, Table 11-12A, shows the difference in a pitch of ⅓ and ¼ for 2″ × 6″ rafters 16″ on center is:

$$\text{Roof pitch } ⅓ = .66A$$
$$¼ = .62A$$
$$\overline{.04A}$$

.04 × A = .04 × 1,568 = 63 FBM

Adjustment for Gable Framing.

Refer to the short-cut formula for computing gable areas, page 28. The factor for a roof pitch $\frac{1}{3}$ for length-to-width ratio of 2:1 is .167.

.167 × 1,568 (area) = 262 sq ft in both gables
From Table 14A, .50 × 262 = 131 FBM
(Table 14A gives the factor to multiply sq ft by to get FBM)

Total Adjusted FBM for This Dwelling.

As determined from specification "G" formula......................... 10,593 FBM
" per roof pitch adjustment for rafters.................................... 63   "
"   " gable framing 131   "
                                                                                     10,787   "

NAILS

For estimating purposes an acceptable average quantity of nails for all framing is 10 to 15 lbs per 1,000 FBM of 8d, 10d, 16d and 20d. See Table 14B for the nail requirements of individual framing members.

TABLE 14—TOTAL BOARD FEET (FBM) FOR DWELLINGS   203

TABLE 14

TOTAL NUMBER OF BOARD FEET OF LUMBER FRAMING IN DWELLINGS, BASED ON THE SPECIFICATIONS SHOWN BUT EXCLUDING GABLE FRAMING
(Roof Pitch 1/4 . . . Length to Width Ratio 2:1)

Ground Floor Area	1-Story on a Slab Specification		1-Story & Basement Specification		1 1/2-Story & Basement Specification		2-Story & Basement Specification	
	A	B	C	D	E	F	G	H
200	772	330	1042	640	1728	1032	1868	1064
300	991	495	1456	960	2406	1548	2588	1596
400	1230	660	1850	1280	3050	2064	3267	2128
500	1462	825	2237	1600	3682	2580	3933	2660
600	1687	990	2617	1920	4302	3096	4586	3192
700	1905	1155	2990	2240	4912	3612	5225	3724
800	2124	1320	3363	2560	5420	4128	5864	4256
900	2335	1485	3730	2880	6119	4644	6490	4788
1000	2548	1650	4098	3200	6715	5160	7116	5320
1100	2760	1815	4465	3520	7312	5676	7741	5852
1200	2965	1980	4825	3840	7965	6192	8354	6384
1300	3170	2145	5185	4160	8483	6708	8966	6916
1400	3375	2310	5545	4480	9068	7224	9580	7448
1500	3575	2475	5900	4800	9642	7740	10178	7980
1600	3780	2640	6260	5120	10228	8256	10790	8512
1700	3977	2805	6612	5440	10802	8772	11389	9044
1800	4176	2970	6966	5760	11376	9288	11988	9576
1900	4375	3135	7320	6080	11950	9804	12587	10108
2000	4573	3300	7673	6400	12524	10320	13186	10640
2100	4765	3465	8020	6720	13086	10836	13770	11171
2200	4963	3630	8373	7040	13661	11352	14370	11704
2300	5515	3795	8720	7360	14223	11868	14956	12236
2400	5354	3960	9074	7680	14797	12384	15555	12768
2500	5545	4125	9420	8000	15360	12900	16140	13300
2600	5737	4290	9767	8320	15922	13416	16726	13832
2700	5929	4455	10114	8640	16484	13932	17312	14364
2800	6120	4620	10460	8960	17046	14448	17898	14896
2900	6313	4785	10808	9280	17609	14964	18483	15428
3000	6510	4950	11160	9600	18183	15480	19082	15960

TABLE 14A

FBM OF FRAMING IN DWELLINGS PER SQUARE FOOT OF WALL, FLOOR OR ROOF SURFACE AREA

Size of Framing Member In Inches	FBM Per Square Foot	
	16″ On Center	24″ On Center
2″ × 3″	.375	.250
*2″ × 4″	*.500	*.333
2″ × 6″	.750	.500
2″ × 8″	1.000	.667
2″ × 10″	1.250	.830
2″ × 12″	1.500	1.000

Special Note:

The figures shown in Table 14A represent the actual FBM for each square foot of wall, floor or roof surface area. There is no allowance for cutting, fitting or waste.

*For 2″ × 4″ framing of studs in a wall use .67 FBM per square foot of wall when they are on 16″ centers; use .50 FBM when the studs are on 24″ centers. This will allow a sufficient amount for shoe, plate, framing at corners and around openings plus cutting and fitting waste.

BOARD MEASURE

Nearly all lumber, from the time it is surveyed in the forest until it is sawed from the logs into timbers and boards, is measured and sold by the unit of the *board foot*. Special millwork—moldings, window and door trim, lattice, handrail, balusters, closet pole, shelf cleats, some types of baseboard, molded exterior trim, wood gutters, and fence pickets—are sold by the lineal foot. Plywood, particle board, flakeboard, etc., as distinguished from lumber, is sold by the square foot.

A board foot is one square foot of wood one inch thick. The symbol for board feet is FBM (feet board measure).

The number of board feet in a piece of wood is obtained by multiplying the width times the thickness in inches, times the length in feet, and dividing by 12.

Table 14C shows the number of board feet in various sizes of lumber of different lengths. Table 14D gives the factor to multiply a piece of lumber by to determine the number of board feet it contains.

TABLE 14—TOTAL BOARD FEET (FBM) FOR DWELLINGS   205

TABLE 14B

APPROXIMATE QUANTITY AND THE SIZE OF NAILS REQUIRED PER 1,000 FBM OF VARIOUS KINDS OF FRAMING

Kind of Framing and Size of Lumber	Size of Nails Used	Lbs Per 1,000 FBM
Sills and plates	10d, 16d & 20d	8
Wall and partition stud	10d & 16d	10
Joists and rafters		
2″ × 6″	16d, some 20d	9
2″ × 8″	″ ″ ″	8
2″ × 10″	″ ″ ″	7
2″ × 12″	″ ″ ″	6
Average for total house framing	8d, 10d, 16d, 20d	15
Wood cross bridging, 1″ ×3″	8d	1 lb per 12 sets
Furring (100 sq ft) on masonry	8d	1
″ ″ ″ studding	8d	¹/₂
Roof trusses	10d, 20d and 40d	10

Where a mix of nails is shown it indicates that judgment is to be exercised as to the different sizes of lumber.

TABLE 14C

NUMBER OF BOARD FEET IN VARIOUS SIZES OF LUMBER
Length of Piece

Size Inches	8′	10′	12′	14′	16′	18′	20′	22′
2 × 3	4	5	6	7	8	9	10	11
2 × 4	5$\frac{1}{3}$	6$\frac{2}{3}$	8	9$\frac{1}{3}$	10$\frac{2}{3}$	12	13$\frac{1}{3}$	14$\frac{2}{3}$
2 × 6	8	10	12	14	16	18	20	22
2 × 8	10$\frac{2}{3}$	13$\frac{1}{3}$	16	18$\frac{2}{3}$	21$\frac{1}{3}$	24	26$\frac{2}{3}$	29$\frac{1}{3}$
2 × 12	16	20	24	28	32	36	40	44
3 × 4	8	10	12	14	16	18	20	22
3 × 6	12	15	18	21	24	27	30	33
3 × 8	16	20	24	28	32	36	40	44
3 × 10	20	25	30	35	40	45	50	55
3 × 12	24	30	36	42	48	54	60	66
4 × 4	10$\frac{2}{3}$	13$\frac{1}{3}$	16	18$\frac{2}{3}$	21$\frac{1}{3}$	24	26$\frac{2}{3}$	29$\frac{1}{3}$

TABLE 14C
(Continued)

NUMBER OF BOARD FEET IN VARIOUS SIZES OF LUMBER
Length of Piece

Size Inches	8'	10'	12'	14'	16'	18'	20'	22'
4 × 6	16	20	24	28	32	36	40	44
4 × 8	$21^{1}/_3$	$26^{2}/_3$	32	$37^{1}/_3$	$42^{2}/_3$	48	$53^{1}/_3$	$58^{2}/_3$
6 × 6	24	30	36	42	48	54	60	66
6 × 8	32	40	48	56	64	72	80	88
6 × 10	40	50	60	70	80	90	100	110
8 × 8	$42^{2}/_3$	$53^{1}/_3$	64	$74^{2}/_3$	$85^{1}/_3$	96	$106^{2}/_3$	$117^{1}/_3$
8 × 10	$53^{1}/_3$	$66^{2}/_3$	80	$93^{1}/_3$	$106^{2}/_3$	120	$133^{1}/_3$	$146^{2}/_3$
8 × 12	64	80	96	112	128	144	160	176
10 × 10	$66^{2}/_3$	$83^{1}/_3$	100	$116^{2}/_3$	$133^{1}/_3$	150	$166^{2}/_3$	$183^{1}/_3$
10 × 12	80	100	120	140	160	180	200	220
12 × 14	112	140	168	196	224	252	280	308

$$\frac{\text{Width in inches} \times \text{Thickness in inches} \times \text{Length in feet}}{12}$$

Illustrative Example

A 2″ × 6″ × 10′ contains 10 FBM

$$\frac{2'' \times 6'' \times 10'}{12} = 10 \text{ FBM}$$

The total number of FBM in a list of framing lumber would be obtained as follows:

$$6 \text{ pieces } 2'' \times 4'' \times 8' = \frac{\cancel{6} \times \cancel{2} \times 4 \times 8}{\cancel{12}_{\;2}} = 32 \text{ FBM}$$

$$10 \text{ pieces } 2'' \times 6'' \times 12' = \frac{10 \times 2 \times 6 \times \cancel{12}}{\cancel{12}} = 120 \text{ FBM}$$

$$4 \text{ pieces } 2'' \times 10'' \times 10' = \frac{\cancel{4} \times 2 \times 10 \times 10}{\cancel{12}} = 66^{2}/_3 \text{ FBM}$$

$$8 \text{ pieces } 4'' \times 4'' \times 18' = \frac{8 \times 4 \times 4 \times \cancel{18}^{\;6}}{\cancel{12}_{\;\cancel{3}}} = 192 \text{ FBM}$$

Total = $410^{2}/_3$ FBM

TABLE 14—TOTAL BOARD FEET (FBM) FOR DWELLINGS 207

TABLE 14D

MULTIPLIERS TO COMPUTE THE NUMBER OF BOARD FEET IN ANY LENGTH OF DIMENSION LUMBER

Nominal Size In Inches	Multiply Length By	Nominal Size In Inches	Multiply Length By
2 × 2	0.333	4 × 4	1.333
2 × 3	0.500	4 × 6	2.000
2 × 4	0.667	4 ×8	2.667
2 × 6	1.000	4 × 10	3.333
2 × 8	1.333	4 × 12	4.000
2 × 10	1.667		
2 × 12	2.000	6 × 6	3.000
		6 × 8	4.000
3 × 3	0.750	6 × 10	5.000
3 × 4	1.000	6 × 12	6.000
3 × 6	1.500		
3 × 8	2.000	8 × 8	5.333
3 × 10	2.500	8 × 10	6.667
3 × 12	3.000	8 × 12	8.000

TABLES 15 TO 20

Roof Decking Materials for All Dwellings
Including Milling and Cutting Waste

These Tables show the quantities of various kinds of roof decking for all dwellings. They include the following roof pitches.

Table No.	Roof Pitch	Inches-rise-per-foot-of-run
15	1/8	3
16	1/6	4
17	5/24	5
18	1/4	6
19	1/3	8
20	1/2	12

MILLING AND CUTTING WASTE

The percentages that have been added to the square foot areas to be covered in these Tables for milling, cutting and fitting waste are as follows:

TABLE 15-20A

Item	Percent Added	Multiply Square Foot Area By
Shiplap		
1″ × 6″ & 1″ × 8″	22%	1.22
1″ × 10″	18	1.18
Tongue & Groove Boards		
1″ × 4″	33	1.33
1″ × 6″, and 1″ × 8″	22	1.22
1″ × 10″	18	1.18
Square edge Boards		
1″ × 4″	19	1.19
1″ × 6″ & 1″ × 8″	15	1.15
Plywood, Plyscore, Insulation Board, etc.	10	1.10

208

HOW TO USE THESE TABLES

Determine the *ground-floor* area of your dwelling as outlined under Computation of Areas, page 17. Read the number of board feet directly from the Tables. No adjustment for length-to-width ratio is necessary.

Special Note:

An alternate area computation is shown and explained on page 17 for roof framing, decking and roofing, where the horizontal area of a roof extends over carports, breezeways, driveways, decks and porches and other areas beyond the perimeter of the main dwelling. When using this alternate area computation, the horizontal square foot area (covered by the roof) developed is substituted for the *ground-floor* area in the Tables.

Overhang

The quantities in the Tables do not allow for overhang at the eaves or gables. For each 12″ of horizontal overhang at the eaves, add 5% to the Table quantities.

Dormers

Roof decking for dormers is approximately the quantity taken up in the main roof by the dormer. The only additional amount of decking is dormer overhang.

Hip and Gable Roofs

The surface area of a hip roof is identical to that of a gable roof of the same pitch and covering the same horizontal area.

Nails Required

For estimating purposes an acceptable average quantity of nails for various types of roof decking is shown in Table 30-38E, page 261. This includes shiplap, tongue and groove boards, square edge boards, plywood and plyscore.

TABLE 15

ROOF DECKING FOR ALL DWELLINGS WITH A ROOF PITCH OF 1/8
(Includes Milling and Cutting Waste)

Ground Floor Area Sq Ft	Roof Surface Area Sq Ft	Shiplap 1" by 6" & 8" Board Ft	Shiplap 1" by 10" Board Ft	Tongue & Groove Boards 1" by 4" Board Ft	Tongue & Groove Boards 1" by 6" & 8" Board Ft	Tongue & Groove Boards 1" by 10" Board Ft	Square Edge Boards 1" by 4" Board Ft	Square Edge Boards 1" by 6" & 8" Board Ft	Plywood, Insulation & Particleboard Square Feet
200	206	252	244	274	252	244	246	236	226
300	309	378	366	411	378	366	369	354	339
400	412	504	488	548	504	488	492	472	452
500	515	630	610	685	630	610	615	590	565
600	618	756	632	822	756	732	738	708	678
700	721	882	854	959	882	854	861	826	791
800	824	1008	976	1096	1008	976	984	944	904
900	927	1134	1098	1233	1134	1098	1107	1062	1017
1000	1030	1260	1220	1370	1260	1220	1230	1180	1130
1100	1133	1386	1342	1507	1386	1342	1353	1298	1243
1200	1236	1512	1464	1644	1512	1464	1476	1416	1356
1300	1339	1638	1586	1781	1638	1586	1600	1534	1469
1400	1442	1764	1708	1918	1764	1708	1722	1652	1582
1500	1545	1890	1830	2055	1890	1830	1845	1770	1695
1600	1648	2016	1952	2192	2016	1952	1968	1888	1808
1700	1751	2142	2074	2329	2142	2074	2091	2006	1921
1800	1854	2268	2196	2466	2268	2196	2214	2124	2034
1900	1957	2394	2318	2603	2394	2318	2337	2242	2147
2000	2060	2520	2440	2740	2520	2440	2460	2360	2260
2100	2163	2646	2562	2877	2646	2562	2583	2478	2373
2200	2266	2772	2684	3014	2772	2684	2706	2596	2486
2300	2369	2898	2806	3151	2898	2806	2829	2714	2600
2400	2472	3024	2928	3288	3024	2928	2953	2832	2712
2500	2575	3150	3050	3425	3150	3050	3075	2950	2825
2600	2678	3276	3172	3562	3276	3172	3198	3068	2938
2700	2781	3402	3294	3699	3402	3294	3321	3186	3051
2800	2884	3528	3416	3836	3528	3416	3440	3304	3164
2900	2987	3654	3538	3973	3654	3538	3567	3422	3277
3000	3090	3780	3660	4110	3780	3660	3690	3540	3390

TABLE 16

ROOF DECKING FOR ALL DWELLINGS WITH A ROOF PITCH OF 1/6
(Includes Milling and Cutting Waste)

Ground Floor Area Sq Ft	Roof Surface Area	Shiplap 1" by		Tongue & Groove Boards 1" by			Square Edge Boards 1" by		Plywood, Insulation & Particleboard
	Sq Ft	6" & 8" Board Ft	10" Board Ft	4" Board Ft	6" & 8" Board Ft	10" Board Ft	4" Board Ft	6" & 8" Board Ft	Square Feet
200	212	258	250	282	258	250	252	244	234
300	318	387	375	423	387	375	378	366	351
400	424	516	500	564	516	500	504	488	468
500	530	645	625	705	645	625	630	610	585
600	636	774	750	846	774	750	756	732	702
700	742	900	875	987	900	875	882	854	819
800	848	1030	1000	1128	1030	1000	1008	976	936
900	954	1160	1125	1269	1160	1125	1134	1098	1053
1000	1060	1290	1250	1410	1290	1250	1260	1220	1170
1100	1166	1420	1375	1551	1420	1375	1386	1342	1287
1200	1272	1551	1500	1692	1550	1500	1512	1464	1404
1300	1378	1680	1625	1833	1680	1625	1638	1586	1521
1400	1484	1810	1750	1974	1810	1750	1764	1708	1638
1500	1590	1935	1875	2115	1935	1875	1890	1830	1755
1600	1696	2064	2000	2256	2064	2000	2016	1952	1872
1700	1802	2195	2125	2397	2195	2125	2142	2074	1989
1800	1908	2322	2250	2538	2322	2250	2268	2196	2106
1900	2014	2450	2375	2679	2450	2375	2394	2318	2223
2000	2120	2580	2500	2820	2580	2500	2520	2440	2340
2100	2226	2710	2625	2961	2710	2625	2646	2562	2457
2200	2332	2840	2750	3102	2840	2750	2772	2684	2574
2300	2438	2970	2875	3243	2970	2875	2898	2806	2691
2400	2544	3100	3000	3384	3100	3000	3024	2928	2808
2500	2650	3225	3125	3525	3225	3125	3150	3050	2925
2600	2756	3354	3250	3666	3354	3250	3276	3172	3042
2700	2862	3483	3375	3807	3483	3375	3402	3294	3159
2800	2968	3610	3500	3948	3610	3500	3528	3416	3276
2900	3074	3740	3625	4089	3740	3625	3654	3528	3393
3000	3180	3870	3750	4230	3870	3750	3780	3660	3510

TABLE 17

ROOF DECKING FOR ALL DWELLINGS WITH A ROOF PITCH OF 5/24
(Includes Milling and Cutting Waste)

Ground Floor Area Sq Ft	Roof Surface Area	Shiplap 1" by		Tongue & Groove Boards 1" by			Square Edge Boards 1" by		Plywood, Insulation & Particleboard
	Sq Ft	6" & 8" Board Ft	10" Board Ft	4" Board Ft	6" & 8" Board Ft	10" Board Ft	4" Board Ft	6" & 8" Board Ft	Square Feet
200	218	266	258	290	266	258	260	250	240
300	327	400	387	435	400	387	390	375	360
400	426	532	516	580	532	516	520	500	480
500	546	665	645	725	665	645	650	625	600
600	654	800	774	870	800	774	780	750	720
700	763	930	900	1015	930	900	910	875	840
800	872	1064	1030	1160	1064	1030	1040	1000	960
900	981	1200	1160	1305	1200	1160	1170	1125	1080
1000	1090	1330	1290	1450	1330	1290	1300	1250	1200
1100	1199	1463	1420	1595	1463	1420	1430	1375	1320
1200	1308	1600	1550	1740	1600	1550	1560	1500	1440
1300	1417	1730	1680	1885	1730	1680	1690	1625	1560
1400	1526	1860	1810	2030	1860	1810	1820	1750	1680
1500	1635	2000	1935	2175	2000	1935	1950	1875	1800
1600	1744	2130	2064	2320	2130	2064	2080	2000	1920
1700	1853	2260	2195	2465	2260	2195	2210	2125	2040
1800	1962	2400	2322	2610	2400	2322	2340	2250	2160
1900	2071	2530	2450	2755	2530	2450	2470	2375	2280
2000	2180	2660	2580	2900	2660	2580	2600	2500	2400
2100	2289	2800	2710	3045	2800	2710	2730	2625	2520
2200	2398	2930	2840	3190	2930	2840	2860	2750	2640
2300	2507	2060	2970	3335	3060	2970	2990	2875	2760
2400	2616	3200	3100	3480	3200	3100	3120	3000	2880
2500	2725	3325	3225	3625	3325	3225	3250	3125	3000
2600	2834	3460	3354	3770	3460	3354	3380	3250	3120
2700	2943	3590	3483	3915	3590	3483	3510	3375	3240
2800	3052	3724	3610	4060	3724	3610	3640	3500	3360
2900	3161	3860	3740	4205	3860	3740	3770	3625	3480
3000	3270	3990	3870	4350	3990	3870	3900	3750	3600

TABLE 18

ROOF DECKING FOR ALL DWELLINGS WITH A ROOF PITCH OF 1/4
(Includes Milling and Cutting Waste)

Ground Floor Area Sq Ft	Roof Surface Area	Shiplap 1" by		Tongue & Groove Boards 1" by			Square Edge Boards 1" by		Plywood Insulation & Particleboard
	Sq Ft	6" & 8" Board Ft	10" Board Ft	4" Board Ft	6" & 8" Board Ft	10" Board Ft	4" Board Ft	6" & 8" Board Ft	Square Feet
200	224	274	264	298	274	264	266	258	246
300	336	411	396	447	411	396	400	387	369
400	448	548	528	600	548	528	532	516	492
500	560	685	660	745	685	660	665	645	615
600	672	822	792	894	822	792	800	774	738
700	784	959	924	1043	959	924	930	900	861
800	896	1096	1056	1192	1096	1056	1064	1030	984
900	1008	1233	1188	1340	1233	1188	1200	1160	1107
1000	1120	1370	1320	1490	1370	1320	1330	1290	1230
1100	1232	1507	1452	1639	1507	1452	1463	1420	1353
1200	1344	1644	1584	1788	1644	1584	1600	1550	1476
1300	1456	1781	1716	1937	1781	1716	1730	1680	1600
1400	1568	1918	1848	2086	1918	1848	1860	1810	1722
1500	1680	2055	1980	2235	2055	1980	2000	1935	1845
1600	1792	2192	2112	2384	2192	2112	2130	2064	1968
1700	1904	2329	2244	2533	2329	2244	2260	2195	2091
1800	2016	2466	2376	2682	2466	2376	2400	2322	2214
1900	2128	2603	2508	2830	2603	2508	2530	2450	2337
2000	2240	2740	2640	2980	2740	2640	2660	2580	2460
2100	2352	2877	2772	3130	2877	2772	2800	2710	2583
2200	2464	3014	2904	3278	3014	2904	2930	2840	2706
2300	2576	3151	3036	3427	3151	3036	3060	2970	2829
2400	2688	3288	3168	3576	3288	3168	3200	3100	2952
2500	2800	3425	3300	3725	3425	3300	3325	3225	3075
2600	2912	3562	3432	3874	3562	3432	3460	3354	3198
2700	3024	3700	3564	4023	3700	3564	3590	3483	3321
2800	3136	3836	3696	4172	3836	3696	3724	3610	3440
2900	3248	3973	3828	4321	3973	3828	3860	3740	3567
3000	3360	4110	3960	4470	4110	3960	3990	3870	3690

TABLE 19

ROOF DECKING FOR ALL DWELLINGS WITH A ROOF PITCH OF 1/3
(Includes Milling and Cutting Waste)

Ground Floor Area Sq Ft	Roof Surface Area Sq Ft	Shiplap 1" by		Tongue & Groove Boards 1" by			Square Edge Boards 1" by		Plywood, Insulation & Particleboard Square Feet
		6" & 8" Board Ft	10" Board Ft	4" Board Ft	6" & 10" Board Ft	10" Board Ft	4" Board Ft	6" & 8" Board Ft	
200	240	292	284	320	292	284	286	276	264
300	360	438	426	480	438	426	429	414	396
400	480	584	569	640	584	568	572	552	528
500	600	730	710	800	730	710	715	690	660
600	720	876	852	960	876	852	858	828	792
700	840	1022	994	1120	1022	994	1000	966	924
800	960	1170	1136	1280	1170	1136	1144	1104	1056
900	1080	1314	1278	1440	1314	1278	1287	1242	1188
1000	1200	1460	1420	1600	1460	1420	1430	1380	1320
1100	1320	1610	1562	1760	1610	1562	1573	1518	1452
1200	1440	1752	1704	1920	1752	1704	1716	1656	1584
1300	1560	1900	1846	2080	1900	1846	1859	1794	1716
1400	1680	2044	1990	2240	2044	1990	2000	1932	1848
1500	1800	2190	2130	2400	2190	2130	2145	2070	1980
1600	1920	2336	2272	2560	2336	2272	2288	2208	2112
1700	2040	2480	2414	2720	2480	2414	2430	2346	2244
1800	2160	2630	2556	2880	2630	2556	2574	2484	2376
1900	2280	2774	2700	3040	2774	2700	2717	2622	2508
2000	2400	2920	2840	3200	2920	2840	2860	2760	2640
2100	2520	3066	2982	3360	3066	2982	3000	2898	2772
2200	2740	3212	3124	3520	3212	3124	3146	3036	2904
2300	2760	3358	3266	3680	3358	3266	3290	3174	3036
2400	2880	3504	3410	3840	3504	3410	3430	3312	3168
2500	3000	3650	3550	4000	3650	3550	3575	3450	3300
2600	3120	3800	3692	4160	3800	3692	3720	3588	3432
2700	3240	3942	3834	4320	3942	3834	3860	3726	3564
2800	3360	4090	3976	4480	4090	3976	4000	3864	3696
2900	3480	4234	4118	4640	4234	4118	4150	4000	3828
3000	3600	4380	4260	4800	4380	4260	4290	4140	3960

TABLE 20

ROOF DECKING FOR ALL DWELLINGS WITH A ROOF PITCH OF 1/2
(Includes Milling and Cutting Waste)

Ground Floor Area Sq Ft	Roof Surface Area	Shiplap 1″ by		Tongue & Groove Boards 1″ by			Square Edge Boards 1″ by		Plywood, Insulation & Particleboard
	Sq Ft	6″ & 8″ Board Ft	10″ Board Ft	4″ Board Ft	6″ & 8″ Board Ft	10″ Board Ft	4″ Board Ft	6″ & 8″ Board Ft	Square Feet
200	284	346	336	378	346	336	338	326	312
300	426	520	504	567	520	504	507	489	468
400	568	690	672	756	690	672	676	652	624
500	710	865	840	945	865	840	845	815	780
600	852	1040	1008	1134	1040	1008	1014	978	936
700	994	1210	1176	1323	1210	1176	1183	1141	1092
800	1136	1385	1344	1512	1385	1344	1352	1304	1248
900	1278	1560	1512	1700	1560	1512	1521	1467	1404
1000	1420	1730	1680	1890	1730	1680	1690	1630	1560
1100	1562	1900	1848	2080	1900	1848	1859	1793	1716
1200	1704	2076	2016	2268	2076	2016	2028	1956	1872
1300	1846	2250	2184	2457	2250	2184	2200	2119	2028
1400	1990	2422	2352	2646	2422	2352	2370	2282	2184
1500	2130	2595	2520	2835	2595	2520	2535	2445	2340
1600	2272	2770	2688	3024	2770	2688	2705	2608	2500
1700	2414	2940	2856	3213	2940	2856	2875	2771	2652
1800	2556	3115	3024	3400	3115	3024	3040	2934	2810
1900	2700	3290	3192	3590	3290	3192	3210	3097	2964
2000	2840	3460	3360	3780	3460	3360	3380	3260	3120
2100	2982	3633	3528	3970	3633	3528	3550	3423	3276
2200	3124	3810	3696	4158	3810	3696	3720	3586	3432
2300	3266	3980	3864	4350	3980	3864	3890	3749	3590
2400	3410	4150	4032	4536	4150	4032	4056	3912	3744
2500	3550	4325	4200	4725	4325	4200	4225	4075	3900
2600	3692	4500	4368	4914	4500	4368	4395	4238	4056
2700	3834	4670	4536	5100	4670	4536	4565	4400	4212
2800	3976	4845	4704	5292	4845	4704	4730	4564	4368
2900	4118	5020	4872	5480	5020	4872	4900	4727	4524
3000	4260	5190	5040	5670	5190	5040	5070	4890	4680

TABLE 15-20B

BASIC FORMULAS FOR ESTIMATING ROOF AREAS
AND THE QUANTITY OF ROOF DECKING

Areas of both gable and hip type roofs can be rapidly obtained by multiplying the horizontal area covered by the roof by the following appropriate factor shown for the pitch of the roof under consideration. Overhang must be added. An approximate amount to be added for overhang is 5% for each 12 inches of horizontal overhang at the eaves. Quantities of materials are easily obtained from the areas.

When Roof Pitch equals	Multiply the Horizontal Area of the Roof By
1/8 (3″ rise-per-foot-of-run)	1.03
1/6 (4″ ″ ″ ″ ″ ″)	1.06
5/24 (5″ ″ ″ ″ ″ ″)	1.09
1/4 (6″ ″ ″ ″ ″ ″)	1.12
1/3 (8″ ″ ″ ″ ″ ″)	1.20
1/2 (12″ ″ ″ ″ ″ ″)	1.42

Milling and cutting waste is shown in Table 15-20A, page 208. This should be added.

Illustrative Example

A dwelling 30 × 70 feet has a gable roof with a pitch of 1/3. From the above Table 15-20B the roof area, excluding overhang, is 30′ × 70′ × 1.20 = 2,520 sq ft. If the roof decking is to be 1″ × 8″ shiplap, milling and cutting waste is 22% as shown on page 208. The total FBM of decking is therefore 2,520 × 1.22 = 3,074 FBM.

TABLES 21 THROUGH 26

Roofing Materials for All Dwellings
Including Cutting and Fitting Waste

These Tables show the quantities of various kinds of roofing for all dwellings. They cover the following roof pitches:

Table No.	Roof Pitch	Inches-rise-per-foot-of-run
21	1/8	3
22	1/6	4
23	5/24	5
24	1/4	6
25	1/3	8
26	1/2	12

CUTTING AND FITTING WASTE

The percentages that are to be added to the areas to be covered in these Tables for cutting and fitting waste, starters, ridge caps, etc., are:

TABLE 21-26A

Roofing Material	Percentage Added	Multiply Area By
Asphalt strip and Asbestos Shingles	10%	1.10
18" Wood Shingles ———— 4" exposure	35	1.35
18" " " ———— 5 1/2" "	10	1.10
24" " " ———— 6" "	38	1.38
24" " " ———— 7 1/2" "	10	1.10
Clay Tile Roofing	5	1.05
15 Lb Saturated Felt	10	1.10
30 " " "	10	1.10

217

HOW TO USE THESE TABLES

Determine the *ground-floor* area of your dwelling as outlined under Computation of Areas, page 17. Read quantities directly from the Tables.

Special Note:

An alternate area computation is shown and explained on page 17 for roof framing, decking and roofing where the horizontal of a roof extends over carports, breezeways, driveways, decks and porches and other areas beyond the perimeter of the main dwelling. When using this alternate area computation, the square foot area developed is to be substituted for the ground-floor area in the Tables.

Overhang

The quantities in the Tables do not allow for overhang at the eaves or gables. For each 12″ horizontal overhang at eaves, add 5% to the Table quantities.

Dormers

Roofing for dormers is approximately the quantity taken up in the main roof by the dormer. The only additional amount of decking is dormer overhang.

Hip and Gable Roofs

The surface area of a hip roof is identical to that of a gable roof of the same pitch and covering the same horizontal area.

Nails Required

Asphalt strip shingles	2 lbs - 1¼ inch nail	
Asphalt individual shingles	3 lbs - ″ ″ ″	
Asbetos cement shingles	3-4 - 3d ″ ″	
Slate 10″ × 20″, 3″ lap shingle	3 - 3d or 4d ″	
Clay tile	3 - 1¾ inch nail	
Wood, 16″ - 18″ shingle	2 - 3d ″ ″	
″ 24″ ″	2 - 4d ″ ″	
″ handsplit shakes	2 - 6d ″ ″	

FORMULAS FOR ESTIMATING ROOF AREAS AND
THE QUANTITY OF ROOFING MATERIAL

The areas of gable and hip roofs can be quickly obtained by multiplying the horizontal area to be covered by the roof, by one of the following factors corresponding to the particular roof pitch.

TABLE 21-26B

Roof Pitch	Multiply Horizontal Area By:
$^1/_8$ (3″ rise-per-foot-of-run)	1.03
$^1/_6$ (4″ rise-per-foot-of-run)	1.06
$^5/_{24}$ (5″ rise-per-foot-of-run)	1.09
$^1/_4$ (6″ rise-per-foot-of-run)	1.12
$^1/_3$ (8″ rise-per-foot-of-run)	1.20
$^1/_2$ (12″ rise-per-foot-of-run)	1.42

Multiply the roof area by the percentage of cutting and fitting waste shown in Tables 21-26A, page 217.

Illustrative Example

A dwelling 30′ × 60′ has a gable roof with a pitch of $^5/_{24}$ and is surfaced with asphalt strip shingles.

The area of the roof with this pitch is 1,800 sq ft × 1.09 = 1962 sq ft

The percentage to be added for cutting, fitting, etc., (page 217) is 10%.

The number of squares of shingles required is:

1,962 × 1.10 = 2158 sq ft

= 21.58 squares rounded out to 22 squares.

TABLE 21

ROOFING FOR ALL DWELLINGS WITH A ROOF PITCH OF ¹/₈
(Figures Include Cutting and Fitting Waste)

Ground Floor Area Sq. Ft.	Roof Surface Area Square Ft.	Asphalt Strip Shingles Square Ft.	Wood Shingles				Asbestos Cement Shingles Square Ft.	Clay Roofing Tile Square Ft.	Number of Rolls of Saturated Felt Roofing Paper	
			18" Long		24" Long				15-Lb.	30-Lb.
			4" Expo. Square Ft.	5¹/₂" Expo. Square Ft.	6" Expo. Square Ft.	7¹/₂" Expo. Square Ft.				
200	206	226	278	226	284	226	226	216	.57	1.14
300	309	339	417	339	426	339	339	324	.85	1.70
400	412	452	556	452	568	452	452	432	1.13	2.27
500	515	565	695	565	710	565	565	540	1.42	2.84
600	618	678	834	678	852	678	678	648	1.70	3.40
700	721	791	973	791	994	791	791	756	1.98	3.97
800	824	904	1112	904	1136	904	904	864	2.27	4.54
900	927	1010	1251	1010	1278	1010	1010	972	2.55	5.10
1000	1030	1130	1390	1130	1420	1130	1130	1080	2.83	5.66
1100	1133	1243	1529	1243	1562	1243	1243	1188	3.11	6.22
1200	1236	1356	1668	1356	1704	1356	1356	1296	3.40	6.80
1300	1339	1469	1810	1469	1846	1469	1469	1404	3.68	7.36
1400	1442	1582	1946	1582	1990	1582	1582	1512	3.96	7.92
1500	1545	1695	2085	1695	2130	1695	1695	1620	4.25	8.50
1600	1648	1808	2224	1808	2272	1808	1808	1728	4.53	9.06
1700	1751	1921	2363	1921	2414	1921	1921	1836	4.81	9.62
1800	1854	2034	2500	2034	2556	2034	2034	1944	5.09	10.18
1900	1957	2147	2640	2147	2700	2147	2147	2052	5.38	10.76
2000	2060	2260	2780	2260	2840	2260	2260	2160	5.66	11.32
2100	2163	2378	2920	2378	2982	2378	2378	2268	5.94	11.88
2200	2266	2486	3058	2486	3124	2486	2486	2376	6.23	12.46
2300	2369	2600	3200	2600	3266	2600	2600	2484	6.51	13.02
2400	2472	2712	3336	2712	3410	2712	2712	2592	6.80	13.58
2500	2575	2825	3475	2825	3550	2825	2825	2700	7.08	14.16
2600	2678	2938	3615	2938	3692	2938	2938	2808	7.36	14.72
2700	2781	3051	3753	3051	3834	3051	3051	2916	7.64	15.28
2800	2884	3164	3892	3164	3976	3164	3164	3024	7.92	15.84
2900	2987	3277	4030	3277	4118	3277	3277	3132	8.21	16.42
3000	3090	3390	4170	3390	4260	3390	3390	3240	8.49	16.98

TABLE 22

ROOFING FOR ALL DWELLINGS WITH A ROOF PITCH OF $\frac{1}{6}$
(Figures Include Cutting and Fitting Waste)

| Ground Floor Area Sq. Ft. | Roof Surface Area Square Ft. | Asphalt Strip Shingles Square Ft. | Wood Shingles | | | | Asbestos Cement Shingles Square Ft. | Clay Roofing Tile Square Ft. | Number of Rolls of Saturated Felt Roofing Paper | |
| | | | 18" Long | | 24" Long | | | | | |
			4" Expo. Square Ft.	5½" Expo. Square Ft.	6" Expo. Square Ft.	7½" Expo. Square Ft.			15-Lb.	30-Lb.
200	212	234	286	234	292	234	234	224	.59	1.17
300	318	351	429	351	438	351	351	336	.88	1.76
400	424	468	472	468	584	468	468	448	1.17	2.34
500	530	585	715	585	730	585	585	560	1.46	2.93
600	636	702	858	702	876	702	702	672	1.76	3.51
700	742	819	1000	819	1022	819	819	784	2.05	4.10
800	848	936	1144	936	1170	936	936	896	2.34	4.68
900	954	1053	1287	1050	1314	1050	1050	1008	2.63	5.27
1000	1060	1170	1430	1170	1460	1170	1170	1120	2.93	5.85
1100	1166	1287	1573	1287	1610	1287	1287	1232	3.22	6.44
1200	1272	1404	1716	1404	1752	1404	1404	1344	3.51	7.02
1300	1378	1521	1859	1521	1900	1521	1521	1456	3.80	7.61
1400	1484	1638	2000	1638	2044	1638	1638	1568	4.10	8.19
1500	1590	1755	2145	1755	2190	1755	1755	1680	4.39	8.78
1600	1696	1872	2288	1872	2336	1872	1872	1792	4.68	9.36
1700	1802	1989	2430	1989	2480	1989	1989	1904	4.97	9.95
1800	1908	2106	2574	2106	2630	2106	2106	2016	5.27	10.53
1900	2014	2223	2717	2223	2774	2223	2223	2128	5.56	11.12
2000	2120	2340	2860	2340	2920	2340	2340	2240	5.85	11.70
2100	2226	2457	3000	2457	3066	2457	2457	2352	6.14	12.29
2200	2332	2574	3146	2574	3212	2574	2574	2464	6.44	12.87
2300	2438	2691	3290	2691	3358	2691	2691	2576	6.73	13.46
2400	2544	2808	3430	2808	3504	2808	2808	2688	7.02	14.04
2500	2650	2925	3575	2925	3650	2925	2925	2800	7.31	14.63
2600	2756	3042	3720	3042	3800	3042	3042	2912	7.61	15.21
2700	2862	3159	3860	3159	3942	3159	3159	3024	7.90	15.80
2800	2968	3276	4000	3276	4090	3276	3276	3136	8.19	16.38
2900	3074	3393	4150	3393	4234	3393	3393	3248	8.48	16.96
3000	3180	3510	4290	3510	4380	3510	3510	3360	8.78	17.55

TABLE 23

ROOFING FOR ALL DWELLINGS WITH A ROOF PITCH OF $^5/_{24}$
(Figures Include Cutting and Fitting Waste)

Ground Floor Area Sq. Ft.	Roof Surface Area Square Ft.	Asphalt Strip Shingles Square Ft.	Wood Shingles				Asbestos Cement Shingles Square Ft.	Clay Roofing Tile Square Ft.	Number of Rolls of Saturated Felt Roofing Paper	
			18″ Long		24″ Long					
			4″ Expo. Square Ft.	5½″ Expo. Square Ft.	6″ Expo. Square Ft.	7½″ Expo. Square Ft.			15-Lb.	30-Lb.
200	218	240	294	240	300	240	240	228	.60	1.20
300	327	360	441	360	450	360	360	342	.90	1.80
400	426	480	588	480	600	480	480	456	1.20	2.40
500	545	600	735	600	750	600	600	570	1.50	3.00
600	654	720	882	720	900	720	720	684	1.80	3.60
700	763	840	1029	840	1050	840	840	798	2.10	4.20
800	872	960	1176	960	1200	960	960	912	2.40	4.80
900	981	1080	1323	1080	1350	1080	1080	1026	2.70	5.40
1000	1090	1200	1470	1200	1500	1200	1200	1140	3.00	6.00
1100	1199	1320	1617	1320	1650	1320	1320	1254	3.30	6.60
1200	1308	1440	1764	1440	1800	1440	1440	1368	3.60	7.20
1300	1417	1560	1911	1560	1950	1560	1560	1482	3.90	7.80
1400	1526	1680	2058	1680	2100	1680	1680	1596	4.20	8.40
1500	1635	1800	2205	1800	2250	1800	1800	1710	4.50	9.00
1600	1744	1920	2352	1920	2400	1920	1920	1824	4.80	9.60
1700	1853	2040	2500	2040	2550	2040	2040	1938	5.10	10.20
1800	1962	2160	2646	2160	2700	2160	2160	2052	5.40	10.80
1900	2071	2280	2793	2280	2850	2280	2280	2166	5.70	11.40
2000	2180	2400	2940	2400	3000	2400	2400	2280	6.00	12.00
2100	2289	2520	3087	2520	3150	2520	2520	2394	6.30	12.60
2200	2398	2640	3234	2640	3300	2640	2640	2508	6.60	13.20
2300	2507	2760	3381	2760	3450	2760	2760	2622	6.90	13.80
2400	2616	2880	3528	2880	3600	2880	2880	2736	7.20	14.40
2500	2725	3000	3675	3000	3750	3000	3000	2850	7.50	15.00
2600	2834	3120	3822	3120	3900	3120	3120	2964	7.80	15.60
2700	2943	3240	3969	3240	4050	3240	3240	3078	8.10	16.20
2800	3052	3360	4116	3360	4200	3360	3360	3192	8.40	16.80
2900	3161	3480	4263	3480	4350	3480	3480	3306	8.70	17.40
3000	3270	3600	4410	3600	4500	3600	3600	3420	9.00	18.00

TABLE 24

ROOFING FOR ALL DWELLINGS WITH A ROOF PITCH OF 1/4
(Figures Include Cutting and Fitting Waste)

Ground Floor Area Sq. Ft.	Roof Surface Area Square Ft.	Asphalt Strip Shingles Square Ft.	Wood Shingles 18" Long 4" Expo. Square Ft.	5½" Expo. Square Ft.	24" Long 6" Expo. Square Ft.	7½" Expo. Square Ft.	Asbestos Cement Shingles Square Ft.	Clay Roofing Tile Square Ft.	Number of Rolls of Saturated Felt Roofing Paper 15-Lb.	30-Lb.
200	224	246	300	246	310	246	246	236	.62	1.24
300	336	369	450	369	465	369	369	354	.93	1.86
400	448	492	600	492	620	492	492	472	1.24	2.48
500	560	615	750	615	775	615	615	590	1.55	3.10
600	672	738	900	738	930	738	738	708	1.86	3.72
700	784	861	1050	861	1085	861	861	826	2.17	4.34
800	896	984	1200	984	1240	984	984	944	2.48	4.96
900	1008	1107	1350	1107	1395	1107	1107	1062	2.79	5.58
1000	1120	1230	1500	1230	1550	1230	1230	1180	3.10	6.20
1100	1232	1353	1650	1353	1705	1353	1353	1298	3.41	6.82
1200	1344	1476	1800	1476	1860	1476	1476	1416	3.72	7.44
1300	1456	1600	1950	1600	2015	1600	1600	1534	4.03	8.06
1400	1568	1722	2100	1722	2170	1722	1722	1652	4.34	8.68
1500	1680	1845	2250	1845	2325	1845	1845	1770	4.65	9.30
1600	1793	1968	2400	1968	2480	1968	1968	1888	4.96	9.92
1700	1904	2091	2550	2091	2635	2091	2091	2006	5.27	10.54
1800	2016	2214	2700	2214	2790	2214	2214	2124	5.58	11.16
1900	2128	2337	2850	2337	2945	2337	2337	2242	5.89	11.78
2000	2240	2460	3000	2460	3100	2460	2460	2360	6.20	12.40
2100	2352	2583	3150	2583	3255	2583	2583	2478	6.51	13.02
2200	2464	2706	3300	2706	3410	2706	2706	2596	6.82	13.64
2300	2576	2829	3450	2829	3565	2829	2829	2714	7.13	14.26
2400	2688	2952	3600	2952	3720	2952	2952	2832	7.44	14.88
2500	2800	3075	3750	3075	3875	3075	3075	2950	7.75	15.50
2600	2912	3198	3900	3198	4030	3198	3198	3068	8.06	16.12
2700	3024	3321	4050	3321	4185	3321	3321	3186	8.37	16.74
2800	3136	3440	4200	3440	4340	3440	3440	3304	8.68	17.36
2900	3248	3567	4350	3567	4495	3567	3567	3422	9.00	18.00
3000	3360	3690	4500	3690	4650	3690	3690	3540	9.30	18.60

TABLE 25

ROOFING FOR ALL DWELLINGS WITH A ROOF PITCH OF $1/3$
(Figures Include Cutting and Fitting Waste)

Ground Floor Area Sq. Ft.	Roof Surface Area Square Ft.	Asphalt Strip Shingles Square Ft.	Wood Shingles				Asbestos Cement Shingles Square Ft.	Clay Roofing Tile Square Ft.	Number of Rolls of Saturated Felt Roofing Paper	
			18" Long		24" Long					
			4" Expo. Square Ft.	5½" Expo. Square Ft.	6" Expo. Square Ft.	7½" Expo. Square Ft.			15-Lb.	30-Lb.
200	240	264	324	264	332	264	264	252	.66	1.32
300	360	396	486	396	498	396	396	378	.99	1.98
400	480	528	648	528	664	528	528	504	1.32	2.64
500	600	660	810	660	830	660	660	630	1.65	3.30
600	720	792	972	792	1000	792	792	756	1.98	3.96
700	840	924	1134	924	1162	924	924	882	2.31	4.62
800	960	1056	1296	1056	1328	1056	1056	1008	2.64	5.28
900	1080	1188	1458	1188	1494	1188	1188	1134	2.97	5.94
1000	1200	1320	1620	1320	1660	1320	1320	1260	3.30	6.60
1100	1320	1452	1782	1452	1826	1452	1452	1386	3.63	7.26
1200	1440	1584	1944	1584	1992	1584	1584	1512	3.96	7.92
1300	1560	1716	2106	1716	2158	1716	1716	1638	4.29	8.58
1400	1680	1848	2268	1848	2324	1848	1848	1764	4.62	9.24
1500	1800	1980	2430	1980	2490	1980	1980	1890	4.95	9.90
1600	1920	2112	2592	2112	2656	2112	2112	2016	5.28	10.56
1700	2040	2244	2754	2244	2822	2244	2244	2142	5.61	11.22
1800	2160	2376	2916	2376	2990	2376	2376	2268	5.94	11.88
1900	2280	2508	3078	2508	3154	2508	2508	2394	6.27	12.54
2000	2400	2640	3240	2640	3320	2640	2640	2520	6.60	13.20
2100	2520	2772	3400	2772	3486	2772	2772	2646	6.93	13.86
2200	2640	2904	3564	2904	3652	2904	2904	2772	7.26	14.52
2300	2760	3036	2726	3036	3820	3036	3036	2898	7.59	15.18
2400	2880	3168	3888	3168	3984	3168	3168	3024	7.92	15.80
2500	3000	3300	4050	3300	4150	3300	3300	3150	8.25	16.50
2600	3120	3432	4212	3432	4316	3432	3432	3276	8.58	17.16
2700	3240	3564	4374	3564	4482	3564	3564	3402	8.91	17.82
2800	3360	3696	4536	3696	4648	3696	3696	3528	9.24	18.48
2900	3480	3828	4700	3828	4814	3828	3828	3654	9.57	19.14
3000	3600	3960	4860	3960	4980	3960	3960	3780	9.90	19.80

TABLE 26

ROOFING FOR ALL DWELLINGS WITH A ROOF PITCH OF $1/2$
(Figures Include Cutting and Fitting Waste)

Ground Floor Area Sq. Ft.	Roof Surface Area Square Ft.	Asphalt Strip Shingles Square Ft.	Wood Shingles				Asbestos Cement Shingles Square Ft.	Clay Roofing Tile Square Ft.	Number of Rolls of Saturated Felt Roofing Paper	
			18" Long		24" Long					
			4" Expo. Square Ft.	5½" Expo. Square Ft.	6" Expo. Square Ft.	7½" Expo. Square Ft.			15-Lb.	30-Lb.
200	284	312	384	312	392	312	312	298	.78	1.55
300	426	468	576	468	588	468	468	447	1.16	2.32
400	568	624	768	624	784	624	624	600	1.55	3.10
500	710	780	960	780	980	780	780	745	1.94	3.88
600	852	936	1152	936	1176	936	936	894	2.33	4.65
700	994	1092	1344	1092	1372	1092	1092	1043	2.71	5.43
800	1136	1248	1536	1248	1568	1248	1248	1192	3.10	6.20
900	1278	1404	1728	1404	1764	1404	1404	1340	3.49	6.98
1000	1420	1560	1920	1560	1960	1560	1560	1490	3.88	7.75
1100	1562	1716	2112	1716	2156	1716	1716	1639	4.26	8.53
1200	1704	1872	2304	1872	2352	1872	1872	1788	4.65	9.30
1300	1846	2028	2496	2028	2548	2028	2028	1937	5.04	10.08
1400	1990	2184	2688	2184	2744	2184	2184	2086	5.43	10.85
1500	2130	2340	2880	2340	2940	2340	2340	2235	5.81	11.63
1600	2272	2500	3072	2500	3136	2500	2500	2384	6.20	12.40
1700	2414	2652	3264	2652	3332	2652	2652	2533	6.59	13.18
1800	2556	2810	3456	2810	3528	2810	2810	2682	6.98	13.95
1900	2700	2964	3648	2964	3724	2964	2964	2830	7.36	14.93
2000	2840	3120	3840	3120	3920	3120	3120	2980	7.75	15.50
2100	2982	3276	4032	3276	4116	3276	3276	3130	8.14	16.28
2200	3124	3432	4224	3432	4312	3432	3432	3278	8.53	17.05
2300	3266	3590	4416	3590	4508	3590	3590	3427	8.91	17.83
2400	3410	3744	4608	3744	4704	3744	3744	3576	9.30	18.60
2500	3550	3900	4800	3900	4900	3900	3900	3725	9.69	19.38
2600	3692	4056	4992	4056	5096	4056	4056	3874	10.08	20.15
2700	3834	4212	5184	4212	5292	4212	4212	4023	10.46	20.93
2800	3976	4368	5376	4368	5488	4368	4368	4172	10.85	21.70
2900	4118	4524	5568	4524	5684	4524	4524	4321	11.24	22.48
3000	4260	4680	5760	4680	5880	4680	4680	4470	11.63	23.25

TABLES 27, 28, and 29

Interior Surface Materials for Walls, Ceilings and Floors

These Tables give the quantities, including all cutting, fitting or milling waste applicable, for the various materials shown which are used on the interior walls, ceilings and rough and finished floors. The Tables also include the square foot and square yard areas of wall, ceiling and floor surfaces. This enables an estimator to quickly determine quantities of those materials that are not provided for in the Tables. All wall quantities are based on a floor to ceiling height of 8 feet.

HOW TO USE THESE TABLES

1. Determine the *ground-floor* area of your dwelling following the method outlined under Computation of Areas in General Instructions, page 17.
2. Determine the lineal feet of perimeter of your dwelling following the method outlined under Perimeter Measurement in General Instructions, page 18.
3. Using Table A, check the *ground-floor* area and the lineal feet of perimeter to obtain the length-to-width ratio of your dwelling.

These Tables are based on a length-to-width ratio of 2:1. If the length-to-width ratio of your dwelling is significantly different, adjust the EXTERIOR WALL QUANTITIES ONLY upward or downward by the percentages under Table A, page 22.

Illustrative Example

A two-story dwelling 30′ × 90′ has a *ground-floor* area of 2,700 sq ft and a length-to-width ratio of 3:1 (length is 3 times the width).

The exterior sidewall area for a dwelling with a 2,700 sq ft *ground-floor* area is shown in Table 29 to be 3,520 sq ft.

This, however, is for a dwelling with a length-to-width ratio of 2:1. Table A, page 22, shows that if the length-to-width ratio is 3:1, 9% must be added to the quantities in the Tables.

226

$$3,520 \times 1.09 = 3,837 \text{ sq ft}$$

The interior partition area for this dwelling is 8,640 sq ft and the ceiling area is 5,400 sq ft (Table 29). The total interior wall and ceiling area is:

Sidewalls	3,837 sq ft	
Partitions	8,640	"
Ceilings	5,400	"
Total	17,877	"

WINDOW AND DOOR OPENINGS

Deductions, in part or in full, for window and door openings is left to the discretion of the estimator. Some deduct openings in full when estimating lath and plaster or drywall: others deduct one half the area; still others do not deduct any openings. Those who deduct nothing or half the area of the openings believe this method will take care of the waste and the additional labor to work around the openings. If openings are deducted in full, a percentage must be added for waste. **NO WASTE HAS BEEN CONSIDERED IN TABLES 27, 28 and 29 FOR WALL OR CEILING MATERIALS.**

AREAS OF ROOMS OF KNOWN SIZE

Table 27-29D, pages 235-237, shows the square foot areas of walls and ceilings in rooms with floor to ceiling heights of 8′ to 10′, with no openings deducted.

ROUGH AND FINISHED FLOORS

Quantities for rough and finished floors may be read directly from the Tables. Assume a dwelling 25′ × 75′ with *ground-floor* area of 1875 sq ft has 1″ × 6″ tongue and groove boards for rough floor and 1″ × 3″ matched oak finished floor. It is a 2-story dwelling. Waste percentages for finish flooring is shown on page 228. The quantity of nails required is shown in Table 27-29A, page 228.

Tongue and groove boards 1″ × 6″
Ground-floor area 1,875 sq ft
    Interpolating in Table 29   4,575 FBM
    Nails required, Tables 27-29A, 30 lbs per 1,000 FBM

              $30 \times 4.575 =$ 137 lbs 8d nails

Matched oak flooring 1″ × 3″
Ground-floor area 1,875 sq ft
    Interpolating in Table 29,
    Nails required, Tables 27-29A, 50 lbs per 1,000 FBM 5,175 FBM

              $50 \times 5.175 =$ 259 lbs 7d and 8d screw
                                                           type nails

TABLE 27-29A

NAILS REQUIRED FOR INTERIOR SURFACE MATERIALS

Drywall	Thickness	Type Nail	Lbs. per 1,000 sq ft
Gypsum board	$1/4''$	$1\frac{1}{4}''$ coated	3
" "	$3/8''$ and $1/2''$	$1\frac{5}{8}''$ "	5
" "	$5/8''$	$1\frac{7}{8}''$ "	5
Gypsum lath	$3/8''$ and $1/2''$	$1\frac{1}{8}''$ blued	15
Plywood, plyscore and insulation board	$5/16''$ and $3/8''$	6d	10
	$5/8''$ and $3/4''$	8d	20

Shiplap and square edge or tongue and groove boards	Size		Lbs. per 1,000 FBM
"	$1'' \times 4''$	8d	30-35
"	$1'' \times 6''$	"	25-30
"	$1'' \times 8''$	"	20-25
"	$1'' \times 10''$	"	15-20
Matched oak floor	$1'' \times 3''$	7d & 8d screw type	50
" " "	$1'' \times 4''$		35

MILLING AND CUTTING WASTE
FOR FINISH FLOORING

Nominal Size In Inches	Actual Size In Inches	Milling and Cutting Waste	Multiply Area By	Flooring Needed Per 1,000 Sq Ft
1×2	$25/32 \times 1\frac{1}{2}$	55%	1.55	1,500 FBM
$1 \times 2\frac{1}{2}$	$\times 2$	42	1.42	1,420 "
1×3	$\times 2\frac{1}{4}$	38	1.38	1,380 "
1×4	$\times 3\frac{1}{4}$	29	1.29	1,290 "

The percentage of waste should be added to the square foot area to be covered. Quantities in the Tables include milling and cutting waste.

TABLE 27

INTERIOR SURFACE MATERIALS FOR WALLS, CEILINGS AND FLOORS
FOR 1-STORY DWELLINGS WITH 8′ CEILINGS

Ground Floor Area Sq Ft	Drywall, Lath & Plaster, Wall Boards, Painting & Decorating.						Rough Flooring, Incl. Milling and Cutting Waste				Fin. Floor Incl. Milling & Cutting Waste	
	Square Feet			Square Yards			Shiplap & Tongue & Groove Bds.	Square Edge Boards		Plywood, Particle-Board, etc.		
	Walls		Clgs.	Walls		Clgs.	1″×6″, 1″×8″	1″×4″	1″×6″		1″×3″	1″×4″
	Exter	Part'n		Exter	Part'n		Board Ft	Board Ft	Board Ft	Square Ft	Bd Ft	Bd Ft
200	480	320	200	53	36	22	242	238	228	220	276	258
300	592	480	300	66	53	33	363	357	342	330	414	387
400	680	640	400	76	71	44	484	476	456	440	552	516
500	760	800	500	84	89	56	605	595	570	550	690	645
600	832	960	600	92	107	67	726	714	684	660	828	774
700	896	1120	700	100	124	78	847	833	800	770	966	900
800	960	1280	800	107	142	89	968	952	912	880	1104	1030
900	1016	1440	900	113	160	100	1089	1071	1026	990	1242	1160
1000	1072	1600	1000	119	178	111	1210	1190	1140	1100	1380	1290
1100	1128	1760	1100	125	196	122	1331	1309	1254	1210	1518	1420
1200	1176	1920	1200	131	213	133	1452	1428	1368	1320	1656	1550
1300	1224	2080	1300	136	231	144	1573	1547	1482	1430	1794	1680
1400	1272	2240	1400	141	249	156	1694	1666	1600	1540	1932	1800
1500	1312	2400	1500	146	267	167	1815	1785	1710	1650	2070	1935
1600	1360	2560	1600	151	284	178	1936	1904	1824	1760	2208	2064
1700	1400	2720	1700	156	302	189	2057	2023	1938	1870	2346	2195
1800	1440	2880	1800	160	320	200	2178	2142	2052	1980	2484	2322
1900	1480	3040	1900	164	338	211	2300	2261	2166	2090	2622	2450
2000	1520	3200	2000	169	356	222	2420	2380	2280	2200	2760	2580
2100	1552	3360	2100	172	373	233	2541	2500	2400	2310	2898	2710
2200	1592	3520	2200	177	391	244	2662	2618	2500	2420	3036	2840
2300	1624	3680	2300	180	409	256	2783	2737	2622	2530	3174	2970
2400	1664	3840	2400	185	427	267	2904	2856	2736	2640	3312	3100
2500	1696	4000	2500	188	444	278	3025	2975	2850	2750	3450	3225
2600	1728	4160	2600	192	462	289	3146	3094	2964	2860	3580	3354
2700	1760	4320	2700	196	480	300	3267	3213	3078	2970	3726	3483
2800	1792	4480	2800	199	498	311	3388	3332	3200	3080	3864	3610
2900	1824	4640	2900	203	516	322	3509	3450	3300	3190	4000	3740
3000	1864	4800	3000	207	533	333	3630	3570	3420	3300	4140	3870

TABLE 28

INTERIOR SURFACE MATERIALS FOR WALLS, CEILINGS AND FLOORS
FOR 1 ½-STORY DWELLINGS WITH 8′ CEILINGS

Ground Floor Area	Drywall, Lath & Plaster, Wall Boards, Painting & Decorating.						Rough Flooring, Incl. Milling and Cutting Waste				Fin. Floor Incl. Milling & Cutting Waste	
	Square Feet			Square Yards			Shiplap & Tongue & Groove Bds.	Square Edge Boards		Plywood, Particle-Board, etc.		
	Walls		Clgs.	Walls		Clgs.	1″×6″, 1″×8″	1″×4″	1″×6″		1″×3″	1″×4″
Sq Ft	Exter	Part'n		Exter	Part'n		Board Ft	Board Ft	Board Ft	Square Ft	Bd Ft	Bd Ft
200	960	480	400	107	53	44	488	476	456	440	552	516
300	1184	720	600	132	80	66	732	714	684	660	828	774
400	1360	960	800	151	107	88	976	952	912	880	1104	1032
500	1520	1200	1000	169	133	112	1220	1190	1140	1100	1380	1290
600	1664	1440	1200	185	160	134	1464	1428	1368	1320	1656	1548
700	1792	1680	1400	199	187	156	1708	1666	1596	1540	1932	1806
800	1920	1920	1600	213	213	178	1952	1904	1824	1760	2208	2064
900	2032	2160	1800	226	240	200	2196	2142	2052	1980	2484	2322
1000	2144	2400	2000	238	267	222	2440	2380	2280	2200	2760	2580
1100	2256	2640	2200	251	293	244	2684	2618	2500	2420	3036	2838
1200	2352	2880	2400	261	320	266	2928	2856	2736	2640	3312	3096
1300	2448	3120	2600	272	347	288	3172	3094	2964	2860	3588	3354
1400	2544	3360	2800	283	373	312	3416	3332	3192	3080	3864	3612
1500	2624	3600	3000	202	400	334	3660	3570	3420	3300	4140	3870
1600	2720	3840	3200	302	427	356	3904	3808	3648	3520	4416	4128
1700	2800	4080	3400	311	453	378	4148	4046	3876	3740	4692	4386
1800	2880	4320	3600	320	480	400	4392	4284	4100	3960	4968	4644
1900	2960	4560	3800	329	507	422	4636	4522	4332	4180	5244	4900
2000	3040	4800	4000	338	533	444	4880	4760	4560	4400	5520	5160
2100	3104	5040	4200	345	560	466	5124	5000	4788	4620	5796	5418
2200	3184	5280	4400	354	587	488	5368	5239	5016	4840	6072	5676
2300	3248	5520	4600	361	613	512	5612	5474	5244	5060	6348	5934
2400	3328	5760	4800	370	640	534	5856	5712	5472	5280	6624	6192
2500	3392	6000	5000	377	667	556	6100	5950	5700	5500	6900	6450
2600	3456	6240	5200	384	693	578	6344	6188	5928	5720	7176	6707
2700	3520	6480	5400	391	720	600	6588	6426	6156	5940	7452	6966
2800	3584	6720	5600	398	747	622	6832	6664	6284	6160	7728	7224
2900	3648	6960	5800	405	773	644	7076	6900	6612	6380	8000	7482
3000	3728	7200	6000	414	800	666	7320	7140	6840	6600	8280	7740

TABLE 29

INTERIOR SURFACE MATERIALS FOR WALLS, CEILINGS AND FLOORS FOR 2-STORY DWELLINGS WITH 8' CEILINGS

Ground Floor Area	Drywall, Lath & Plaster, Wall Boards, Painting & Decorating.						Rough Flooring, Incl. Milling and Cutting Waste				Fin. Floor Incl. Milling & Cutting Waste	
	Square Feet			Square Yards			Shiplap & Tongue & Groove Bds.	Square Edge Boards		Plywood, Particle-Board, etc.		
	Walls		Clgs.	Walls		Clgs.						
Sq Ft	Exter	Part'n		Exter	Part'n		1"×6", 1"×8"	1"×4"	1"×6"		1"×3"	1"×4"
							Board Ft	Board Ft	Board Ft	Square Ft	Bd Ft	Bd Ft
200	960	640	400	107	71	44	488	476	456	440	552	516
300	1184	960	600	132	106	66	732	714	684	660	828	774
400	1360	1280	800	151	142	88	976	952	912	880	1104	1032
500	1520	1600	1000	169	178	112	1220	1190	1140	1100	1380	1290
600	1664	1920	1200	185	214	134	1464	1428	1368	1320	1656	1548
700	1792	2240	1400	199	248	156	1708	1666	1596	1540	1932	1806
800	1920	2560	1600	213	285	178	1952	1904	1824	1760	2208	2064
900	2032	2880	1800	226	320	200	2196	2142	2052	1980	2484	2322
1000	2144	3200	2000	238	356	222	2440	2380	2280	2200	2760	2580
1100	2256	3520	2200	251	392	244	2684	2618	2500	2420	3036	2838
1200	2352	3840	2400	261	426	266	2928	2856	2736	2640	3312	3096
1300	2448	4160	2600	272	462	288	3172	3094	2964	2860	3588	3354
1400	2544	4480	2800	283	498	312	3416	3332	3192	3080	3864	3612
1500	2624	4800	3000	292	534	334	3660	3570	3420	3300	4140	3870
1600	2720	5120	3200	302	568	356	3904	3808	3648	3520	4416	4128
1700	2800	5440	3400	311	604	378	4148	4046	3876	3740	4692	4386
1800	2880	5760	3600	320	640	400	4392	4284	4100	3960	4968	4644
1900	2960	6080	3800	329	676	422	4636	4522	4332	4180	5244	4900
2000	3040	6400	4000	338	712	444	4880	4760	4560	4400	5520	5160
2100	3104	6720	4200	345	746	466	5124	5000	4788	4620	5796	5418
2200	3184	7040	4400	354	782	488	5368	5239	5016	4840	6072	5676
2300	3248	7360	4600	361	818	512	5612	5474	5244	5060	6348	5934
2400	3328	7680	4800	370	854	534	5856	5712	5472	5280	6624	6192
2500	3392	8000	5000	377	888	556	6100	5950	5700	5500	6900	6450
2600	3456	8320	5200	384	924	578	6344	6188	5928	5720	7176	6708
2700	3520	8640	5400	391	960	600	6588	6426	6156	5940	7452	6966
2800	3584	8960	5600	398	996	622	6832	6664	6384	6160	7728	7224
2900	3648	9280	5800	405	1032	644	7076	6900	6612	6380	8000	7482
3000	3728	9600	6000	414	1066	666	7320	7140	6840	6600	8280	7740

TABLE 27-29B

FORMULAS FOR ESTIMATING INTERIOR SURFACE MATERIALS
(Floors, walls and ceilings)
WHERE A = AREA,   P = PERIMETER

Surface Material			1-Story	1 ½-Story	2-Story
Drywall, Lath & Plaster, Painting, etc.					
Sidewall Area, (number of sq ft)			8 P	16 P	16P
Partition " " " " "			1.6 A	2.4 A	3.2 A
Ceiling " " " " "			A	2 A	2 A
Totals			2.6 A + 8 P	4.4 A + 16 P	5.2 A + 16 P
Sidewall Area, (number sq yds)			.89 P	1.78 P	1.78 P
Partition " " " "			.178 A	.27 A	.356 A
Ceiling " " " "			.11 A	.22 A	.22 A
Totals			.29 A + .89 P	.49 A + 1.78 P	.576 A + 1.78 P
Rough Flooring (including waste)					
Shiplap	1" × 6", FBM		1.22 A	2.44 A	2.44 A
	1" × 8" "		1.21 A	2.42 A	2.42 A
Tongue & Groove Bds.	1" × 6" "		1.22 A	2.44 A	2.44 A
	1" × 8" "		1.20 A	2.40 A	2.40 A
Square Edge Bds.	1" × 4" "		1.19 A	2.38 A	2.38 A
	1" × 6" "		1.14 A	2.28 A	2.28 A
Plywood, Particle-board, etc.,		Sq Ft	1.10 A	2.20 A	2.20 A
Matched Oak, Maple, Pine Flooring	1" × 3"		1.38 A	2.76 A	2.76 A
	1" × 4"		1.29 A	2.58 A	2.58 A

HOW TO USE THESE FORMULAS

Substitute in these formulas the *ground-floor* area and the perimeter of the dwelling to estimate the quantity of the particular material being considered. The formulas for the sq ft and sq yd areas are shown for materials not in the Table.

DRYWALL

Gypsum board panels are available in 5/8″, 1/2″ and 3/8″ thicknesses in sheets 4′ wide and 8′, 9′, 12′ and 14′ long. The 5/8′ is recommended for single layer drywall construction. Edges of the sheets are tapered on the face side for joint reinforcement when the joints are taped and filled with joint compound.

The quantity of gypsum board is estimated from the surface area, less window and door openings. Ten percent fitting and cutting waste is generally added unless sketches of the walls and ceilings are made and the number and size of each piece of wall board is then determined.

Nails, 5d, are spaced 6 to 8 inches. If adhesive is used the spacing is much greater.

The quantity of joint compound and rolls of tape are shown below.

Illustrative Example

Assume that a two-story dwelling is 32′ × 60′, which gives it a *ground-floor* area of 1,920 sq ft and a perimeter of 184 lin ft. The foregoing formulas show for a two-story dwelling 3.2A + 16P is the sq ft surface area of the side walls and partitions, and 2A for the area of the ceilings.

Side wall and partition area =   3.2 × 1,920 + 16 × 184′ =   9,088 sq ft
Ceiling area =   2 × 1,920   =   3,840 ″ ″
Total interior surface area   12,928 sq ft

Note that in the formula 3.2A + 16P

3.2A is the surface area of the partitions
16P is the surface area of the side walls

The partition area can be taken out and the actual lineal feet of partition estimated. this formula is for a dwelling with a 2:1 length-to-width ratio. If the length-to-width ratio is other than 2:1, such as 4:1 the side wall should be adjusted by using Table A, page 22. In this example the area of the side walls is 16P or 16 × 184 = 2,944 sq ft.

Table A shows that 18% is to be added for a 4:1 length-to-width ratio.

.18 × 2,944 = 530 sq ft
12,928 + 530 = 13,458 sq ft

DRYWALL TAPE AND JOINT COMPOUND

Square Feet of Wallboard	Joint Compound	Rolls of Tape	
100-200	1 gallon	2-60′ rolls	
300-400	2 ″	3-60′ ″	
500-600	3 ″	1-250′ ″	
700-800	4 ″	1-250′ ″	& 1-60′ roll
900-1,000	*5 ″	1-500′ ″	

*50-lbs of powder joint compound per 1,000 sq ft may be substituted.

TABLE 27-29C

APPROXIMATE NUMBER OF SACKS OF PREPARED GYPSUM PLASTER REQUIRED FOR COVERING 100 SQ YDS

Base	Plaster Thickness In Inches	Number of Sacks
Wood lath	$5/8$	22 (80 lb sacks)
Metal lath	$5/8$	35 "
Gypsum lath	$1/2$	20 "
Masonry walls	$5/8$	24 (67 lb sacks)

APPROXIMATE QUANTITIES OF MATERIALS REQUIRED FOR 100 SQ YDS OF WHITE COAT FINISH, $1/16''$ THICK

Kind of Finish	100 lb Sacks Neat Gypsum	100 lb Sacks Keene Cement	50 lb Sacks Hydrated Lime
Lime Putty	2	—	8
Keene's Cement	—	4	4

Based on ASA mix of 1 (100-lb) sack neat gypsum gauging plaster to 4 (50-lb) sacks hydrated lime, and 1 (100-lb) sack of Keene's cement to 1 (50-lb) sack hydrated lime for medium hard finish

TABLE 27-29D

This Table, is a group of Tables showing the square feet in the walls and ceilings of rooms up to 24 feet by 22 feet and having ceiling heights of 8 feet to 10 feet. No openings are considered. Room sizes that are between even feet may be estimated by interpolating in the Table.

TABLE 27-29D

TOTAL SQUARE FEET OF WALL AND CEILING AREA

ROOMS WITH CEILINGS 8 FEET

	3'	4'	5'	6'	7'	8'	9'	10'	11'	12'	13'	14'	15'	16'	17'	18'	19'	20'	21'	22'
3'	105	124	143	162	181	200	219	238	257	276	295	314	333	352	371	390	409	428	447	466
4'	124	144	164	184	204	224	244	264	284	304	324	344	364	384	404	424	444	464	484	504
5'	143	164	185	206	227	248	269	290	311	332	353	374	395	416	437	458	479	500	521	542
6'	162	184	206	228	250	272	294	316	338	360	382	404	426	448	470	492	514	536	558	580
7'	181	204	227	250	273	296	319	342	365	388	411	434	457	480	503	526	549	572	595	618
8'	200	224	248	272	296	320	344	368	392	416	440	464	488	512	536	560	584	608	632	656
9'	219	244	269	294	319	344	369	394	419	444	469	494	519	544	569	594	619	644	669	694
10'	238	264	290	316	342	368	394	420	446	472	498	524	550	576	602	628	654	680	706	732
11'	257	284	311	338	365	392	419	446	473	500	527	554	581	608	635	662	689	716	743	770
12'	276	304	332	360	388	416	444	472	500	528	556	584	612	640	668	696	724	752	780	808
13'	295	324	353	382	411	440	469	498	527	556	585	614	643	672	701	730	759	788	817	846
14'	314	344	374	404	434	464	494	524	554	584	614	644	674	704	734	764	794	824	854	884
15'	333	364	395	426	457	488	519	550	581	612	643	674	705	736	767	798	829	860	891	922
16'	352	384	416	448	480	512	544	576	608	640	672	704	736	768	800	832	864	896	928	960
17'	371	404	437	470	503	536	569	602	635	668	701	734	767	800	833	866	899	932	965	998
18'	390	424	458	492	526	560	594	628	662	696	730	764	798	832	866	900	934	968	1002	1036
19'	409	444	479	514	549	584	619	654	689	724	759	794	829	864	899	934	969	1004	1039	1074
20'	428	464	500	536	572	608	644	680	716	752	788	824	860	896	932	968	1004	1040	1076	1112
21'	447	484	521	558	595	632	669	706	743	780	817	854	891	928	965	1002	1039	1076	1113	1150
22'	466	504	542	580	618	656	694	732	770	808	846	884	922	960	998	1036	1074	1112	1150	1188
23'	485	524	563	602	641	680	719	758	797	836	875	914	953	992	1031	1070	1109	1148	1187	1226
24'	504	544	584	624	664	704	744	784	824	864	904	944	984	1024	1064	1104	1144	1184	1224	1264

TABLE 27-29D

TOTAL SQUARE FEET OF WALL AND CEILING AREA

ROOMS WITH CEILINGS 9 FEET

	3'	4'	5'	6'	7'	8'	9'	10'	11'	12'	13'	14'	15'	16'	17'	18'	19'	20'	21'	22'
3'	117	138	159	180	201	222	243	264	285	306	327	348	369	390	411	432	453	474	495	516
4'	138	160	182	204	226	248	270	292	314	336	358	380	402	424	446	468	490	512	534	556
5'	159	182	205	228	251	274	297	320	343	366	389	412	435	458	481	504	527	550	573	596
6'	180	204	228	252	276	300	324	348	372	396	420	444	468	492	516	540	564	588	612	636
7'	201	226	251	276	301	326	351	376	401	426	451	476	501	526	551	576	601	626	651	676
8'	222	248	274	300	326	352	378	404	430	456	482	508	534	560	586	612	638	664	690	716
9'	243	270	297	324	351	378	405	432	459	486	513	540	567	594	621	648	675	702	729	756
10'	264	292	320	348	376	404	432	460	488	516	544	572	600	628	656	684	712	740	768	796
11'	285	314	343	372	401	430	459	488	517	546	575	604	633	662	691	720	749	778	807	836
12'	306	336	366	396	426	456	486	516	546	576	606	636	666	696	726	756	786	816	846	876
13'	327	358	389	420	451	482	513	544	575	606	637	668	699	730	761	792	823	854	885	916
14'	348	380	412	444	476	508	540	572	604	636	668	700	732	764	796	828	860	892	924	956
15'	369	402	435	468	501	534	567	600	633	666	699	732	765	798	831	864	897	930	963	996
16'	390	424	458	492	526	560	594	628	662	696	730	764	798	832	866	900	934	968	1002	1036
17'	411	446	481	516	551	586	621	656	691	726	761	796	831	866	901	936	971	1006	1041	1076
18'	432	468	504	540	576	612	648	684	720	756	792	828	864	900	936	972	1008	1044	1080	1116
19'	453	490	527	564	601	638	675	712	749	786	823	860	897	934	971	1008	1045	1082	1119	1156
20'	474	512	550	588	626	664	702	740	778	816	854	892	930	968	1006	1044	1082	1120	1158	1196
21'	495	534	573	612	651	690	729	768	807	846	885	924	963	1002	1041	1080	1119	1158	1197	1236
22'	516	556	596	636	676	716	756	796	836	876	916	956	996	1036	1076	1116	1156	1196	1236	1276
23'	537	578	619	660	701	742	783	824	865	906	947	988	1029	1070	1111	1152	1193	1234	1275	1316
24'	558	600	642	684	726	768	810	852	894	936	978	1020	1062	1104	1146	1188	1230	1272	1314	1356

236

TABLE 27-29D

TOTAL SQUARE FEET OF WALL AND CEILING AREA

ROOMS WITH CEILINGS 10 FEET

	3'	4'	5'	6'	7'	8'	9'	10'	11'	12'	13'	14'	15'	16'	17'	18'	19'	20'	21'	22'
3'	129	152	175	198	221	244	267	290	313	336	359	382	405	428	451	474	497	520	543	566
4'	152	176	200	224	248	272	296	320	344	368	392	416	440	464	488	512	536	560	584	608
5'	175	200	225	250	275	300	325	350	375	400	425	450	475	500	525	550	575	600	625	650
6'	198	224	250	276	302	328	354	380	406	432	458	484	510	536	562	588	614	640	666	692
7'	221	248	275	302	329	356	383	410	437	464	491	518	545	572	599	626	653	680	707	734
8'	244	272	300	328	356	384	412	440	468	496	524	552	580	608	636	664	692	720	748	776
9'	267	296	325	354	383	412	441	470	499	528	557	586	615	644	673	702	731	760	789	818
10'	290	320	350	380	410	440	470	500	530	560	590	620	650	680	710	740	770	800	830	860
11'	313	344	375	406	437	468	499	530	561	592	623	654	685	716	747	778	809	840	871	902
12'	336	368	400	432	464	496	528	560	592	624	656	688	720	752	784	816	848	880	912	944
13'	359	392	425	458	491	524	557	590	623	656	689	722	755	788	821	854	887	920	953	986
14'	382	416	450	484	518	552	586	620	654	688	722	756	790	824	858	892	926	960	994	1028
15'	405	440	475	510	545	580	615	650	685	720	755	790	825	860	895	930	965	1000	1035	1070
16'	428	464	500	536	572	608	644	680	716	752	788	824	860	896	932	968	1004	1040	1076	1112
17'	451	488	525	562	599	636	673	710	747	784	821	858	895	932	969	1006	1043	1080	1117	1154
18'	474	512	550	588	626	664	702	740	778	816	854	892	930	968	1006	1044	1082	1120	1158	1196
19'	497	536	575	614	653	692	731	770	809	848	887	926	965	1004	1043	1082	1121	1160	1199	1238
20'	520	560	600	640	680	720	760	800	840	880	920	960	1000	1040	1080	1120	1160	1200	1240	1280
21'	543	584	625	666	707	748	789	830	871	912	953	994	1035	1076	1117	1158	1199	1240	1281	1322
22'	566	608	650	692	734	776	818	860	902	944	986	1028	1070	1112	1154	1196	1238	1280	1322	1364
23'	589	632	675	718	761	804	847	890	933	976	1019	1062	1105	1148	1191	1234	1277	1320	1363	1406
24'	612	656	700	744	788	832	876	920	964	1008	1052	1096	1140	1184	1228	1272	1316	1360	1404	1448

PAINTING AND PAPERHANGING

PAINTING

When estimating the number of square feet of painting, the actual surface to be painted should be measured as accurately as possible because the cost of the material and the number of hours of labor will be determined from the surface area to be covered. The painting or decorating of flat wall surfaces, such as ceiling and floor areas, presents no special problem in measurement, but questions frequently arise as to how to obtain the areas for windows, trimmed openings, stairs and balustrades, doors, exterior cornices, lattices and so forth. Rules-of-thumb are employed by most painters and, while there are differences in the methods used, each one strives to reasonably approximate the actual surface to be covered. The following methods for the measurement of flat and irregular surfaces are recommended.

Interior Walls and Ceilings

To obtain the area of the ceiling, multiply the length times the width. The area of the walls is obtained by measuring the distance around the room (the perimeter) and multiplying by the height from the floor to the ceiling. When walls are to be painted only above or below a wainscoting, the height measurement should be only for that portion to be painted.

Whether or not window and door openings are to be deducted will depend on the particular method used to estimate. When openings are deducted, the cost of material and labor to paint openings is added separately. If window and door openings are not deducted, then the additional time for cutting in windows and doors is included in the labor allowance for the room or per square foot area. Actually it requires no additional paint, even though different colors are used for the finish coat. It does require more time than painting a flat surface.

Windows and Doors

Measure the width and height from the outside of the trim of the opening. Add 2 feet to the width and height of a window. Add 2 feet to the width and 1 foot to the height of a door. This will allow for moldings, edges and frames. A window that measures $3' \times 6'$ would be figured as $5' \times 8'$ or 40 square feet. ($3' + 2' = 5'$ and $6' + 2' = 8'$.) A door measuring $3' \times 7'$ would be figured $5' \times 8' = 40$ square feet ($3' + 2' = 5'$ and $7' + 1' = 8'$). Many painters use the unit of 40 square feet for all average sized openings when figuring windows and doors.

Windows or doors with sash having more than one light of glass, are figured at 2 square feet for each additional light. A 6-light sash would add 10 square feet to the window area.

The proper measurement of window and door areas is very important when estimating brick, masonry, or other surfaces where the painting of such opening is strictly an individual operation.

Floors

The number of square feet in a floor is obtained by multiplying the length times the width. Openings less than $10' \times 10'$ in the floor are not deducted.

Wainscoting

If a wainscoting is painted on a flat surface such as plaster, the area is obtained by multiplying the length times the width. When the wainscoting is paneled, the area should be multiplied by 1 1/2 or 2, depending on the form of the surface.

Stairs and Balustrades

To obtain the surface area of stairs that are to be painted, allow 1 foot for the width of the tread, and 1 foot for the width of the riser to take care of the nosing and molding. Multiply this width by the length of the treads or risers, plus 2 feet for stair strings. A stairway with treads and risers 3'6" wide would have 3'6" + 2' = 5 1/2 square feet for each tread and riser. Multiply the area of the tread and the riser by the number of each.

A stairway with 18 risers 4 feet wide would have an area as follows:

$$\text{Risers} = 18 \times 1' \times (4' + 2')$$
$$= 18 \times 1' \times 6' \qquad\qquad = 108 \text{ sq ft}$$

Treads (1 less than number of risers)
$$= 17 \times 1' \times (4' + 2')$$
$$= 17 \times 1' \times 6' \qquad\qquad = \underline{102} \text{ sq ft}$$
$$\text{Total} = 210 \text{ sq ft}$$

Some authorities count risers and multiply by 8 times the width.

The area calculation for a balustrade is obtained by measuring the height from the tread to the top of the handrail. Multiply this height by the length of the balustrade. The area of square edge and relatively simply designed balustrades should be multiplied by four. Turned and fancy balustrade areas should be multiplied by five. This takes care of both sides.

A balustrade that measures 2'6" $\times$ 18' has a plane area of 45 square feet. The paint area for a simple balustrade would be 45 square feet $\times$ 4 or 180 square feet. For a turned and fancy balustrade the paint area would be 45 square feet $\times$ 5 or 225 square feet.

Baseboard, Chair-rail, Picture Moldings, etc.

The paint area of baseboards, chair-rails, plate rails, picture moldings and other individual trim members should be estimated on the basis of one square foot per lineal foot.

Trimmed Openings

The paint area of two sides of a *trimmed* opening (one without a door) is obtained by measuring the lineal feet around the two sides and top of the opening and multiplying by three.

A trimmed opening 8 feet wide and 7 feet high would have a paint area of 8′ + 7′ + 7′ = 22′ × 3 = 66 square feet. This area is for both sides of the opening. If it is computed in this manner for one room, care should be taken not to include it in the adjoining room also.

Built-in Shelving, Cupboards, and Cases

To obtain the paint area for built-in shelves, cupboards, book cases and cabinets, measure the front area (width × height). Multiply the front area by 3 for open-front units. Multiply the front area by 5 for units having doors. The total area obtained includes the complete finishing of the interior and exterior.

Exterior Shingles and Siding (Wood, Metal and Composition)

To obtain the paint area of exterior shingles and siding, measure the actual wall area including gables, but do not deduct window or door openings less than 10′ × 10′. For narrow clapboard exposures, and for all shingles, add 20 percent to the actual area. For wide clapboard exposures (over 5 inches) add 10 percent to the actual area.

Exterior Cornices and Eaves

Measure the length and width of the cornice to obtain the area. Multiply this area by 2 for relatively simple cornices, and multiply it by 3 for fancy or ornate cornices.

Where cornices are open, with exposed rafters, multiply the cornice area (length times overhang) by 3 to obtain the paint area.

For open cornices or eaves that do not have the rafters exposed, add 50 percent to the area.

Exterior Masonry Walls

To obtain the paint area of brick, stucco, cement block, and other exterior masonry walls, measure the actual wall area including gables. Do not deduct window or door openings less than $10' \times 10'$.

Fences

To obtain the paint area of a solid board fence, measure the length and height. Multiply the length times the height to obtain the area of *one side*. Multiply by 2 if it is to be painted on two sides.

The paint area of *one side* of a picket fence is determined by multiplying the length times the height by 2. Two sides, multiply by 4. Chain link fences, measure one side, multiply by 3.

Lattice

To obtain the paint area of lattice work, multiply the length times the width. To paint *one side* multiply the actual area by 3.

ESTIMATING MATERIALS

Painting and finishing is one of the least difficult of building trades to estimate, because the quantities of material, and the numbers of hours of labor are both determined directly from the area to be covered.

When the paint area has been measured and calculated, the quantity of material required per coat is obtained by dividing that area by the number of square feet a gallon of paint will cover.

Illustrative Example No. 1

A room $14' \times 18' \times 9'$ is to be given *one* coat of flat paint on sheet rock walls and ceiling.

Ceiling area	$14' \times 18' = 252$ sq ft
Wall area	$2 (14' + 18') \times 9' = \underline{576}$ sq ft
	Total $= \overline{828}$ sq ft

(From Table 27-29E)

$$\text{Paint required for one coat} = \frac{828}{450} = 1.84 \text{ gallons}$$

If only one room is to be painted the quantity would be rounded out to 2 gallons. Where other rooms are to be painted, any adjustment to whole or half gallons is made at the end of the entire painting estimate.

Illustrative Example No. 2

A room 10′ × 16′ × 8′6″ is to be painted *two* coats of flat on plastered walls and ceiling.

Ceiling area	10′ × 16′ = 160 sq ft
Wall area	2 (10′ + 16′) × 8½ = 442 sq ft
	602
	(Two coats) × 2
	1,204 sq ft

Table 27-29D may also be used

(From Table 27-29E)

$$\text{Paint required} = \frac{1,204}{450} = 2.68 \text{ gallons}$$

Table 27-29E shows the approximate number of square feet that a gallon of painting materials will cover on the most frequently encountered surfaces. When the surfaces are unusually rough or porous, the number of square feet should be reduced accordingly.

TABLE 27-29E

APPROXIMATE COVERING CAPACITY OF PAINTING MATERIALS USING BRUSH APPLICATION

USE OF PAINT MATERIALS	First Coat	Sq Ft Per Gallon Second Coat	Third Coat
Interior			
Flat paint on smooth plaster	450	450	450
Flat paint on sand finish plaster	300	300	350
Flat paint on texture finish plaster	300	300	300
Gloss or semi-gloss on smooth plaster	400	400	500
Gloss or semi-gloss on sand plaster	300	400	400
Gloss or semi-gloss on texture plaster	250	350	400
Calcimine-Watersize-size	720		
Calcimine	240		
Calcimine-Oilsize-size	225		
Calcimine	240		
Concrete block-Resin Emulsion	200		
Wood veneer-Lacquer	500	540	

USE OF PAINT MATERIALS	First Coat	Sq Ft Per Gallon Second Coat	Third Coat
Wood veneer-Synthetic resin	600	675	
Penetrating wax	600	675	
Enamel on wood floors	400	400	
Stainwax on floors or trim	500	600	
Shellac (4 lb cut)	500	500	500
Varnish over shellac	500		
Varnish remover	150		
Exterior			
Wood siding and trim-flat or semi-gloss	450	550	600
Staining shingle roofs and siding	200	300	
Oil Paint-asbestos shingles	200	300	
Cedar shakes-Latex	200	300	400
Brick -Latex	200	300	400
Concrete floors and steps-enamel	300	400	400
Link fences	750		
Gutters and leaders	200-250 lin ft per coat		

PAPERHANGING

Estimating Materials (See also Table 27-29F)

When hanging wallpaper, some allowance must be made for the waste which results from cutting, fitting around openings and built-in units, and for matching patterns. As a general rule the waste averages between 15 percent and 20 percent. A single roll of paper contains 36 square feet. A practical and acceptable method for allowing waste is to figure the rolls at 30 square feet. Double rolls are figured at 60 square feet to take care of waste.

The cost of material and labor for papering is estimated by the roll. If the cost per square foot or square yard is desired, it may be obtained in two ways: by dividing the cost of papering a room by the wall area, and by computing the cost of hanging one roll of paper and dividing by 30 square feet.

To obtain the number of rolls of paper required, the distance around the room (perimeter) is multiplied by the height from the top of the baseboard to the ceiling. *All window and door openings are deducted.* The result is the wall area to be papered. That area is divided by 30 to obtain the number of single rolls of paper. Paper is sold in full rolls and the number of rolls needed must be carried out to the next whole roll. If double rolls are used, the area should be divided by 60.

Where walls are papered above a chair rail only, or above a wainscoting, the height measurement should be taken from where the paper starts to the ceiling. When a single wall is to be papered the length of that wall is measured and multiplied by the height.

Where ceilings are to be papered, the area is obtained by multiplying the length of the ceiling by the width.

If a border is required, the distance around the room divided by 3 will give the number of yards required.

Illustrative Example

Find the number of single rolls of paper and the number of yards of border required for the walls of a room 14' × 18' × 8'6". The baseboard is 6" high. Openings consist of two windows 3' × 5' and two doors 3'6" × 7'.

Area of Walls (above baseboard)
2(14' + 18') × 8'   = 512 sq ft
Deduct openings
2 windows 3' × 5' = 30 sq ft
2 doors 3½' × 7' = 49 sq ft

$$\hspace{8cm} - \ 79 \text{ sq ft}$$
Area to be papered   = 433 sq ft

Rolls of paper = $\dfrac{433}{30}$ = 14.4 = 15 rolls

Yards of border = $\dfrac{2(14' + 18')}{3}$ = $\dfrac{64}{3}$ = 22 yards

The amount of paste needed to hang paper varies with the type and weight of the paper. Heavy or rough textured papers require more than lightweight papers. For average estimating purposes a pound of paste makes 2 gallons, which will hang approximately 10 single rolls of paper.

Estimating Labor

A paperhanger will hang paper at the rate of 3 single rolls per hour under normal conditions. This rate is for butt-jointed work. If the joints are lapped, the rate should be increased at about 3 1/2 or 4 rolls per hour.

Where workmanship and materials are of the highest grade, a paperhanger will hang paper at the rate of 2 rolls per hour.

Paper borders can be hung at the rate of approximately 30 yards per hour.

Labor Table 21 shows the approximate labor hours required for various paperhanging operations.

SANITAS AND WALLTEX

Sanitas and Walltex come in rolls containing 9 square yards. They are frequently used on the walls of bathrooms and kitchens because they are water-resistant and washable. The area is obtained in the same manner as for wallpaper. The quantity of Sanitas or Walltex required is equal to the area to be covered plus 10 percent for waste. Because they are expensive, measurements for Sanitas and Walltex should be taken with care.

A paperhanger can hang approximately 2 rolls of Sanitas or Walltex per hour.

TABLE 27-29 F

ESTIMATING QUANTITIES FOR PAPERHANGING WALLS AND CEILINGS:

Measure straight area to secure number of square feet and divide by 30. (This allows 6 sq. ft. for waste.) Deduct ½ roll for every opening. Or, for the following standard-size rooms use this handy chart:

Size of Room	Single Rolls of Side Wall Height of Ceiling			Yards of Border	Rolls of Ceiling
	8 feet	9 feet	10 feet		
4 × 8	6	7	8	9	2
4 × 10	7	8	9	11	2
4 × 12	8	9	10	12	2
6 × 10	8	9	10	12	2
6 × 12	9	10	11	13	3
8 × 12	10	11	13	15	4
8 × 14	11	12	14	16	4
10 × 14	12	14	15	18	5
10 × 16	13	15	16	19	6
12 × 16	14	16	17	20	7
12 × 18	15	17	19	22	8
14 × 18	16	18	20	23	8
14 × 22	18	20	22	26	10
15 × 16	15	17	19	23	8
15 × 18	16	18	20	24	9
15 × 20	17	20	22	25	10
15 × 23	19	21	23	28	11
16 × 18	17	19	21	25	10
16 × 20	18	20	22	26	10
16 × 22	19	21	23	28	11

Size of Room	Single Rolls of Side Wall Height of Ceiling			Yards of Border	Rolls of Ceiling
	8 feet	9 feet	10 feet		
16 × 24	20	22	25	29	12
16 × 26	21	23	26	31	13
17 × 22	19	22	24	28	12
17 × 25	21	23	26	31	13
17 × 28	22	25	28	32	15
17 × 32	24	27	30	35	17
17 × 35	26	29	32	37	18
18 × 22	20	22	25	29	12
18 × 25	21	24	27	31	14
18 × 28	23	26	28	33	16
20 × 26	23	28	28	33	17
20 × 28	24	27	30	34	18
20 × 34	27	30	33	39	21

Deduct one single roll of side wall for every two ordinary sized doors or windows or every 36 square feet of opening. Yard goods with no match such as wide vinyls, measure area, take out for openings and allow 10" for waste.

Courtesy of Painting and Decorating Contractors of America, Falls Church, Va. 22046.

TABLES 30 THROUGH 38

Exterior Sidewall Materials

These Tables give the quantities, including all cutting, fitting and milling waste applicable, for the various materials shown. They also show the exterior sidewall surface area. Areas and material quantities are shown with and without gable ends included to take in flat, hip and gable type roofs. Tables 30, 32 and 34 include gable areas. Tables 31, 33 and 35 THROUGH 38 exclude gables.

HOW TO USE THESE TABLES

1. Determine the *ground-floor* area of your dwelling following the method outlined under Computation of Areas in General Instructions, page 17.

2. Determine the lineal feet of perimeter of your dwelling following the method outlined under Perimeter Measurement in General Instructions, page 18.

3. Using Table A, check the *ground-floor* area and the lineal feet of perimeter to obtain the length-to-width ratio of your dwelling.

These Tables are based on a length-to-width ratio of 2:1. If the length-to-width ratio of your dwelling is significantly different, adjust the Table quantities upward or downward by the percentages under Table A, page 22.

Illustrative Example

A 1-story dwelling 40′ × 40′ has a *ground-floor* area of 1,600 sq ft. The length-to-width ratio is 1:1 (length equals width). Since the Tables are based on a length-to-width ratio of 2:1, Table A, page 22, shows that an adjustment of 5% has to be made.

Table 30 shows that there are 1,730 sq ft of exterior sidewall area in a 1-story dwelling with a *ground-floor* area of 1,600 sq ft. Adjusting for the difference in L:W ratio.

1,730 × .95 = 1,644 sq ft area of sidewalls

247

If 1″ × 8″ bevel siding is applied, Table 30 shows it will require 2,336 FBM.
The adjustment for a 1:1 length-to-width ratio would be 2,336 × .95 = 2,219 FBM.

EXTERIOR WALL HEIGHT ADJUSTMENT

The exterior wall heights in these Tables are assumed as follows:

1- story dwellings	9 ft
1 1/2-story dwellings	15 ft
2-story dwellings	18 ft

To adjust the Table quantities for walls higher or lower than assumed, a simple adjustment upward or downward is shown on page 27, Table B.

GABLE QUANTITY ADJUSTMENT

When the roof pitch is other than 1/4, on which the Tables are based, an adjustment of the gable area or material may be desired. To make such an adjustment proceed as follows:

Step 1.

Use Tables 31, 33 and 35 to 38 for material quantities without gables.

Step 2.

From Tables C1 or C2, or from the shortcut Formula, page 28, determine the gable area of your dwelling.

Step 3.

Multiply the gable area determined in step 2 by the factor for the particular material to be used, page 259. Table 30-38A

Step 4.

Add the results of step 1 and step 3.

Illustrative Example

A 1-story dwelling 30′ × 60′ has a gable roof pitch of ¹/₂ (12″ rise-per-foot-of-run). The *ground-floor* area is 1,800 sq ft.

Step 1. and Step No. 2 Combined

Table 31 (gables excluded) shows that there are 1,620 sq ft in the exterior sidewalls of this dwelling. Using the short-cut formula on page 28, the *ground-floor* area is multiplied by .25 where the length-to-width ratio is 2:1.

1,800 sq ft × .25 = 450 sq ft

(Table C2 gives the same result)

Step 3.

Because in this illustration the number of sq ft of exterior wall surface is being sought, this Step 3 will be bypassed.

Step 4.

By adding Steps 1 and 2 the total exterior wall surface is found to be:

1,620 + 450 = 2,070 sq ft

Illustrative Example No. 2

In the foregoing illustration assume that it is desired to determine the number of FBM of 1″ × 10″ bevel siding in this dwelling.

Table 31 shows 2,106 FBM excluding the gable ends. The gable area in the above illustration was determined to be 450 sq ft. To determine the amount of bevel siding, including cutting, fitting and cutting waste, the Table 30-38A, page 259, shows that the area is to be multiplied by 1.30 which gives 585 FBM. Adding this to the quantity shown in Table 31, excluding gables, we have

2,106 + 585 = 2,691 FBM of bevel siding

TABLE 30

EXTERIOR SIDEWALL MATERIALS FOR 1-STORY DWELLINGS
(Includes Milling and Cutting Waste) (Window & Door Openings Not Deducted)
Gable Included; Wall Height 9′

Ground Floor Area Sq Ft	Exterior Surface Area		Shiplap, Tongue & Groove Boards		Insulation Board, Plywood, Particle-Board Etc.	Bevel Siding			Drop Siding	
	Gable Ends			1″×6″ 1″×8″		1″×6″ 1″ Lap	1″×8″ 1¼″ Lap	1″×10″ 1½″ Lap	1″×6″	1″×8″
	Included Square Ft	Excluded Square Ft	1″×4″ Bd. Ft.	1″×8″ Bd. Ft.	Sq. Ft.	Bd. Ft.	Bd. Ft.	Bd. Ft.	Bd. Ft.	Bd. Ft.
200	565	540	751	689	622	763	763	734	706	678
300	704	666	936	859	774	950	950	915	880	845
400	815	765	1084	994	896	1100	1100	1060	1019	978
500	917	855	1220	1119	1008	1238	1238	1192	1146	1100
600	1011	936	1345	1233	1112	1365	1365	1314	1264	1213
700	1096	1008	1458	1337	1206	1480	1480	1425	1370	1315
800	1180	1080	1569	1440	1298	1593	1593	1534	1475	1416
900	1255	1143	1669	1531	1380	1694	1694	1632	1569	1506
1000	1330	1206	1769	1623	1463	1796	1796	1729	1663	1596
1100	1407	1269	1871	1717	1548	1900	1900	1829	1759	1688
1200	1474	1323	1960	1798	1621	1990	1990	1916	1843	1769
1300	1540	1377	2048	1879	1694	2079	2079	2002	1925	1848
1400	1607	1431	2137	1961	1768	2170	2170	2089	2009	1928
1500	1663	1476	2212	2029	1829	2245	2245	2162	2079	1996
1600	1730	1530	2300	2110	1903	2336	2336	2249	2163	2076
1700	1787	1575	2377	2180	1966	2412	2412	2323	2234	2144
1800	1845	1620	2454	2250	2030	2490	2490	2399	2306	2214
1900	1903	1665	2531	2322	2093	2569	2569	2474	2379	2284
2000	1960	1710	2606	2391	2156	2646	2646	2548	2450	2352
2100	2008	1746	2671	2450	2209	2711	2711	2610	2510	2410
2200	2066	1791	2748	2521	2273	2789	2789	2686	2583	2479
2300	2113	1827	2810	2578	2324	2853	2853	2747	2641	2536
2400	2172	1872	2889	2650	2389	2932	2932	2824	2715	2606
2500	2220	1908	2953	2708	2442	2997	2997	2886	2775	2664
2600	2269	1944	3018	2768	2496	3063	3063	2950	2836	2723
2700	2318	1980	3083	2845	2550	3129	3129	3013	2898	2782
2800	2366	2016	3147	2887	2603	3194	3194	3076	2958	2839
2900	2413	2052	3209	2944	2654	3258	3258	3137	3016	2896
3000	2473	2097	3289	3017	2720	3338	3338	3215	3091	2968

TABLE 31

EXTERIOR SIDEWALL MATERIALS FOR 1-STORY DWELLINGS
(Includes Milling and Cutting Waste) (Window & Door Openings Not Deducted)
Gables Excluded; Wall Height 9′

Ground Floor Area Sq. Ft.	Exterior Surface Area		Shiplap, Tongue & Groove Boards		Insulation Board, Plywood, Particle-Board Etc.	Bevel Siding			Drop Siding	
	Gable Ends		1″×4″	1″×6″ 1″×8″		1″×6″ 1″ Lap	1″×8″ 1¼″ Lap	1″×10″ 1½″ Lap	1″×6″	1″×8″
	Included Square Ft	Excluded Square Ft	Bd. Ft.	Bd. Ft.	Sq. Ft.	Bd. Ft.	Bd. Ft.	Bd. Ft.	Bd. Ft.	Bd. Ft.
200	565	540	718	659	594	729	729	702	675	648
300	704	666	886	813	733	900	900	866	833	800
400	815	765	1017	933	842	1033	1033	995	956	918
500	917	855	1137	1043	940	1154	1154	1111	1069	1026
600	1011	936	1245	1142	1030	1264	1264	1217	1170	1123
700	1096	1008	1341	1230	1109	1360	1360	1310	1260	1210
800	1180	1080	1436	1318	1188	1458	1458	1404	1350	1296
900	1255	1143	1520	1394	1257	1543	1543	1486	1428	1372
1000	1330	1206	1604	1471	1327	1628	1628	1568	1508	1447
1100	1407	1269	1688	1548	1396	1713	1713	1650	1586	1523
1200	1474	1323	1760	1614	1455	1786	1786	1720	1654	1588
1300	1540	1377	1831	1680	1515	1859	1859	1790	1721	1652
1400	1607	1431	1903	1746	1574	1932	1932	1860	1788	1717
1500	1663	1476	1963	1800	1624	1993	1993	1918	1845	1771
1600	1730	1530	2035	1867	1683	2066	2066	1989	1912	1836
1700	1787	1575	2095	1922	1733	2126	2126	2048	1968	1890
1800	1845	1620	2155	1976	1782	2187	2187	2106	2025	1944
1900	1903	1665	2214	2031	1832	2248	2248	2165	2081	1998
2000	1960	1710	2274	2086	1881	2308	2308	2223	2138	2052
2100	2008	1746	2322	2130	1921	2357	2357	2270	2182	2095
2200	2066	1791	2382	2185	1970	2418	2418	2328	2239	2149
2300	2113	1827	2430	2229	2010	2466	2466	2375	2284	2192
2400	2172	1872	2490	2284	2059	2527	2527	2434	2340	2246
2500	2220	1908	2598	2328	2099	2576	2576	2480	2385	2290
2600	2269	1944	2586	2372	2138	2625	2625	2527	2430	2333
2700	2318	1980	2633	2416	2178	2673	2673	2574	2475	2376
2800	2366	2016	2681	2460	2218	2722	2722	2620	2520	2419
2900	2413	2052	2729	2503	2257	2770	2700	2668	2565	2462
3000	2473	2097	2789	2558	2307	2830	2830	2726	2621	2516

TABLE 32

EXTERIOR SIDEWALL MATERIALS FOR 1½ STORY DWELLINGS
(Includes Milling and Cutting Waste—Window & Door Openings Not Deducted)
Gables Included; Wall Height 9′

Ground Floor Area Sq Ft	Exterior Surface Area Gable Ends Included Square Ft	Gable Ends Excluded Square Ft	Shiplap, Tongue & Groove Boards 1″×4″ Bd. Ft.	1″×6″ 1″×8″ Bd. Ft.	Insulation Board Plywood, Particle-Board Etc. Sq. Ft.	Bevel Siding 1″×6″ 1″ Lap Bd. Ft.	1″×8″ 1¼ Lap Bd. Ft.	1″×10″ 1½ Lap Bd. Ft.	Drop Siding 1″×6″ Bd. Ft.	1″×8″ Bd. Ft.
200	925	900	1230	1128	1018	1250	1250	1202	1156	1110
300	1148	1110	1527	1397	1263	1550	1550	1492	1435	1378
400	1325	1275	1762	1616	1458	1790	1790	1723	1656	1590
500	1487	1425	1978	1814	1636	2007	2007	1933	1859	1784
600	1635	1560	2175	1995	1800	2207	2207	2126	2044	1962
700	1768	1680	2351	2157	1945	2387	2387	2298	2210	2122
800	1900	1800	2527	2318	2090	2565	2565	2470	2375	2280
900	2017	1905	2683	2461	2219	2723	2723	2622	2521	2420
1000	2134	2010	2838	2603	2347	2880	2880	2774	2668	2561
1100	2253	2115	2996	2749	2478	3042	3042	2930	2816	2704
1200	2356	2205	3133	2874	2592	3180	3180	3063	2945	2827
1300	2458	2295	3269	3000	2704	3318	3318	3195	3073	2950
1400	2561	2385	3406	3124	2817	3457	3457	3329	3200	3073
1500	2647	2460	3520	3229	2912	3573	3573	3441	3309	3176
1600	2750	2550	3658	3355	3025	3713	3713	3575	3438	3300
1700	2837	2625	3773	3461	3121	3830	3830	3688	3546	3404
1800	2925	2700	3890	3569	3218	3950	3950	3802	3656	3510
1900	3013	2775	4007	3676	3314	4068	4068	3917	3766	3616
2000	3100	2850	4123	3782	3410	4185	4185	4030	3875	3720
2100	3172	2910	4218	3870	3489	4282	4282	4124	3965	3806
2200	3260	2985	4336	3977	3586	4400	4400	4238	4075	3912
2300	3331	3045	4430	4064	3664	4497	4497	4330	4164	4000
2400	3420	3120	4549	4172	3762	4617	4617	4446	4275	4104
2500	3492	3180	4644	4260	3841	4714	4714	4540	4365	4190
2600	3565	3240	4741	4349	3922	4813	4813	4635	4456	4278
2700	3638	3300	4838	4438	4000	4911	4911	4729	4548	4366
2800	3710	3360	4934	4526	4081	5008	5008	4823	4638	4452
2900	3781	3420	5029	4613	4160	5104	5104	4915	4726	4537
3000	3871	3495	5148	4723	4258	5226	5226	5032	4838	4645

TABLE 33

EXTERIOR SIDEWALL MATERIALS FOR 1½ STORY DWELLINGS
(Includes Milling and Cutting Waste—Window & Door Openings Not Deducted)
Gables Excluded; Wall Height 9'

Ground Floor Area Sq. Ft.	Exterior Surface Area		Shiplap, Tongue & Groove Boards		Insulation Board Plywood, Particle-Board Etc.	Bevel Siding			Drop Siding	
	Gable Ends		1"×4"	1"×6" 1"×8"		1"×6" 1" Lap	1"×8" 1¼" Lap	1"×10" 1½" Lap	1"×6"	1"×8"
	Included Square Ft	Excluded Square Ft	Bd. Ft	Bd. Ft.	Sq. Ft.	Bd. Ft.	Bd. Ft.	Bd. Ft.	Bd. Ft.	Bd. Ft.
200	925	900	1200	1098	990	1215	1215	1170	1125	1080
300	1148	1110	1476	1354	1221	1500	1500	1443	1388	1332
400	1325	1275	1696	1556	1402	1721	1721	1658	1594	1530
500	1487	1425	1900	1738	1568	1924	1924	1853	1781	1710
600	1635	1560	2075	1903	1716	2106	2106	2028	1950	1872
700	1768	1680	2234	2050	1848	2268	2268	2184	2100	2016
800	1900	1800	2394	2196	1980	2430	2430	2340	2250	2160
900	2017	1905	2540	2324	2096	2572	2572	2476	2381	2286
1000	2134	2010	2673	2452	2211	2714	2714	2613	2512	2412
1100	2253	2115	2813	2580	2327	2855	2855	2750	2644	2538
1200	2356	2205	2933	2690	2425	2977	2977	2866	2756	2646
1300	2458	2295	3052	2800	2525	3098	3098	2984	2869	2754
1400	2561	2385	3172	2910	2624	3220	3220	3100	2981	2862
1500	2647	2460	3272	3000	2706	3321	3321	3198	3075	2952
1600	2750	2550	3392	3111	2805	3443	3443	3315	3188	3060
1700	2837	2625	3491	3203	2928	3544	3544	3413	3281	3150
1800	2925	2700	3591	3294	2970	3645	3645	3510	3375	3240
1900	3013	2775	3691	3386	3052	3746	3646	3608	3469	3330
2000	3100	2850	3790	3477	3135	3848	3848	3705	3562	3420
2100	3172	2910	3870	3550	3200	3929	3929	3783	3638	3492
2200	3260	2985	3970	3642	3284	4030	4030	3880	3731	3582
2300	3331	3045	4050	3715	3350	4110	4110	3958	3806	3654
2400	3420	3120	4150	3806	3432	4212	4212	4056	3900	3744
2500	3492	3180	4230	3880	3500	4293	4293	4134	3975	3816
2600	3565	3240	4310	3953	3564	4374	4374	4212	4050	3888
2700	3638	3300	4390	4026	3630	4455	4455	4290	4125	3960
2800	3710	3360	4469	4100	3696	4536	4536	4368	4200	4032
2900	3781	3420	4550	4172	3762	4617	4617	4446	4275	4104
3000	3871	3495	4648	4264	3845	4718	4718	4544	4369	4194

TABLE 34

EXTERIOR SIDEWALL MATERIALS FOR 2-STORY DWELLINGS
(Includes Milling and Cutting Waste; Window and Door Openings Not Deducted)
Gables Included; Wall Height 9′

Ground Floor Area Sq. Ft.	Exterior Surface Area Gable Ends Included Square Ft	Exterior Surface Area Gable Ends Included Square Ft	Shiplap, Tongue & Groove Boards 1″×4″ Bd. Ft.	Shiplap, Tongue & Groove Boards 1″×6″ 1″×8″ Bd. Ft.	Insulation Board, Plywood, Particle-Board Etc. Sq. Ft.	Bevel Siding 1″×6″ 1″ Lap Bd. Ft.	Bevel Siding 1″×8″ 1¼″ Lap Bd. Ft.	Bevel Siding 1″×10″ 1½″ Lap Bd. Ft.	Drop Siding 1″×6″ Bd. Ft.	Drop Siding 1″×8″ Bd. Ft.
200	1105	1080	1470	1348	1216	1492	1492	1437	1381	1326
300	1370	1332	1822	1671	1507	1850	1850	1781	1713	1644
400	1580	1530	2100	1928	1738	2133	2133	2054	1975	1896
500	1772	1710	2357	2162	1950	2392	2392	2304	2215	2126
600	1947	1872	2590	2375	2142	2628	2628	2531	2434	2336
700	2104	2016	2798	2567	2314	2840	2840	2735	2630	2525
800	2260	2160	3006	2757	2486	3051	3051	2938	2825	2712
900	2398	2286	3190	2926	2638	3237	3237	3117	2998	2878
1000	2536	2412	3373	3094	2790	3424	3424	3297	3170	3043
1100	2676	2538	3560	3265	2944	3613	3613	3479	3345	3211
1200	2797	2646	3720	3412	3077	3776	3776	3636	3496	3356
1300	2917	2754	3880	3559	3208	3938	3938	3792	3646	3500
1400	3038	2862	4040	3706	3342	4101	4101	3950	3798	3646
1500	3139	2952	4175	3830	3453	4238	4238	4081	3924	3767
1600	3260	3060	4336	3977	3586	4401	4401	4238	4075	3912
1700	3362	3150	4471	4102	3698	4539	4539	4371	4203	4034
1800	3465	3240	4608	4227	3811	4678	4678	4505	4331	4158
1900	3568	3330	4745	4353	3925	4817	4817	4638	4460	4282
2000	3670	3420	4881	4477	4037	4955	4955	4771	4588	4404
2100	3754	3492	4993	4580	4129	5068	5068	4880	4692	4505
2200	3857	3582	5130	4706	4243	5207	5207	5014	4821	4628
2300	3940	3654	5240	4807	4114	5319	5319	5122	4925	4728
2400	4044	3744	5379	4934	4448	5459	5459	5257	5055	4853
2500	4128	3816	5490	5036	4541	5573	5573	5366	5160	4953
2600	4213	3888	5603	5140	4634	5688	5688	5477	5266	5056
2700	4298	3960	5716	5244	4728	5802	5802	5587	5373	5158
2800	4382	4032	5828	5346	4820	5916	5916	5697	5478	5258
2900	4465	4104	5938	5447	4912	6028	6028	5805	5581	5358
3000	4570	4194	6078	5575	5027	6170	6170	5941	5713	5480

TABLE 35

EXTERIOR SIDEWALL MATERIALS FOR 2-STORY DWELLINGS
(Includes Milling and Cutting Waste; Window and Door Openings Not Deducted)
Gables Excluded; Wall Height 9′

Ground Floor Area Sq. Ft.	Exterior Surface Area		Shiplap, Tongue & Groove Boards		Insulation Board, Plywood, Particle-Board Etc.	Bevel Siding			Drop Siding	
	Gable Ends					1″×6″ 1″ Lap	1″×8″ 1¼″ Lap	1″×10″ 1½″ Lap		
	Included	Excluded	1″×4″	1″×6″ 1″×8″					1″×6″	1″×8″
	Square Ft	Square Ft	Bd. Ft.	Bd. Ft.	Sq. Ft.	Bd. Ft.	Bd. Ft.	Bd. Ft.	Bd. Ft.	Bd. Ft.
200	1105	1080	1436	1318	1188	1458	1458	1404	1350	1296
300	1370	1332	1772	1625	1465	1798	1798	1732	1665	1598
400	1580	1530	2035	1867	1708	2066	2066	1989	1913	1836
500	1772	1710	2274	2086	1881	2309	2309	2223	2138	2052
600	1947	1872	2490	2284	2059	2527	2527	2434	2340	2246
700	2104	2016	2681	2460	2218	2722	2722	2621	2520	2410
800	2260	2160	2873	2635	2376	2916	2916	2808	2700	2592
900	2398	2286	3040	2789	2515	3086	3086	2972	2858	2743
1000	2536	2412	3208	2943	2653	3256	3256	3136	3015	2894
1100	2676	2538	3376	3096	2792	3426	3426	3300	3173	3046
1200	2797	2646	3520	3228	2911	3572	3572	3440	3308	3175
1300	2917	2754	3663	3360	3029	3718	3718	3580	3443	3305
1400	3038	2862	3806	3492	3148	3864	3864	3720	3578	3434
1500	3139	2952	3926	3600	3247	3985	3985	3838	3690	3542
1600	3260	3060	4070	3733	3366	4131	4131	3978	3825	3672
1700	3362	3150	4190	3843	3465	4253	4253	4095	3938	3780
1800	3465	3240	4310	3953	3564	4374	4374	4212	4050	3888
1900	3568	3330	4429	4063	3663	4496	4496	4329	4163	3996
2000	3670	3420	4549	4172	3762	4617	4617	4446	4275	4104
2100	3754	3492	4644	4224	3841	4714	4714	4540	4365	4190
2200	3857	3582	4764	4370	3940	4836	4836	4657	4478	4298
2300	3940	3654	4860	4458	4019	4933	4933	4750	4568	4385
2400	4044	3744	4980	4568	4118	5054	5054	4867	4680	4493
2500	4128	3816	5075	4655	4198	5151	5151	4961	4770	4580
2600	4213	3888	5171	4743	4277	5249	5249	5054	4860	4666
2700	4298	3960	5267	4831	4356	5346	5346	5148	4950	4752
2800	4382	4032	5362	4919	4435	5443	5443	5242	5040	4838
2900	4465	4104	5458	5007	4514	5540	5540	5335	5130	4925
3000	4570	4194	5578	5117	4613	5662	5662	5452	5242	5033

TABLE 36

EXTERIOR SIDEWALL MATERIALS FOR 1-STORY DWELLINGS CONTINUED
(Window and Door Openings Not Deducted). Unless Otherwise Indicated,
Gables Excluded; Wall Height 9′

Ground Floor Area Sq Ft	Brickwork 4″Veneer Number of Brick	Brickwork 8″ Solid Number of Brick	Concrete Block 8″ × 16″ Number of Block	Stucco or Cement Plaster Square Yards	Stucco or Cement Plaster Square Feet	Exterior Paint Gables Included Square Feet	Exterior Paint Gables Excluded Square Feet
200	3780	7560	608	60	540	565	540
300	4662	9324	750	74	660	704	666
400	5355	10710	861	85	765	815	765
500	5985	11970	962	95	855	917	855
600	6552	13104	1053	104	936	1011	936
700	7056	14112	1134	112	1008	1096	1008
800	7560	15120	1215	120	1080	1180	1080
900	8000	16000	1286	127	1143	1255	1143
1000	8442	16884	1357	134	1206	1330	1206
1100	8883	17766	1428	141	1269	1407	1269
1200	9261	18522	1488	147	1323	1474	1323
1300	9639	19278	1549	153	1377	1540	1377
1400	10017	20034	1610	159	1431	1607	1431
1500	10332	20664	1660	164	1476	1663	1476
1600	10710	21420	1721	170	1530	1730	1530
1700	11025	22050	1772	175	1575	1787	1575
1800	11340	22680	1823	180	1620	1845	1620
1900	11655	23310	1873	185	1665	1903	1665
2000	11970	23940	1924	190	1710	1960	1710
2100	12222	24444	1964	194	1746	2008	1746
2200	12537	25074	2015	199	1791	2066	1791
2300	12789	25578	2055	203	1827	2113	1827
2400	13104	26208	2106	208	1872	2172	1872
2500	13356	26712	2147	212	1908	2220	1908
2600	13608	27216	2187	216	1944	2269	1944
2700	13860	27720	2228	220	1980	2318	1980
2800	14112	28224	2268	224	2016	2366	2016
2900	14364	28728	2309	228	2052	2413	2052
3000	14679	29358	2359	233	2097	2473	2097

TABLE 37

EXTERIOR SIDEWALL MATERIALS FOR 1½ STORY DWELLINGS CONTINUED
(Window and Door Openings Not Deducted). Unless Otherwise Indicated,
Gables Excluded; Wall Height 9′

Ground Floor Area Sq Ft	Brickwork 4″ Veneer Number of Brick	Brickwork 8″ Solid Number of Brick	Concrete Block 8″ × 16″ Number of Block	Stucco or Cement Plaster Square Yards	Stucco or Cement Plaster Square Feet	Exterior Paint Gables Included Square Feet	Exterior Paint Gables Excluded Square Feet
200	6300	12600	1013	100	900	925	900
300	7770	15540	1250	122	1100	1148	1100
400	8925	17850	1434	142	1275	1325	1275
500	9975	19950	1603	158	1425	1487	1425
600	10920	21840	1755	173	1560	1635	1560
700	11760	23520	1890	187	1680	1768	1680
800	12600	25200	2025	200	1800	1900	1800
900	13335	26670	2143	212	1905	2017	1905
1000	14070	28140	2261	223	2010	2134	2010
1100	14805	29610	2380	235	2115	2253	2115
1200	15435	30870	2480	245	2205	2356	2205
1300	16065	32130	2582	255	2295	2458	2295
1400	16695	33390	2683	265	2285	2561	2385
1500	17220	34440	2768	273	2460	2647	2460
1600	17850	35700	2869	283	2550	2750	2550
1700	18375	36750	2953	292	2625	2837	2625
1800	18900	37800	3038	300	2700	2925	2700
1900	19425	38850	3122	308	2775	3013	2775
2000	19950	39900	3206	317	2850	3100	2850
2100	20370	40740	3274	323	2910	3172	2910
2200	20895	41790	3358	332	2985	3260	2985
2300	21315	42630	3426	338	3045	3331	3045
2400	21840	43680	3510	347	3120	3420	3120
2500	22260	44520	3578	353	3180	3492	3180
2600	22680	45360	3645	360	3240	3565	3240
2700	23100	46200	3712	367	3360	3638	3300
2800	23520	47040	3780	373	3360	3710	3360
2900	23940	47880	3848	380	3420	3781	3420
3000	24465	48930	3932	388	3495	3871	3495

TABLE 38

EXTERIOR SIDEWALL MATERIALS FOR 2-STORY DWELLINGS CONTINUED
(Window and Door Openings Not Deducted)
Gables Excluded Unless Otherwise Indicated
Wall Height 9′

Ground Floor Area Sq Ft	Brickwork		Concrete Block 8″ × 16″	Stucco or Cement Plaster		Exterior Paint Gables	
	4″ Veneer Number of Brick	8″ Solid Number of Brick	Number of Block	Square Yards	Square Feet	Included Square Feet	Excluded Square Feet
200	7560	15120	1215	120	1080	1105	1080
300	9324	18648	1498	148	1332	1370	1332
400	10710	21420	1721	170	1530	1580	1530
500	11970	23940	1924	190	1710	1772	1710
600	13104	26280	2106	208	1872	1947	1872
700	14112	28224	2268	224	2016	2104	2016
800	15120	30240	2430	240	2160	2260	2160
900	16000	32000	2572	254	2286	2398	2286
1000	16884	33768	2714	268	2412	2536	2412
1100	17766	35532	2855	282	2538	2676	2538
1200	18522	37044	2977	294	2646	2798	2646
1300	19278	38556	3098	306	2754	2917	2754
1400	20034	40068	3220	318	2862	3038	2862
1500	20664	41328	3321	328	2952	3139	2952
1600	21420	42840	3443	340	3060	3260	3060
1700	22050	44100	3544	350	3150	3362	3150
1800	22680	45360	3645	360	3240	3465	3240
1900	23310	46620	3746	370	3330	3568	3330
2000	23940	47880	3848	380	3420	3670	3420
2100	24444	48888	3828	388	3492	3754	3492
2200	25074	50148	4030	398	3582	3857	3582
2300	25578	51156	4110	406	3654	3980	3654
2400	26208	52416	4212	416	3744	4044	3744
2500	26712	53424	4293	424	3816	4128	3816
2600	27216	54432	4374	432	3888	4213	3888
2700	27720	55440	4455	440	3960	4298	3960
2800	28224	56448	4536	448	4032	4382	4032
2900	28728	57456	4617	456	4104	4365	4104
3000	29358	58716	4718	466	4194	4570	4194

TABLE 30-38A

FACTORS BY WHICH WALL AREAS ARE MULTIPLIED TO OBTAIN QUANTITIES OF MATERIAL INCLUDING ALL FITTING, CUTTING AND MILLING WASTE APPLICABLE

Sidewall Material		Applicable Waste	Factor
Shiplap	1″ × 6″ & 1″ × 8″	.22	1.22
Tongue & groove boards	1″ × 4″	.33	1.33
″ ″ ″	1″ × 6″ & 1″ × 8″	.22	1.22
Insulation board ....)			
		.10	1.10
Plywood, particle board, etc. ....)			
Bevel siding	1″ × 6″, 1″ lap	.35	1.35
″ ″	1″ × 8″, 1¼″ lap	.35	1.35
″ ″	1″ × 10″, 1½″ lap	.30	1.30
Drop siding	1″ × 6″	.25	1.25
″ ″	1″ × 8″	.20	1.20
Brickwork 4″ veneer (to obtain number of)			7
8″ ″ ″			14
12″ ″ ″ ″			21
Concrete block 8″ ×16″ ″ ″			1.125
Stucco, Cement plaster, etc. ....number of sq yds divide by 9			
Painting (no openings deducted) ....number of sq ft multiply by 1			
″ ″ ″ ″ ....″ ″ sq yds divide by 9			

Important Note: Tables 30 to 38.

For painting, use the Tables that include gables if the roof is a gable roof. Otherwise use the Tables that exclude gables.

TABLE 30-38B

FORMULAS FOR APPROXIMATING EXTERIOR SIDEWALL MATERIALS *WITH GABLE ENDS EXCLUDED* AND WHERE P = PERIMETER
(Compute gable areas from Table C1 or C2, APPLY waste factors on page 251)

Item of Construction	1-Story	1½-Story	2-Story
Exterior wall surface area . . . in square feet	9P	15P	18P
Sheathing & Siding Including Waste . . . FBM			
Shiplap 1″ × 6″ & 1″ × 8″	11P	18.3P	22P

Item of Construction	1-Story	1½-Story	2-Story
Tongue & groove boards 1″ × 4″	12P	20P	24P
" " " 1″ × 6″ & 1″ × 8″	11P	18.3P	22P
Bevel siding 1″ × 6″, 1″ lap	12P	20.3P	24.3P
" " 1″ × 8″, 1¼″ lap	12P	20.3P	25.7P
" " 1″ × 10″, 1½″ lap	11.7P	19.5P	23.4P
Drop siding 1″ × 6″	11.25P	18.8P	22.5P
" 1″ × 8″	11P	18P	21.6P
Insulation board, plywood, particleboard, etc. (number of square feet)	10P	16.5P	20P
Brick veneer 4″ thick, (number of)	63P	105P	126P
Solid brick 8″ " " "	126P	210P	252P
Concrete block 8″ × 16″ " "	10.125P	16.875P	20.25P
Stucco or cement plaster ....(number of square yards)	1P	1.67P	2P
Painting exterior . . . net square foot area, add proper percentage for type materials such as bevel siding etc.	9P	15P	18P

Note: There is no deduction for openings in these formulas.

Adjust for exterior wall heights other than used in the Tables. (see Table B)

Illustrative Example

In the previous example, the dwelling is one-story, 30′ × 60′, and has a perimeter of 180 lin ft. From Table 30-38B, under one-story dwellings, the formula for 1″ × 10″ bevel siding with a 1½″ lap, is 11.7P.

$$11.7 \times 180' = 2,106 \text{ FBM}$$

This corresponds with the quantity in Table 31 as in the previous example. By adding 585 FBM for the gables the total is 2,691 FBM.

The formulas in Table 30-38B are most convenient when the ground-floor areas lie between those shown in the Tables.

MORTAR FOR BRICK MASONRY

TABLE 30-38C

Type of Wall (³/₈″ Joint)	Nominal Size of Brick in Inches	Cu Yds Mortar Per 1,000 Brick	Cu Ft Mortar Per 1,000 Brick
4″ Brick veneer	2¼ × 3¾ × 8	.33	9.0
8″ " wall	" " "	.50	13.5
12″ " "	" " "	.60	16.2

Divide the above quantities by 10 to obtain amount of mortar per 100 brick.

MORTAR MIXES

For estimating purposes a commonly used mortar mix is shown on page 167, under Table 3A. This mix is for concrete block and brickwork.

TABLE 30-38D

CUBIC YARDS OF CEMENT PLASTER (STUCCO) FOR 100 SQUARE YARDS OF VARIOUS THICKNESSES (1:3 MIX)*

Plaster Thickness In Inches	Cubic Yards On Masonry Base	Cubic Yards On Wire Lath Base
1/4	0.75	0.90
1/2	1.50	1.80
5/8	1.37	1.64
3/4	2.25	2.70
1	3.00	3.60

*See Mortar Mix (1:3), page 167.

TABLE 30-38E

NAILS REQUIRED FOR EXTERIOR WALL MATERIALS

Kind of Material	Size of Material	Size of Nail Used	Lbs Per 1,000 FBM
Shiplap, tongue & groove and square edge boards	1" × 4"	8d	30-35
"	1" × 6"	8d	25-30
"	1" × 8"	8d	20-25
"	1" × 10"	8d	15-20
Bevel siding	1" × 6", 1" lap	6d	25
" "	1" × 8", 1¼" lap	8d	20
" "	1" × 10" 1½" lap	8d	20
Drop siding, Matched rustic	1" × 4"	8d	40
" " " "	1" × 6"	8d	30
" " " "	1" × 8"	8d	25
Insulation board	½" × 4' × 8'	2" galvanized	10 per M sq ft
Plywood and Plyscore	5/16", 3/8"	6d	10
	5/8", 3/4"	8d	20

TABLE 39

Insulation for Ceilings—
Loose-Fill Mineral Wool or Fiberglass

This Table shows the number of 40-lb bags of loose-fill mineral wool or fiberglass insulation required for ceilings of dwellings for various densities and depth of fill.

HOW TO USE THIS TABLE

1. Determine the *ground-floor* area of your dwelling following the method outlined under Computation of Areas in General Instructions, page 17.

   No perimeter measurement is necessary in using this Table nor is a length-to-width ratio needed. Gable ends are not included in these Tables.

2. Select the density and depth of fill from Table 39 and read the number of bags required; use the *ground-floor* area of your dwelling.

Illustrative Example

A 1-story dwelling, 30′ × 50′, has a *ground-floor* area of 1,500 sq ft. At a density of 6 lbs per cubic foot and a depth of 3¹/₂″ it would take 61.7 or 62 40-lb bags of insulation (Table 39). As the Table indicates, this includes the area taken up by the joists.

TABLE 39—INSULATION FOR CEILINGS 263

TABLE 39

LOOSE FILL INSULATION FOR THE CEILINGS OR FLOORS OF DWELLINGS
(Mineral Wool or Fiberglass)
NUMBER OF 40 LB BAGS REQUIRED FOR THE DEPTH & DENSITY SHOWN
(No openings have been deducted)

Ground Floor Area Sq Ft	Density 6 Lb/Cubic Foot Depth of Fill						Density 8 Lb/Cubic Foot Depth of Fill						Density 10 Lb/Cubic Foot Depth of Fill					
	1"	2"	3"	3½"	4"	6"	1"	2"	3"	3½"	4"	6"	1"	2"	3"	3½"	4"	6"
200	2.4	4.7	7.0	8.2	9.4	14.1	3.1	6.3	9.4	10.9	12.5	18.9	3.9	7.8	11.8	13.8	15.7	23.5
300	3.5	7.1	10.6	12.3	14.2	21.1	4.7	9.4	14.1	16.4	18.8	28.3	5.9	11.8	17.6	20.7	23.6	35.3
400	4.7	9.4	14.0	16.5	18.9	28.2	6.3	12.5	18.8	21.9	25.0	37.7	7.8	15.7	23.5	27.6	31.5	47.0
500	5.9	11.8	17.6	20.6	26.6	35.2	7.8	15.7	23.5	27.3	31.3	47.2	9.8	19.6	29.4	34.5	39.4	58.8
600	7.1	14.1	21.1	24.7	28.3	42.3	9.4	18.8	28.2	32.8	37.5	56.6	11.8	23.5	35.3	41.4	47.2	70.6
700	8.2	16.5	24.7	28.8	33.0	49.3	11.0	21.9	32.9	38.3	43.8	66.0	13.7	27.5	41.2	48.3	55.0	82.4
800	9.4	18.8	28.2	32.9	37.7	56.3	12.5	25.1	37.6	43.7	50.0	75.5	15.7	31.4	47.0	55.2	63.0	94.0
900	10.6	21.2	31.7	37.0	42.5	63.4	14.1	28.2	42.3	49.2	56.3	84.9	17.6	35.3	53.0	62.0	71.0	106
1000	11.8	23.5	35.2	41.2	47.2	70.4	15.7	31.3	47.0	54.6	62.5	94.3	19.6	39.2	58.8	69.0	78.7	118
1100	13.0	25.9	38.7	45.3	51.9	77.5	17.2	34.5	51.6	60.1	68.8	104	21.6	43.0	64.7	76.0	86.6	129
1200	14.1	28.2	42.3	49.4	56.6	84.5	18.8	37.6	56.3	65.6	75.0	113	23.5	47.0	70.6	83.0	94.5	141
1300	15.3	30.6	45.8	53.5	61.3	91.5	20.4	40.8	61.0	71.0	81.3	122	25.5	51.0	76.5	89.7	102	153
1400	16.5	33.0	49.3	57.6	66.0	98.6	22.0	43.9	65.7	76.5	87.5	132	27.5	55.0	82.4	96.6	110	165
1500	17.6	35.3	52.8	61.7	70.8	106	23.5	47.0	70.4	82.0	93.8	141	29.4	59.0	88.2	104	118	177
1600	18.8	37.6	56.3	65.8	75.5	113	25.1	50.2	75.1	87.4	100	151	31.4	63.0	94.0	110	126	188
1700	20.0	40.0	60.0	70.0	80.2	120	26.6	53.3	79.8	92.9	106	160	33.3	66.7	100	117	134	200
1800	21.2	42.4	63.4	74.1	84.9	127	28.2	56.4	84.5	98.4	113	170	35.3	70.6	106	124	142	212
1900	22.4	44.7	66.9	78.2	89.6	134	29.8	59.6	89.2	104	119	179	37.3	74.5	112	131	150	224
2000	23.5	47.0	70.4	82.3	94.3	141	31.3	62.7	93.9	109	125	189	39.2	78.4	118	138	158	235
2100	24.7	49.4	73.9	86.4	99.1	148	32.9	65.8	98.6	115	131	198	41.2	82.4	124	145	165	247
2200	25.9	51.8	77.5	90.5	104	155	34.5	69.0	103	120	138	208	43.0	86.3	129	152	173	259
2300	27.1	54.1	81.0	94.7	109	162	36.1	72.1	108	126	144	217	45.0	90.2	135	158	181	271
2400	28.2	56.5	84.5	98.8	113	169	37.6	75.2	113	131	150	226	47.0	94.0	141	166	189	282
2500	29.4	58.8	88.0	103	118	176	39.2	78.4	117	137	156	236	49.0	98.0	147	172	197	294
2600	30.6	61.2	91.5	107	123	183	40.8	81.5	122	142	163	245	51.0	102	153	179	205	306
2700	31.8	63.5	95.1	111	127	190	42.3	84.6	127	148	169	255	53.0	106	159	186	213	318
2800	33.0	65.9	98.6	115	132	197	43.9	87.8	132	153	175	264	55.0	110	165	193	221	329
2900	34.1	68.2	102	119	137	204	45.5	90.9	136	159	181	274	57.0	114	171	200	228	341
3000	35.3	70.6	106	124	142	211	47.0	94.0	141	164	187	283	59.0	118	177	207	236	353

FORMULAS FOR ESTIMATING INSULATION

The quantity of loose fill and batt insulation is readily estimated from the following formulas. Having determined the area to be insulated, walls, floors or ceilings, divide the area by the factors shown in the Table for loose fill insultation; multiply an area by the factors shown, for the number of batts.

TABLE 39A

LOOSE FILL INSULATION
Square feet covered by a 40 lb bag of mineral wool or fiberglass.
(Includes area taken up by studding or joists)

Density of Fill	Depth of Fill							
	1″	2″	3″	3½″	3⅝″	4″	6″	10″
6 Lbs/Cu Ft	85.0	42.5	28.4	24.3	23.5	21.2	14.2	8.5
8 ″ ″ ″	63.8	31.9	21.3	18.3	17.6	16.0	10.6	6.4
10 ″ ″ ″	51.0	25.5	17.0	14.5	14.1	12.7	8.5	5.1

Divide the above factors into the area to obtain the number of bags.

BATT INSULATION

Number of batts of sizes shown per square foot of area to be covered, including area taken up by studding or joists.

	Size of Batt To Be Used					
Batts Per Sq Ft	15″ × 24″	15″ × 48″	19″ × 24″	19″ × 48″	23″ × 24″	23″ × 48″
	.38	.19	.30	.15	.25	.125

Multiply the above factors by the area to obtain the number of batts.

TABLE 39—INSULATION FOR CEILINGS   265

Illustrative Examples

Example No. 1.

An attic floor is to be insulated with 3½″ of loose fill to a density of 6 lbs per cu ft. The gross area to be covered, including the floor joists, is 24′ × 50′ or 1,200 sq ft.
Table 39A shows a factor of 24.3 (1 bag covers 24.3 sq ft).

$$1,200 \div 24.3 = 49.38 \text{ bags needed}$$

Example No. 2.

Assume, in the above example, the floor joists are 2″ × 4″, 16″ on center, which are the lower cords of prefab trusses. Insulating batts 23″ × 48″ are to be used.
Table 39A shows a factor of .125 (.125 of a batt per sq ft).

$$.125 \times 1,000 = 125 \text{ batts needed}$$

Example No. 3.

The sidewalls of a one-story ranch house are to have insulating batts between the exterior wall studs. The studs are 2″ × 4″ and 16″ on center. The batt size is 15″ × 48″. The net area (openings deducted) is 1,040 sq ft.
Table 39A shows a factor .19.

$$.19 \times 1,040 = 198 \text{ batts needed.}$$

TABLES 40, 41 and 42

Insulation for Exterior Walls—
Loose-Fill Mineral Wool or Fiberglass

(Excludes Gable Areas)

These Tables show the number of 40 lb bags of loose-fill mineral wool or fiberglass insulation needed for the sidewalls of dwellings according to density and depth of fill.

HOW TO USE THESE TABLES

1. Determine the *ground-floor* area of your dwelling following the method outlined under Computation of Areas in General Instructions, page 17.

2. Determine the perimeter of your dwelling following the method outlined under Perimeter Measurement in the General Instructions, page 18.

3. Using Table A, check the *ground-floor* of your dwelling and the lineal feet of perimeter to obtain the length-to-width ratio.

4. Tables are based on dwellings that have a length-to-width ratio of 2:1. If the length-to-width ratio of your dwelling is significantly different adjust the quantity in the Tables upward or downward by the percentages under Table A, page 22.

Illustrative Example

A 1-story dwelling, 30′ × 90′, has a length-to-width ratio of 3:1 and a *ground-floor* area of 2700 sq ft. Specifications call for loose-fill insulation in the sidewalls and stipulate a density of 8 lbs per cu ft and the depth of fill between the studs to be ½". Table 40, based on a length-to-width ratio of 2:1, shows that 81.5 bags are required. Table A, page 22, shows that if the length-to-width ratio is 3:1 an adjustment of 9% is to be added to the Table quantities.

$$81.5 \times 1.09 = 89 \text{ bags are required}$$

EXTERIOR WALL HEIGHT ADJUSTMENT

Exterior wall heights on which these Tables are based are 9' for a 1-story dwelling, 15' for one that is 1 1/2-story and 18' for a 2-story dwelling. If the height of the exterior walls of your dwelling is greater or less than stated above, the Table quantities may be adjusted upward or downward as the case may be by referring to Table B, page 27.

Window and Door Openings

There has been no deduction for exterior window or door openings in these Tables. Because of variations in size and number of such openings, this is left to the discretion of the estimator.

TABLE 40

INSULATION FOR THE EXTERIOR WALLS OF 1-STORY DWELLINGS EXCLUDING THE GABLE ENDS.
NUMBER OF 40 LB BAGS OF LOOSE FILL (MINERAL WOOL OR FIBERGLASS) REQUIRED FOR THE DEPTH AND DENSITY SHOWN.
(Quantities are to the nearest full bag)

Ground Floor Area Sq Ft	Ext. wall area S F	Density 6 Lb/Cu Ft — Depth of Fill						Density 8 Lb/Cu Ft — Depth of Fill						Density 10 Lb/Cu Ft — Depth of Fill					
		1″	2″	3″	3½″	3⅝″	4″	1″	2″	3″	3½″	3⅝″	4″	1″	2″	3″	3½″	3⅝″	4″
200	540	6	13	19	22	23	26	9	17	25	30	31	34	11	21	32	37	39	43
300	666	8	16	24	27	28	31	10	21	31	37	38	42	13	26	39	46	47	52
400	765	9	18	27	32	33	36	12	24	36	42	43	48	15	30	45	53	54	60
500	855	10	20	30	35	37	40	13	27	40	47	49	54	17	34	50	59	61	67
600	936	11	22	33	39	40	44	15	29	44	51	53	59	18	37	55	64	67	73
700	1008	12	24	36	42	43	48	16	32	47	55	57	63	20	40	59	69	72	79
800	1080	13	25	38	44	46	51	17	34	51	59	61	68	21	42	63	74	77	85
900	1143	14	27	40	47	49	54	18	36	54	63	65	72	23	45	67	78	82	90
1000	1206	14	28	43	50	52	57	19	38	57	66	69	76	24	47	71	83	86	95
1100	1269	15	30	45	52	54	60	20	40	60	70	72	79	25	50	75	87	90	99
1200	1323	16	31	47	54	57	62	21	42	62	73	75	83	26	52	78	91	94	104
1300	1377	16	32	49	57	59	65	22	43	65	76	78	86	27	54	81	95	98	108
1400	1431	17	34	50	59	61	67	22	45	67	79	81	90	28	56	84	98	102	112
1500	1476	17	35	52	61	63	70	23	46	69	81	84	93	29	58	87	101	105	116
1600	1530	18	36	54	63	65	72	24	48	72	84	87	96	30	60	90	105	109	120
1700	1575	19	37	56	65	67	74	25	49	74	86	89	99	31	62	93	108	112	123
1800	1620	19	38	57	67	69	76	26	51	76	89	92	102	32	64	95	111	115	127
1900	1665	20	39	59	69	71	78	26	52	78	91	95	105	33	65	98	114	118	131
2000	1710	20	40	60	70	73	80	27	54	80	94	97	107	34	67	100	117	122	134
2100	1746	21	41	62	72	74	82	27	55	82	96	99	109	34	68	103	120	124	137
2200	1791	21	42	63	74	77	84	28	56	84	98	102	113	35	70	105	123	128	141
2300	1827	22	43	64	75	78	86	29	57	86	100	104	115	36	72	107	125	130	143
2400	1872	22	44	66	77	80	88	29	59	88	103	106	117	37	73	110	129	133	147
2500	1908	23	45	67	79	82	90	30	60	90	105	109	120	38	75	112	131	136	150
2600	1944	23	46	69	80	83	92	31	61	91	107	111	122	38	76	114	133	138	153
2700	1980	23	47	70	82	85	93	31	62	93	109	113	124	39	78	116	136	141	155
2800	2016	24	47	71	83	86	95	32	63	95	111	115	126	40	79	118	138	143	158
2900	2052	24	48	72	84	88	97	32	65	96	113	117	129	40	81	121	141	146	161
3000	2097	25	49	74	86	90	99	33	66	98	115	119	132	41	82	123	144	149	165

TABLE 41

INSULATION FOR THE EXTERIOR WALLS OF 1¹/₂-STORY DWELLINGS
EXCLUDING THE GABLE ENDS.
NUMBER OF 40 LB BAGS OF LOOSE FILL (MINERAL WOOL OR FIBERGLASS)
REQUIRED FOR THE DEPTH AND DENSITY SHOWN.
(Quantities are to the nearest full bag)

Ground Floor Area Sq Ft	Ext. wall area	Density 6 Lb/Cu Ft						Density 8 Lb/Cu Ft						Density 10 Lb/Cu Ft					
		Depth of Fill						Depth of Fill						Depth of Fill					
	S F	1″	2″	3″	3¹/₂″	3⁵/₈″	4″	1″	2″	3″	3¹/₂″	3⁵/₈″	4″	1″	2″	3″	3¹/₂″	3⁵/₈″	4″
200	900	11	21	32	37	38	42	14	28	42	49	51	56	18	36	54	63	65	72
300	1110	12	26	39	46	47	52	17	35	51	60	62	68	22	44	66	77	80	88
400	1275	15	30	45	53	54	60	20	40	60	70	72	80	25	50	75	88	90	100
500	1425	17	34	50	59	61	67	22	45	66	77	80	88	28	56	84	98	102	112
600	1560	18	37	55	64	67	73	24	49	72	84	87	96	31	62	93	109	112	124
700	1680	20	40	59	69	72	79	26	53	78	92	94	104	33	66	99	116	120	132
800	1800	21	42	64	74	77	85	28	57	84	98	102	112	35	70	105	123	127	140
900	1905	22	45	67	78	81	90	30	60	90	105	109	120	37	74	111	130	134	148
1000	2010	24	47	71	83	86	95	32	63	96	112	116	128	39	78	117	137	141	156
1100	2115	25	50	75	87	90	100	33	66	99	116	120	132	41	82	123	144	149	164
1200	2205	26	52	78	91	94	104	35	69	105	123	127	140	43	86	129	151	156	172
1300	2295	27	54	81	95	98	108	36	72	108	126	131	144	45	90	135	158	163	180
1400	2385	28	56	84	98	102	112	37	75	111	130	134	148	47	94	141	165	170	188
1500	2460	29	58	87	101	105	116	39	77	117	137	141	156	48	96	144	168	174	192
1600	2550	30	60	90	105	109	120	40	80	120	140	145	160	50	100	150	175	181	200
1700	2625	31	62	93	108	112	124	41	82	123	144	149	164	51	102	153	179	185	204
1800	2700	32	64	95	111	115	127	42	85	126	147	153	169	53	106	159	186	192	212
1900	2775	33	65	98	114	118	131	44	87	132	154	160	176	54	108	162	189	196	216
2000	2850	34	67	101	117	122	134	45	89	135	158	163	180	56	112	168	196	203	224
2100	2910	34	69	103	120	124	137	46	91	138	161	167	184	57	114	171	200	207	228
2200	2985	35	70	105	123	127	140	47	93	141	165	170	188	59	118	177	207	214	236
2300	3045	36	72	108	125	130	143	48	95	144	168	174	192	60	120	180	210	218	240
2400	3120	37	73	110	129	133	147	49	98	147	172	178	196	61	122	183	214	221	244
2500	3180	37	75	112	131	136	150	50	100	150	175	181	200	62	124	186	217	225	248
2600	3240	38	76	114	133	138	153	51	102	153	179	185	204	64	128	192	224	232	256
2700	3300	39	78	117	136	141	155	52	104	156	182	189	208	65	130	195	228	236	260
2800	3360	40	79	119	138	143	158	53	105	159	186	192	212	66	132	198	231	239	264
2900	3420	40	81	121	141	146	161	54	107	162	189	196	216	67	134	201	235	243	268
3000	3495	41	82	123	144	149	165	55	110	165	193	199	220	69	138	207	242	250	276

TABLE 42

INSULATION FOR THE EXTERIOR WALLS OF 2-STORY DWELLINGS
EXCLUDING THE GABLE ENDS.
NUMBER OF 40 LB BAGS OF LOOSE FILL (MINERAL WOOL OR FIBERGLASS)
REQUIRED FOR THE DEPTH AND DENSITY SHOWN.
(Quantities are to the nearest full bag)

Ground Floor Area Sq Ft	Ext. wall area S F	Density 6 Lb/Cu Ft — Depth of Fill						Density 8 Lb/Cu Ft — Depth of Fill						Density 10 Lb/Cu Ft — Depth of Fill					
		1"	2"	3'	3½"	3⅝'	4"	1"	2"	3"	3½"	3⅝'	4"	1"	2"	3"	3½"	3⅝"	4"
200	1080	13	25	38	45	46	51	17	34	51	59	61	68	21	42	63	74	78	85
300	1332	16	31	47	55	57	63	21	42	63	73	76	84	26	52	78	92	95	105
400	1530	18	36	54	63	65	72	24	48	72	84	87	96	30	60	90	105	109	120
500	1710	20	40	60	70	73	80	27	53	80	93	97	107	33	66	99	117	121	133
600	1872	22	44	66	77	80	88	29	59	88	103	106	117	37	74	111	128	133	147
700	2016	24	47	71	83	86	95	32	63	95	111	115	127	40	80	120	138	143	158
800	2160	25	51	76	89	92	102	34	68	101	119	123	135	42	84	126	148	153	169
900	2286	27	54	81	94	98	108	36	72	108	125	130	143	45	90	135	157	163	178
1000	2412	28	57	85	99	103	114	38	76	114	133	137	151	47	95	141	166	172	189
1100	2538	30	60	90	105	108	120	40	80	120	140	144	160	50	100	150	175	181	200
1200	2646	31	62	93	109	113	124	42	83	124	145	150	166	52	104	155	182	188	207
1300	2754	32	65	97	113	118	130	43	86	130	151	157	173	54	108	162	189	196	217
1400	2862	34	67	101	118	122	135	45	90	135	157	163	180	56	112	168	197	204	225
1500	2952	35	69	104	122	126	139	46	93	139	162	168	185	58	116	173	203	210	231
1600	3060	36	72	108	126	131	144	48	96	144	168	174	192	60	120	280	210	218	240
1700	3150	37	74	111	130	134	248	49	99	148	173	179	197	62	124	185	216	223	247
1800	3240	38	76	114	133	138	152	51	101	152	177	184	203	63	126	190	222	230	253
1900	3330	39	78	118	137	142	157	52	105	157	183	189	209	65	130	196	229	237	261
2000	3420	40	80	121	141	146	161	54	107	161	188	194	214	67	134	201	235	243	268
2100	3492	41	82	123	144	149	164	55	110	164	192	199	219	69	138	206	240	248	274
2200	3582	42	84	126	147	153	168	56	112	168	196	203	224	70	140	211	246	254	281
2300	3654	43	86	129	151	156	172	57	115	172	201	208	229	72	144	215	251	260	287
2400	3744	44	88	132	154	160	176	59	117	176	205	213	235	73	146	220	257	266	293
2500	3916	45	90	135	157	163	180	60	120	180	209	217	239	75	150	225	262	271	299
2600	3888	46	91	137	160	166	183	61	122	183	213	221	244	76	152	228	267	276	305
2700	3960	47	93	140	163	169	186	62	124	186	217	225	248	78	156	232	272	282	311
2800	4032	47	95	142	166	172	190	63	126	189	221	229	253	79	158	137	277	287	316
2900	4104	48	97	145	169	175	193	64	129	193	225	233	258	81	162	242	282	292	322
3000	4194	49	99	148	173	179	197	66	131	197	230	238	263	82	164	247	288	298	329

TABLE 43

Insulation for Exterior Walls

Batts—Glass, Mineral Wool or Rock Wool

(Excludes Gable Areas)

This Table shows the number of insulation batts of various widths and lengths that are required in the exterior walls of 1, 1 1/2 and 2-story dwellings.

HOW TO USE THIS TABLE

1. Determine the *ground-floor* area of your dwelling following the method outlined under Computation of Areas in General Instructions, page 17.

2. Determine the perimeter of your dwelling following the method outlined under Perimeter Measurement in the General Instructions, page 18.

3. Using Table A, check the *ground-floor* area and lineal feet of perimeter of your dwelling to obtain the length-to-width ratio.

4. This Table is based on dwellings that have a length-to-width ratio of 2:1. If the length-to-width ratio of your dwelling is significantly different adjust the quantity in the Table upward or downward by the percentages shown under Table A, page 22.

Illustrative Example

A 2-story dwelling, 20′ × 60′, has a length-to-width ratio of 3:1 and a *ground-floor* area of 1,200 sq ft. Insulation batts 48″ long are to be placed between studding that is 16″ on center. Table 43 shows that it will require 503 batts 15″ wide.

271

Table A shows that if the length-to-width ratio is 3:1 instead of 2:1 an adjustment of 9% must be made. The number of batts, therefore, is 503 × 1.09 = 548 batts.

EXTERIOR WALL HEIGHT ADJUSTMENT

The exterior wall heights on which this Table is based are 9′ for a 1-story dwelling, 15′ for one that is 1 1/2-story and 18′ for a 2-story dwelling. If the exterior wall height of a dwelling is more or less than stated above, the Table quantities may be adjusted upward or downward as the case may be by referring to Table B, page 27.

Illustrative Example

In the previous example, if the exterior wall height is 16′ instead of 18′ as used in the Table, the quantity computed (548) should be multiplied by the factor in Table B which for 16′ is .89.

548 × .89 = 488 batts required

Window and Door Openings

There has been no deduction for exterior window or door openings in this Table. Because of variations in size and number of such openings, this is left to the discretion of the estimator.

TABLE 43—INSULATION FOR EXTERIOR WALLS (BATTS) 273

TABLE 43

INSULATION BATTS FOR THE SIDEWALLS OF DWELLINGS GLASS, MINERAL OR ROCK WOOL. NO OPENINGS DEDUCTED. NUMBER OF BATTS REQUIRED

Ground Floor Area	1-Story Dwelling						1 1/2-Story Dwelling						2-Story Dwelling					
	Size of Batts						Size of Batts						Size of Batts					
	15" By		19" By		23" By		15" By		19" By		23" By		15" By		19" By		23" By	
	24"	48"	24"	48"	24"	48"	24"	48"	24"	48"	24"	48"	24"	48"	24"	48"	24"	48"
200	205	103	162	81	135	68	342	171	270	135	225	113	410	205	324	162	270	135
300	253	127	200	100	166	83	422	211	332	166	276	138	506	253	400	200	333	166
400	290	145	230	115	191	96	484	242	382	191	319	161	580	290	460	230	383	192
500	325	162	256	128	214	107	542	271	428	214	356	178	650	325	512	256	428	214
600	356	178	280	140	234	117	592	296	468	234	390	195	712	356	562	281	468	234
700	383	192	302	151	252	126	638	319	504	252	420	210	766	383	604	302	504	252
800	410	205	324	162	270	135	648	342	540	270	450	225	820	410	648	324	540	270
900	434	217	343	171	286	143	724	362	572	286	476	238	868	434	686	343	572	286
1000	458	229	362	181	302	151	764	382	604	302	502	251	916	458	724	362	603	302
1100	482	241	380	190	317	159	804	402	634	317	529	265	964	482	762	381	635	318
1200	502	251	396	198	331	166	838	419	662	331	551	275	1006	503	794	397	662	331
1300	524	262	413	207	344	172	872	436	688	344	574	287	1046	523	826	413	688	344
1400	544	272	429	215	358	179	906	453	716	358	596	298	1088	544	858	429	715	358
1500	560	280	442	221	369	185	934	467	738	369	615	308	1122	561	886	443	738	369
1600	580	290	460	230	383	192	970	485	764	382	638	319	1162	581	918	459	765	383
1700	598	299	472	236	394	197	998	499	788	398	656	328	1198	599	944	472	788	394
1800	615	308	486	243	405	203	1026	513	810	405	675	338	1230	615	972	486	810	405
1900	632	316	500	250	416	208	1054	527	832	416	694	347	1266	633	1000	500	832	416
2000	650	325	513	257	428	214	1084	542	854	427	713	356	1300	650	1026	513	855	427
2100	664	332	524	262	437	218	1106	553	874	437	728	364	1326	663	1048	524	873	436
2200	680	340	537	268	448	224	1134	567	896	448	746	373	1360	680	1074	537	896	448
2300	694	347	548	274	457	228	1156	578	914	457	761	380	1388	694	1096	548	914	457
2400	711	356	562	281	468	234	1186	593	936	468	780	390	1422	711	1123	562	936	468
2500	726	363	572	286	477	238	1208	604	954	477	795	398	1450	725	1144	572	954	477
2600	738	369	584	292	486	243	1232	616	972	486	810	405	1476	738	1166	583	972	486
2700	752	376	594	297	495	248	1254	627	990	495	825	413	1504	752	1188	594	990	495
2800	766	383	604	302	504	252	1276	638	1008	504	840	420	1532	766	1210	605	1008	504
2900	780	390	616	308	513	256	1300	650	1026	513	855	428	1560	780	1232	616	1026	513
3000	797	398	630	315	524	262	1328	664	1048	524	874	437	1594	797	1258	629	1048	524

TABLE 44

Insulation for Ceilings and Floors
Batts—Glass, Mineral Wool or Rock Wool

This Table shows the number of insulation batts of various widths and lengths required in the ceilings or floors of dwellings.

HOW TO USE THIS TABLE

Determine the *ground-floor* area of your dwelling following the method outlined under Computation of Areas in General Instructions, page 17.

No perimeter measurement is necessary and length-to-width ratio is not involved because the Table quantities are based solely on the *ground-floor* area. Select the length and width of the batts to be used and read the number needed directly from the Table.

Illustrative Example

The attic floor of a dwelling, 40′ × 60′, requires that insulation batts be placed between the 2″ × 4″ ceiling joists that are 24″ on center. Batts 23″ wide are called for and specifications state the batts are to be 48″ long. Table 44 shows that for a *ground-floor* area of 2,400 sq ft (40 ′ × 60′ = 2,400 sq ft) 300 batts are needed.

Note: The area includes that taken up by the joists.

TABLE 44—INSULATION FOR CEILINGS, FLOORS (BATTS)   275

TABLE 44

INSULATION BATTS FOR THE CEILINGS OF DWELLINGS
(Glass, Mineral or Rock Wool)
NUMBER OF BATTS REQUIRED

Ground Floor Area Sq Ft		Batt Size					
		15" By		19" By		23" By	
		24"	48"	24"	48"	24"	48"
200		76	38	60	30	50	25
300		114	57	90	45	75	38
400		152	76	120	60	100	50
500		190	95	150	75	125	63
600		228	114	180	90	150	75
700		266	133	210	105	175	86
800		304	152	240	120	200	100
900		342	171	270	135	225	113
1000		380	190	300	150	250	125
1100		418	209	330	165	275	137
1200		456	228	360	180	300	150
1300		494	247	390	195	325	163
1400		532	266	420	210	350	175
1500		570	285	450	225	375	188
1600		608	304	480	240	400	200
1700		646	323	510	255	425	212
1800		684	342	540	270	450	225
1900		722	361	570	285	475	238
2000		760	380	600	300	500	250
2100		798	399	630	315	525	263
2200		836	418	660	330	550	275
2300		874	437	690	345	575	288
2400		912	456	720	360	600	300
2500		950	475	750	375	625	313
2600		988	494	780	390	650	325
2700		1026	513	810	405	675	338
2800		1064	532	840	420	700	350
2900		1102	551	870	435	725	363
3000		1140	570	900	450	750	375

One and Two-Car Attached and Detached Garages

Tables 45 through 67 apply to one and two-car garages. The shortcut formulas under the dwelling section of this book may be used in estimating garage materials of construction and therefor are not repeated here.

The Tables for garages are based on a 2:1 length-to-width ratio for one-car garages and on a 1:1 length-to-width ratio for two-car garages. There is no adjustment for different length-to-width ratios because in most cases the effect on the quantity of materials will not be significant.

Any adjustment for gable materials due to roof pitches other than 1/4 on which the tables are based is to be made at the discretion of the estimator, because differences will also be minor in the overall estimate.

The perimeter of an attached garage is the total of the three unattached sides. Table quantities are computed on this basis. Garage door openings are deducted in figuring the Tables; a 9-foot opening for a one-car garage and a 16-foot opening for a two-car garage.

The Labor Tables, the discussion on estimating labor, overhead and profit, and illustrative examples all apply equally to garage construction as well as dwelling construction.

276

TABLE 45

Concrete Footings, Foundation Walls and Floor Slabs for One- and Two-Car Detached Garages

This Table shows the number of cubic yards of concrete for various size footings, foundation walls above the footings, floor slabs and base. "Under Foundation Wall Above Footing" there is also shown the number of 8″ × 16″ concrete block required for walls that are 24″, 32″ and 48″ high. The height of these walls above the footing varies with the frost line in different parts of the country and with local Building laws regulating construction.

HOW TO USE THIS TABLE

1. Determine the *ground-floor* area of the garage.

2. Read quantities directly from the Table according to your specifications. If the area of your garage is between those in the Table, interpolate as explained in General Instructions, pages 19-20.

FORMULAS

It may be desirable to use the formulas shown under each Table in the Dwelling section rather than the Table 45. They will be found as follows:

The procedure to follow in using these basic formulas and Tables is exactly the same as the procedure prescribed under the dwelling section where the formulas and Tables appear. The one difference in the case of an attached garage is that the perimeter is for three sides of the building inasmuch as one side is attached to the dwelling. Therefore, whenever the perimeter P is shown in a formula for attached garages it must be remembered that it is for the three unattached sides of the garage. Table 45 follows on page 278.

TABLE 45

FOOTINGS, FOUNDATION WALLS ABOVE FOOTINGS & FLOOR SLABS FOR 1-CAR, 1-STORY GARAGES, DETACHED, WITH A 9-FOOT DOOR

Ground Floor Area Sq. Ft.	Footing Width & Depth of Concrete 16"x6" CY	18"x8" CY	24"x1' CY	Foundation Wall Above Footing Width & Depth of Concrete 8"x2' CY	8"x3' CY	10"x2' CY	10"x3' CY	10"x4' CY	Concrete Block 8"x16" 24" High units	32" High units	48" High units	Gravel Base Thickness 3" CY	4" CY	5" CY	Conc Slab Thickness 3" CY	4" CY	Topping Thickness 1" CY	1½" CY
200	1.26	1.89	3.77	2.53	3.77	3.16	4.74	6.32	115	153	230	1.86	2.48	3.10	1.86	2.48	0.62	0.92
250	1.43	2.15	4.29	2.88	4.29	3.60	5.39	7.19	131	174	261	2.33	3.10	3.88	2.33	3.10	0.78	1.15
300	1.61	2.41	4.81	3.22	4.81	4.03	6.05	8.06	147	195	293	2.79	3.72	4.65	2.79	3.72	0.93	1.38
350	1.75	2.63	5.25	3.52	5.25	4.40	6.60	8.80	160	213	320	3.26	4.34	5.43	3.26	4.34	1.09	1.61
400	1.88	2.81	5.62	3.77	5.62	4.71	7.07	9.42	171	228	342	3.72	4.96	6.20	3.72	4.96	1.24	1.84
450	2.00	3.00	6.00	4.02	6.00	5.02	7.53	10.0	182	243	365	4.20	4.58	6.98	4.20	4.58	1.40	2.07
500	2.12	3.12	6.36	4.27	6.36	5.33	8.00	10.7	194	258	387	4.64	6.20	7.75	4.65	6.20	1.55	2.30

FOR 2-CAR DETACHED GARAGES WITH 16' DOOR

Ground Floor Area Sq. Ft.	Footing Width & Depth of Concrete 16"x6" CY	18"x8" CY	24"x1' CY	Foundation Wall Above Footing Width & Depth of Concrete 8"x2' CY	8"x3' CY	10"x2' CY	10"x3' CY	10"x4' CY	Concrete Block 8"x16" 24" High units	32" High units	48" High units	Gravel Base Thickness 3" CY	4" CY	5" CY	Conc Slab Thickness 3" CY	4" CY	Topping Thickness 1" CY	1½" CY
200	1.01	1.52	3.03	2.03	3.03	2.54	3.82	5.08	92	123	184	1.86	2.48	3.10	1.86	2.48	0.62	0.92
250	1.16	1.74	3.48	2.33	3.48	2.92	4.37	5.83	106	141	212	2.33	3.10	3.88	2.33	3.10	0.78	1.15
300	1.31	1.96	3.92	2.63	3.92	3.29	4.93	6.57	119	159	238	2.79	3.72	4.65	2.79	3.72	0.93	1.38
350	1.46	2.18	4.37	2.93	4.37	3.66	5.49	7.32	133	177	266	3.26	4.34	5.43	3.26	4.34	1.09	1.61
400	1.58	2.37	4.74	3.18	4.74	3.97	5.95	7.94	144	192	288	3.72	4.96	6.20	3.72	4.96	1.24	1.84
450	1.70	2.55	5.11	3.42	5.11	4.28	6.42	8.56	155	207	310	4.19	5.58	6.98	4.19	5.58	1.40	2.07
500	1.80	2.70	5.40	3.62	5.40	4.53	6.79	9.05	164	219	328	4.65	6.20	7.75	4.65	6.20	1.55	2.30
550	1.93	2.89	5.77	3.87	5.77	4.84	7.25	9.67	176	234	352	5.12	6.82	8.53	5.12	6.82	1.71	2.53
600	2.03	3.03	6.07	4.07	6.07	5.08	7.63	10.2	185	246	370	5.58	7.44	9.30	5.58	7.44	1.86	2.76
650	2.12	3.18	6.36	4.27	6.37	5.33	8.00	10.7	194	258	388	6.05	8.06	10.1	6.05	8.06	2.02	2.99
700	2.22	3.33	6.67	4.46	6.67	5.58	8.37	11.2	203	270	406	6.51	8.68	10.9	6.51	8.68	2.17	3.22
750	2.32	3.48	6.96	4.66	6.96	5.83	8.74	11.7	212	282	424	6.98	9.30	11.6	6.98	9.30	2.33	3.45
800	2.40	3.59	7.18	4.81	7.18	6.02	9.02	12.0	218	291	436	7.44	9.92	12.4	7.44	9.92	2.48	3.68
850	2.50	3.74	7.47	5.01	7.47	6.26	9.39	12.5	227	303	454	7.91	10.5	13.2	7.91	10.5	2.64	3.91
900	2.57	3.85	7.70	5.16	7.70	6.45	9.67	12.9	234	312	468	8.37	11.2	13.9	8.37	11.2	2.79	4.14
950	2.64	3.96	7.92	5.31	7.92	6.62	9.95	13.3	241	321	482	8.84	11.8	14.8	8.84	11.8	2.95	4.37
1000	2.72	4.07	8.14	5.46	8.14	6.82	10.2	13.6	248	330	496	9.30	12.4	15.5	9.30	12.4	3.10	4.60

TABLE 46

Exterior Wall and Ceiling Framing, Including Shoe and Plate

(Number of Board Feet Required)

For 1-Car Detached Garages with 9' Door
For 2-Car Detached Garages with 16' Door

This Table shows the board feet (FBM) of exterior wall and ceiling framing for both 1-car and 2-car detached garages. The door openings are 9' and 16' respectively. Rafter framing is shown in Tables 53 and 54; Trusses in Table 55. Wall studding is shown for garages with gables and without gables as in the case of a hip or shed type roof. Studding is shown for 16" and 24" on center. Ceiling joists may be 2" × 4" or 2" × 6", 24" on center.

HOW TO USE THIS TABLE

1. Determine the *ground-floor* area of your garage.
2. Select the framing specified for your garage. Read quantities directly from the Table for the *ground-floor* area. If the area of the garage falls between those in the Table, interpolate as explained in the General Instructions, pages 19-20.

ADJUSTMENT FOR GABLE FRAMING WHEN ROOF PITCH IS OTHER THAN 1/4, THE PITCH ON WHICH THIS TABLE IS BASED.

Because of the relatively small *ground-floor* area in garages, differences in gable areas, as roof pitches increase or decrease from the 1/4 pitch used in the Table, will be of little significance. If precise quantities are desired refer to pages 29-30 under the Dwelling section.

TABLE 46A

FORMULAS FOR ESTIMATING THE FBM OF FRAMING FOR DETACHED GARAGES

P = Perimeter   A = Ground-Floor Area
Garage Door Openings:
  1-Car 9′ Wide   All Studding 8′ Long
  2-Car 16′ ″

Item of Framing	1-Car Garage	2-Car Garage
Exterior wall area including gables ″ ″ ″ excluding	8 (P-9) + Gable area* 8 (P-9)	8 (P-16) + Gable area* 8 (P-16)
Exterior wall studs including gables 2″ × 4″ - 16″ on center 2″ × 4″ - 24″ ″ ″	.667 × Exterior wall area .44 × ″ ″	.667 × Exterior wall area .44 × ″ ″
Exterior wall studs excluding gables 2″ × 4″ - 16″ on center 2″ × 4″ - 24″ ″ ″	5.33 (P-9) 3.56 (P-9)	5.33 (P-16) 3.56 (P-16)
Sills, plate, door header, etc. Ceiling Joists...2″×6″, 24″ on center 2″×4″, ″ ″ ″	2.5 (P-9) .55 A .35 A	2.7 (P-16) .55 A .35 A

For Rafters see Tables 53 and 54. For Prefab Trusses see Table 55.
*See Tables C1 and C2 for computing the gable areas which are based on *ground-floor* area, pitch of the roof and length-to-width ratio.

TABLE 46—EXTERIOR WALL AND CEILING FRAMING (DETACHED GARAGES)   281

Illustrative Example

To determine the total FBM of framing in a 2-car garage 24' × 25'. The studding is 2" × 4", 16" on center; there is a 2" × 4" sill, a 4" × 4" plate and 2 − 2" ×12" for the door header. Prefab trusses are 24" on center having a 2" × 4" cord and bracing with 2" × 6" rafters. The perimeter is 98 lin ft and the *ground-floor* area is 600 sq ft. The roof is a gable type.

There are three ways to approach the solution and each is shown here.

Method No. 1

Use Table 46 for framing walls and Table 55 for the trusses. Quantities may be read directly from the Tables.

Table 46 ....Studding	537	FBM
" " ....Sill, plate and door header	221	"
" 55 ....Prefab trusses	768	"
	1,526	"

Method No. 2

Using the basic formulas, first determine the exterior wall area excluding gables. Compute the gable areas from Table C2. Use the basic formula for sill, plate and door header.

Exterior wall area excluding gables 8 (P-16) = 8 (98-16)		=	656 sq ft
Gable area from Table C2..,		=	150 "
	Total		806 "
			×.667
			538 FBM

Sill, plate and door header 2.7 (P-16) = 2.7 (98-16)		=	221 "
Prefab trusses...Table 55		=	768 "
	Total		1,527 "

Method No. 3

Determine the FBM of exterior wall studs from basic formula 5.33 (P-16). Compute gable area from Table C2 as in Method No. 2. Add sill, plate and door header from formula 2.7 (P-16) and prefab trusses from Table 55.

Studding excluding gables 5.33 (98-16)....................................... =	437	FBM
Gable area, Table C2 150 sq ft × .667..=	100	"
Sill, plate and door header, 2.7 (P-16) = 2.7 × 82	= 221	"
Prefab trusses, Table 55.. =	768	"

Nails for Framing: See page 205, Table 14-B.   Total   1,526   "

TABLE 46

EXTERIOR WALL & CEILING FRAMING INCLUDING SHOE & PLATE
(Number of Board Feet Required)

FOR 1-CAR DETACHED GARAGES WITH 9′ DOOR

Ground Floor Area	Exterior Wall Area		Sill, Plate Shoe & Door Head	2″ × 4″ Studs Gable Ends Included		2″ × 4″ Studs Gable Ends Excluded		Ceiling Joists 24″ on Center	
	Gable Ends								
	Included	Excluded		16″ Center	24″ Center	16″ Center	24″ Center	2″ × 4″	2″ × 6″
Sq Ft	Bd Ft	Bd Ft	Bd Ft	Bd Ft	Bd Ft	Bd Ft	Bd Ft	Bd Ft	Bd Ft
200	433	408	128	285	190	272	181	70	110
250	494	464	145	325	217	309	206	88	138
300	558	520	163	365	244	346	231	105	165
350	612	568	178	400	267	378	252	123	193
400	658	608	190	430	287	405	270	140	220
450	704	648	203	460	306	432	287	158	248
500	750	688	215	490	327	459	306	175	275

(Note; Rafters and trusses shown in Tables 53 to 55 inclusive)

FOR 2-CAR DETACHED GARAGES WITH 16′ DOOR

Ground Floor Area	Exterior Wall Area		Sill, Plate Shoe & Door Head	2″ × 4″ Studs Gable Ends Included		2″ × 4″ Studs Gable Ends Excluded		Ceiling Joists 24″ on Center	
	Gable Ends								
	Included	Excluded		16″ Center	24″ Center	16″ Center	24″ Center	2″ × 4″	2″ × 6″
Sq Ft	Bd Ft	Bd Ft	Bd Ft	Bd Ft	Bd Ft	Bd Ft	Bd Ft	Bd Ft	Bd Ft
200	379	328	110	252	167	219	146	70	110
250	438	376	127	292	194	251	167	88	138
300	498	424	143	332	221	282	188	105	165
350	559	472	159	372	248	314	209	122	193
400	612	512	173	408	272	341	227	140	220
450	664	552	186	442	294	368	245	158	248
500	708	584	197	472	314	389	259	175	275
550	731	624	210	507	338	416	277	193	303
600	806	656	221	537	358	437	291	210	330
650	851	688	232	567	378	458	305	228	358
700	896	720	243	597	398	480	320	245	385
750	940	752	254	626	417	501	334	263	412
800	976	776	262	650	433	517	344	280	440
850	1021	808	273	680	452	538	358	300	468
900	1057	832	280	704	469	554	369	315	495
950	1093	856	290	728	485	570	380	332	522
1000	1128	880	297	751	500	586	390	350	550

TABLES 47 and 48

Exterior Sidewall Material for 1-Car and 2-Car Detached Garages with 9′ and 16′ Door Openings Respectively

Table 47 Includes Gable Ends
Table 48 Excludes Gable Ends

These Tables show the exterior wall areas and various kinds of exterior wall materials, including rough wood and composition board, brick veneer and solid brick, concrete block, etc. for detached garages. Table 47 includes gable end areas while Table 48 excludes them to provide for hip and flat or shed type roofs. Milling, cutting and fitting waste is included where appropriate.

HOW TO USE THESE TABLES

1. Determine the *ground-floor* area of your garage.
2. Select the exterior wall material according to specifications for your garage.
3. Read off the quantity of material required according to the *ground-floor* area.

Interpolate if the *ground-floor* area of your garage falls between those in the Tables. Interpolating is explained under the Dwelling section, page 20.

ADJUSTMENT FOR GABLE END MATERIALS WHEN ROOF PITCH IS OTHER THAN ¹/₄, THE PITCH ON WHICH THESE TABLES ARE BASED.

Because of the relatively small *ground-floor* area in garages, the differences in quantities of material in gable areas as roof pitches increase or decrease from the 1/4 pitch used in the Tables is generally not significant in the overall estimate. Where precise quantities are desired, refer to pages 29-30, under the Dwelling section.

SHORTCUT FORMULAS FOR ESTIMATING EXTERIOR WALL MATERIAL QUANTITIES WHEN THE SQUARE FOOT AREAS ARE KNOWN

Multiply the number of square feet of wall area by the factor shown in Table 30-38A, page 259, of the Dwelling section for the kind or type of material to be used.

Illustrative Example

The exterior wall surface area is computed from Table 46A, page 280. There is one formula for garages that have a gable roof in order to include the gable area. There is another formula for garages that have no gables, i.e., shed type, flat or hip roofs. The *ground-floor* area is 676 sq ft and the perimeter is 104 lin ft. Assume a 2-car detached garage, 26' × 26', with a hip roof. Determine the quantity of insulation board and also the board feet of 1" × 8" bevel siding. The formula for the exterior surface area of the garage is 8 (P-16) from Table 26A.

$$8 (104' - 16) \ldots\ldots\ldots\ldots = 704 \text{ sq ft}$$

The factor for insulation board per sq ft is 1.10
The factor for 1" × 8" bevel siding per sq ft is 1.35
Multiplying these factors by the surface area:

      Insulation board   1.10 × 704 = 774 sq ft
      Bevel siding   1.35 × 704 = 950 FBM

A second method is to use Table 48 and interpolate between 650 and 700 sq ft

For 700 sq ft *ground-floor* area, insulation board is   792 sq ft
" 650 "   "   "   "   "   "   757 "

                    ²⁶/₅₀ × difference   35 "   = 18 sq ft

      Total insulation board   757 + 18 = 775 sq ft

For 700 sq ft *ground-floor* area, 1" × 8" bevel siding is   972 FBM
" 650 "   "   "   "   "   "   "   929 "

                    ²⁶/₅₀ × difference   43 "   = 22 FBM

      Total 1" × 8" bevel siding   929 + 22 = 951 FBM

Either method may be used although the first method may be easier for most readers.

Nails for exterior wall surface materials: See page 261, Table 30-38E.

TABLE 47

EXTERIOR SIDEWALL MATERIAL INCLUDING MILLING & CUTTING WASTE
WHERE APPLICABLE . . . GABLE ENDS ARE INCLUDED
FOR 1-CAR DETACHED GARAGES WITH 9′ DOOR

Ground Floor Area	Shiplap, Tongue & Groove		Insulation Board Plywood Etc.	Bevel Siding			Drop Siding		Brickwork		8"×16' Conc. Block	Stucco & Cement Plaster	Exterior SF Sidewall Area For Painting Gable Ends	
	1"×4"	1"×6" 1"×8"		1"×6" 1" Lap	1"×8" 1¼" Lap	1"×10" 1½" Lap	1"×6"	1"×8"	4" Veneer	8" Solid			Inc.	Excl.
Sq Ft	Bd Ft	Bd Ft	Sq Ft	Bd Ft	Bd Ft	Bd Ft	Bd Ft	Bd Ft	Units	Units	Units	Sq Yds	Inc.	Excl.
200	576	528	476	585	585	563	541	541	3031	6062	487	48	433	408
250	657	603	543	667	667	642	618	618	3458	6916	556	55	494	464
300	742	681	614	753	753	725	698	698	3906	7812	628	62	558	520
350	814	747	673	826	826	796	765	765	4284	8568	689	68	612	568
400	875	803	724	888	888	855	823	823	4606	9212	740	73	658	608
450	936	859	774	950	950	915	880	880	4928	9856	792	78	704	648
500	998	915	828	1013	1013	975	938	938	5250	10500	844	83	750	688

FOR 2-CAR DETACHED GARAGES WITH 16′ DOOR

Ground Floor Area	Shiplap, Tongue & Groove		Insulation Board Plywood Etc.	Bevel Siding			Drop Siding		Brickwork		8"×16' Conc. Block	Stucco & Cement Plaster	Exterior SF Sidewall Area For Painting Gable Ends	
	1"×4"	1"×6" 1"×8"		1"×6" 1" Lap	1"×8" 1¼" Lap	1"×10" 1½" Lap	1"×6"	1"×8"	4" Veneer	8" Solid			Inc.	Excl.
Sq Ft	Bd Ft	Bd Ft	Sq Ft	Bd Ft	Bd Ft	Bd Ft	Bd Ft	Bd Ft	Units	Units	Units	Sq Yds	Inc.	Excl.
200	504	462	417	512	512	493	474	474	2653	5306	426	42	379	328
250	583	534	482	591	591	569	548	548	3066	6132	493	49	438	376
300	662	608	548	672	672	647	623	623	3486	6972	560	55	498	424
350	743	682	615	755	755	727	699	699	3913	7826	629	63	559	472
400	814	747	673	826	826	796	765	765	4284	8568	689	68	612	512
450	883	810	730	896	896	863	830	830	4648	9296	747	74	664	552
500	942	864	779	956	956	920	885	885	4956	9912	797	79	708	584
550	1012	928	837	1027	1027	989	951	951	5327	10654	856	85	761	624
600	1072	983	887	1088	1088	1048	1008	1008	5642	11284	907	90	806	656
650	1132	1038	936	1149	1149	1106	1064	1064	5957	11914	957	95	851	688
700	1192	1093	986	1210	1210	1165	1020	1120	6272	12544	1008	100	896	720
750	1250	1146	1034	1269	1269	1222	1175	1175	6580	13160	1058	104	940	752
800	1290	1183	1067	1310	1310	1261	1213	1213	6790	13580	1091	108	970	776
850	1358	1246	1123	1378	1378	1327	1276	1276	7147	14294	1149	113	1021	808
900	1406	1290	1163	1427	1427	1374	1321	1321	7400	14798	1189	117	1057	832
950	1454	1333	1202	1476	1476	1421	1366	1366	7651	15302	1230	121	1093	856
1000	1500	1376	1241	1523	1523	1466	1410	1410	7896	15792	1269	125	1128	880

TABLE 48

EXTERIOR SIDEWALL MATERIAL INCLUDING MILLING & CUTTING WASTE WHERE APPLICABLE . . . GABLE ENDS ARE EXCLUDED
FOR 1-CAR DETACHED GARAGES WITH 9' DOOR

Ground Floor Area	Shiplap, Tongue & Groove		Insulation Board Plywood Etc.	Bevel Siding			Drop Siding		Brickwork		8"×16' Conc. Block	Stucco & Cement Plaster	Exterior SF Sidewall Area For Painting Gable Ends	
	1"×4"	1"×6" 1"×8"		1"×6" 1" Lap	1"×8" 1¼" Lap	1"×10" 1½" Lap	1"×6"	1"×8"	4" Veneer	8" Solid				
Sq Ft	Bd Ft	Bd Ft	Sq Ft	Bd Ft	Bd Ft	Bd Ft	Bd Ft	Bd Ft	Units	Units	Units	Sq Yds	Inc.	Excl.
200	543	498	449	550	550	530	510	510	2856	5712	459	45	433	408
250	617	566	510	626	626	603	580	580	3248	6496	522	52	494	464
300	692	634	572	702	702	676	650	650	3640	7280	585	58	558	520
350	755	693	625	767	767	738	710	710	3976	7952	639	63	612	568
400	809	742	669	821	821	790	760	760	4256	8512	684	68	658	608
450	862	790	713	875	875	842	810	810	4536	9072	729	72	704	648
500	915	839	757	929	929	894	860	860	4816	9632	774	76	750	688

FOR 2-CAR DETACHED GARAGES WITH 16' DOOR

Ground Floor Area	Shiplap, Tongue & Groove		Insulation Board Plywood Etc.	Bevel Siding			Drop Siding		Brickwork		8"×16' Conc. Block	Stucco & Cement Plaster	Exterior SF Sidewall Area For Painting Gable Ends	
	1"×4"	1"×6" 1"×8"		1"×6" 1" Lap	1"×8" 1¼" Lap	1"×10" 1½" Lap	1"×6"	1"×8"	4" Veneer	8" Solid				
Sq Ft	Bd Ft	Bd Ft	Sq Ft	Bd Ft	Bd Ft	Bd Ft	Bd Ft	Bd Ft	Units	Units	Units	Sq Yds	Inc.	Excl.
200	436	400	360	443	443	426	410	410	2296	4592	368	36	379	328
250	500	459	414	508	508	489	470	470	2632	5264	423	42	438	376
300	564	517	466	572	572	551	530	530	2968	5936	477	47	498	424
350	628	576	519	637	637	614	590	590	3304	6608	531	52	559	472
400	680	625	563	691	691	666	640	640	3584	7168	576	57	612	512
450	734	673	607	745	745	718	690	690	3864	7728	621	61	664	552
500	776	712	642	788	788	759	730	730	4088	8196	657	65	708	584
550	830	761	686	842	842	811	780	780	4368	8736	702	69	761	624
600	872	800	722	886	886	853	820	820	4592	9184	738	73	806	656
650	915	839	757	929	929	894	860	860	4816	9632	774	76	851	688
700	958	878	792	972	972	936	900	900	5040	10080	810	80	896	720
750	1000	917	827	1015	1015	978	940	940	5264	10528	846	84	940	752
800	1033	947	854	1048	1048	1009	970	970	5432	10864	873	86	970	776
850	1075	986	889	1090	1090	1050	1010	1010	5656	11312	909	90	1021	808
900	1107	1015	915	1123	1123	1082	1040	1040	5824	11648	936	93	1057	832
950	1138	1044	941	1156	1156	1113	1070	1070	5992	11984	963	95	1093	856
1000	1170	1074	968	1188	1188	1144	1100	1100	6160	12320	990	98	1128	880

TABLE 49

Concrete Footings, Foundation Walls and Floor Slabs for 1-Car and 2-Car Attached Garages

This Table shows the cubic yards of concrete for various size footings, foundation walls above the footings, floor slabs and base for 1-car and 2-car attached garages. Under Foundation Wall Above Footing, in the Table, there is also shown the number of 8″ × 16″ concrete blocks required for walls that are 24″, 32″ and 48″ high. The depth of foundation walls above footings varies with the frost line and local building codes. In some parts of the South, 18″ to 24″ is adequate, while in northern climates 4 feet or more may be required.

HOW TO USE THIS TABLE

1. Determine the *ground-floor* area of your garage.
2. Select the size of footing; the width and depth of any foundation wall above the footing, and the thickness of the floor slab and base. Read quantities directly from the Table for your *ground-floor* area. If the area falls between those in the Table, interpolate as explained in General Instructions, page 20.

BASIC FORMULAS

The basic formulas for quickly estimating the materials shown in this Table will be found under the Dwelling section. See, also, page 277, page 295, one and two-car detached garages.

287

The procedure to follow in using these formulas and Tables is the same as the procedure prescribed under the dwelling section where they appear. The one important difference is in the case an attached garage; the perimeter (P) is for the three sides that are not attached to the main dwelling. Therefore, whenever the perimeter, P, appears in a formula or Table, that perimeter is for the three unattached sides of the garage.

TABLE 49

FOOTINGS, FOUNDATIONS & FLOOR SLABS FOR 1-CAR ATTACHED GARAGES

Ground Floor Area Sq. Ft.	Footing Width & Depth of Concrete			Foundation Wall Above Footing Width & Depth of Concrete					Concrete Block 8"x16"			Floor Slab or Base Material Gravel Base Thickness			Conc Slab Thickness		Topping Thickness	
	16"x6" CY	18"x8" CY	24"x1' CY	8"x2' CY	8"x3' CY	10"x2' CY	10"x3' CY	10"x4' CY	24" High units	32" High units	48" High units	3" CY	4" CY	5" CY	3" CY	4" CY	1" CY	1½" CY
200	.77	1.15	2.29	1.54	2.29	1.92	2.88	3.84	70	93	140	1.86	2.48	3.10	1.86	2.48	.62	.92
250	.89	1.33	2.66	1.79	2.66	2.23	3.35	4.46	81	108	162	2.33	3.10	3.88	2.33	3.10	.78	1.15
300	1.00	1.48	2.96	1.98	2.96	2.48	2.72	4.96	90	120	180	2.79	3.72	4.65	2.79	3.72	.93	1.38
350	1.09	1.63	3.26	2.18	3.26	2.73	4.09	5.46	99	132	198	3.26	4.34	5.43	3.26	4.34	1.09	1.61
400	1.19	1.78	3.55	2.38	3.55	2.98	4.46	5.95	108	144	216	3.72	4.96	6.20	3.72	4.96	1.24	1.84
450	1.26	1.89	3.77	2.53	3.77	3.16	4.74	6.32	115	153	230	4.19	5.58	6.98	4.19	5.58	1.40	2.07
500	1.33	2.00	4.00	2.68	4.00	3.35	5.02	6.70	122	162	244	4.65	6.20	7.75	4.65	6.20	1.55	2.30

FOR 2-CAR ATTACHED GARAGES

Ground Floor Area Sq. Ft.	Footing Width & Depth of Concrete			Foundation Wall Above Footing Width & Depth of Concrete					Concrete Block 8"x16"			Floor Slab or Base Material Gravel Base Thickness			Conc Slab Thickness		Topping Thickness	
	16"x6" CY	18"x8" CY	24"x1' CY	8"x2' CY	8"x3' CY	10"x2' CY	10"x3' CY	10"x4' CY	24" High units	32" High units	48" High units	3" CY	4" CY	5" CY	3" CY	4" CY	1" CY	1½" CY
200	.67	1.00	2.00	1.34	2.00	1.67	2.51	3.35	61	81	122	1.86	2.48	3.10	1.86	2.48	.62	.92
250	.77	1.15	2.29	1.54	2.29	1.92	2.88	3.84	70	93	140	2.33	3.10	3.88	2.33	3.10	.78	1.15
300	.89	1.33	2.66	1.79	2.66	2.23	3.35	4.46	81	108	162	2.79	3.72	4.65	2.79	3.72	.93	1.38
350	1.00	1.48	2.96	1.98	2.96	2.48	3.72	4.96	90	120	180	3.26	4.34	5.43	3.26	4.34	1.09	1.61
400	1.09	1.63	3.26	2.18	3.26	2.73	4.09	5.46	99	132	198	3.72	4.96	6.20	3.72	4.96	1.24	1.84
450	1.19	1.78	3.55	2.38	3.55	2.98	4.46	5.95	108	144	216	4.19	5.58	6.98	4.19	5.58	1.40	2.07
500	1.26	1.89	3.77	2.53	3.77	3.16	4.74	6.32	115	153	230	4.65	6.20	7.75	4.65	6.20	1.55	2.30
550	1.36	2.00	4.07	2.73	4.07	3.41	5.12	6.82	124	165	248	5.12	6.82	8.53	5.12	6.82	1.71	2.53
600	1.43	2.15	4.29	2.88	4.29	3.60	5.39	7.19	131	174	261	5.58	7.44	9.30	5.58	7.44	1.86	2.76
650	1.51	2.26	4.51	3.03	4.51	3.78	5.67	7.56	137	183	275	6.05	8.06	10.1	6.05	8.06	2.02	3.00
700	1.58	2.37	4.74	3.17	4.74	3.97	5.96	7.94	144	192	288	6.51	8.68	10.9	6.51	8.68	2.17	3.22
750	1.65	2.48	4.96	3.32	4.96	4.15	6.23	8.31	151	201	302	6.98	9.30	11.6	6.98	9.30	2.33	3.45
800	1.70	2.55	5.11	3.42	5.11	4.28	6.42	8.56	155	207	311	7.44	9.92	12.4	7.44	9.92	2.48	3.68
850	1.78	2.66	5.33	3.57	5.33	4.46	6.70	8.93	162	216	324	7.91	10.5	13.2	7.91	10.5	2.64	3.91
900	1.83	2.74	5.48	3.67	5.48	4.59	6.88	9.18	167	222	333	8.37	11.2	13.9	8.37	11.2	2.79	4.14
950	1.88	2.81	5.62	3.77	5.62	4.71	7.07	9.42	171	228	342	8.84	11.8	14.7	8.84	11.8	2.95	4.37
1000	1.95	2.92	5.85	3.92	5.85	4.90	7.35	9.80	178	237	356	9.30	12.4	15.5	9.30	12.4	3.10	4.60

TABLE 50

Exterior Wall and Ceiling Framing
Including Shoe and Plate
(Number of Board Feet Required)

For 1-Car Attached Garages with 9′ Door
For 2-Car Attached Garages with 16′ Door

This Table shows the Board Feet (FBM) of exterior wall and ceiling framing for both 1-car and 2-car attached garages. The door openings are 9′ and 16′ respectively. Rafter framing is shown in Tables 53 and 54; Trusses in Table 55. Wall studding is shown for garages with gables and without gables as in the case of a hip or shed type roof. Studding is also shown for 16″ and 24″ on center. Ceiling joists may be 2″ × 4″ or 2″ × 6″, on 24″ centers.

HOW TO USE THIS TABLE

1. Determine the *ground-floor* area of your garage.
2. Select the framing specified for your garage. Read quantities directly from the Table for the *ground-floor* area. If the area of the garage falls between those in the Table, interpolate as explained in General Instructions, page 20.

ADJUSTMENT FOR GABLE FRAMING WHEN ROOF PITCH IS OTHER THAN 1/4, THE PITCH ON WHICH THIS TABLE IS BASED

Because of the relatively small *ground-floor* area in garages, differences in gable areas as roof pitches increase or decrease from the 1/4 pitch used in the Table are of little significance in the overall estimate. If precise quantities are desired, refer to pages 29-30, under the Dwelling section.

290

TABLE 50

EXTERIOR WALL & CEILING FRAMING INCLUDING SHOE & PLATE
(Number of Board Feet Required)
FOR 1-CAR ATTACHED GARAGES WITH 9′ DOOR

Ground Floor Area Sq Ft	Exterior Wall Area Gable Ends		Sill, Plate Shoe & Door Head	2″ × 4″ Studs Gable Ends Included		2″ × 4″ Studs Gable Ends Excluded		Ceiling Joists 24″ on Center	
	Included Bd Ft	Excluded Bd Ft	Bd Ft	16″ Center Bd Ft	24″ Center Bd Ft	16″ Center Bd Ft	24″ Center Bd Ft	2″ × 4″ Bd Ft	2″ × 6″ Bd Ft
200	261	248	87	174	116	165	110	70	110
250	304	288	100	203	135	192	128	88	138
300	339	320	112	226	151	213	142	105	165
350	374	352	124	249	166	235	157	123	193
400	409	384	134	273	182	256	170	140	220
450	436	408	143	291	194	272	181	158	248
500	463	432	151	309	206	288	192	175	275

(Note: Rafters and trusses are shown in Tables 53 to 55 inclusive)

FOR 2-CAR ATTACHED GARAGES WITH 16′ DOOR

Ground Floor Area Sq Ft	Exterior Wall Area Gable Ends		Sill, Plate Shoe & Door Head	2″ × 4″ Studs Gable Ends Included				Ceiling Joists 24″ on Center	
	Included Bd Ft	Excluded Bd Ft	Bd Ft	16″ Center Bd Ft	24″ Center Bd Ft			2″ × 4″ Bd Ft	2″ × 6″ Bd Ft
200	242	216	81	161	107	144	97	70	110
250	279	248	93	186	124	165	110	88	138
300	325	288	108	217	145	192	128	105	165
350	364	320	120	243	162	213	142	123	193
400	402	352	132	268	179	235	157	140	220
450	440	384	144	293	195	256	170	158	248
500	470	408	153	313	209	272	181	175	275
550	509	440	165	340	227	293	195	193	300
600	539	464	174	360	240	309	206	210	240
650	570	488	183	380	253	325	216	228	358
700	600	512	192	400	267	341	227	245	385
750	630	536	201	420	280	357	238	263	413
800	652	552	207	435	290	368	245	280	440
850	683	576	216	456	304	384	256	298	468
900	705	592	222	470	313	394	262	315	495
950	725	608	228	484	323	405	270	333	522
1000	756	632	237	504	336	421	280	350	550

TABLE 50A

BASIC FORMULAS FOR ESTIMATING THE FBM OF
FRAMING FOR ATTACHED GARAGES

P = The Perimeter of an Attached Garage which excludes the
side that is attached to the dwelling.

A = Ground-floor Area   Garage Door Openings, 1-Car 9', 2-Car 16'

Item of Framing	1-Car Garage	2-Car Garage
Exterior wall surface area including gable " " " " excluding "	8(P-9) + Gable area* 8 (P-9)	8(P-16) + Gable area* 8 (P-16)
Exterior wall studs including gable end 2" × 4", 16" on center " 24" " "	.667 × Ext. wall area .44 × " " "	.667 × Ext. wall area .44 × " " "
Exterior wall studs excluding gable end 2" × 4", 16" on center " 24" " "	5.33 (P-9) 3.56 (P-9)	5.33 (P-16) 3.56 (P-16)
Sill, plate, door header, etc.	2.8P	3.0P
Ceiling joists, 2" × 4", 24" on center 2" × 6", 24" " "	.35A .55A	.35A .55A

Rafters—See Tables 53 and 54. Prefab Trusses—See Table 55

*To determine the one gable area of an attached garage, use Tables C1 and C2 which are a function of the *ground-floor* area, the pitch of the roof, and the length-to-width ratio of the garage. Use 1/2 of the area in these Tables since the areas shown are for two gables. The shortcut formula may also be used if more convenient.

Illustrative Examples

To determine the total FBM of framing for a 1-car attached garage 13' × 26'. The pitch of the roof is ¹/₄; studding is 2" × 4", 16" on center; ceiling joists are 2" × 4", 24" on

TABLE 50—EXTERIOR WALL AND CEILING FRAMING (ATTACHED GARAGES)   293

center, and the rafters are 2″ × 6″, 24″ on center. The *ground-floor* area is 13′ × 26′ = 338 sq ft and the perimeter, P, is 52 lin ft for the three unattached sides, the 13 ft side being attached to the dwelling.

The framing may be obtained from Table 50 and Table 54 (Rafters) by interpolating between *ground-floor* areas of 300 and 350 sq ft.

Exterior wall studs	Table 50	243 FBM
Ceiling joists	″ ″	113 ″
Sill, plate and door header	″ ″	120 ″
Rafters	″ 54	210 ″
Total framing		686 ″

The framing may also be obtained by using the basic formulas in Tables 50A and 11-12A (Rafters). The formula for the exterior wall area is 8 (52 − 9) + the area of the gable end.

8 (52 − 9)	344 sq ft (Table 50A)
$\frac{1}{2}$ (.125 × 338) Gable	+21 ″ ″ (Table C1 and C2, page 28)
Total exterior wall area	365 ″ ″

1. Exterior wall studs = .667 × exterior wall area   = .667 × 365 = 243 FBM
2. Ceiling joists, 2″ × 4″, 24″ on center = .35A   = .35 × 338 = 118 ″
3. Sill, plate and door header = 2.8 (P − 9)   = 2.8 × 43 = 120 ″
4. Rafters, 2″ × 6″, 24″ on center = .62 × A   = .62 × 338 = 210 ″

   Total framing 691 ″

1, 2 and 3 from Table 50A
4 from Table 11-12A
Nails for framing: See page 205, Table 14B.

TABLES 51 and 52

Exterior Sidewall Materials for
One-and Two-Car Attached Garages
with 9′ and 16′ Door Openings Respectively

(Gables Excluded in Table 52;
Included in Table 51)

These Tables show the exterior wall areas of attached garages, and various kinds of exterior wall materials including rough wood and composition board, brick veneer, solid brick, concrete block, etc. There is one gable end as a rule in attached garages; Table 51 includes the gable while Table 52 excludes it. Milling, cutting and fitting waste is included where appropriate.

HOW TO USE THESE TABLES

Determine the *ground-floor* area of the garage. Select the exterior wall material according to specifications and read quantities directly from the Tables for the *ground-floor* area. If the area is between those in the Tables, interpolate as explained under the Dwelling section, page 20.

ADJUST FOR GABLE END MATERIALS IF ROOF PITCH
IS OTHER THAN 1/4 ON WHICH TABLES ARE BASED.

Because the area of garages is relatively small compared to the dwelling, the difference in quantities of materials is not usually significant as the roof pitch increases or decreases from the 1/4 pitch used in the Tables. Where it is necessary to be precise, refer to pages 29-30, under Dwelling section.

ESTIMATING QUANTITIES BY FORMULA

Determine the wall area directly from Tables 47 and 48 for detached garages, and from Table 50 for attached garages. Actual area may also be used. Multiply that area by the factor shown on Table 30-38A, page 259, for the kind of type material to be used.

Illustrative Example

An attached garage is 24′ × 25′ and has a *ground-floor* area of 600 sq ft. The perimeter of the three unattached sides is 74 lin ft. It has a hip roof and the exterior walls are 4″ brick veneer. Determine the number of brick required.

From Table 50* we find there are 464 sq ft of exterior surface where gables are excluded which is the case in the problem since the roof is a hip type. Table 30-38A shows a factor of 7 (brick per sq ft).

$$7 \times 464 = 3{,}248 \text{ brick required}$$

If the quantity is to be read directly from Table 52 (gables excluded), we find the same number of brick, 3,248.

*Actually, Tables 50, 51 and 52 each show the exterior wall area.

Mortar required for brickwork: See Table 30-38C. For mortar materials per cu ft or cu yd, see Table 3A.

TABLE 51

EXTERIOR SIDEWALL MATERIAL INCLUDING MILLING & CUTTING WASTE WHERE APPLICABLE . . . GABLE ENDS ARE INCLUDED
FOR 1-CAR ATTACHED GARAGES WITH 9' DOOR

Ground Floor Area	Shiplap, Tongue & Groove		Insulation Board Plywood Etc.	Bevel Siding			Drop Siding		Brickwork		8"×16" Conc. Block	Stucco & Cement Plaster	Exterior SF Sidewall Area For Painting	
	1"×4"	1"×6" 1"×8"		1"×6" 1" Lap	1"×8" 1¼" Lap	1"×10" 1½" Lap	1"×6"	1"×8"	4" Veneer	8" Solid			Gable Ends	
Sq Ft	Bd Ft	Bd Ft	Sq Ft	Bd Ft	Bd Ft	Bd Ft	Bd Ft	Bd Ft	Units	Units	Units	Sq Yds	Inc.	Excl.
200	347	318	287	352	352	339	326	326	1827	3654	294	29	261	248
250	404	371	334	410	410	395	380	380	2128	4256	342	34	304	288
300	451	414	373	458	458	440	424	424	2373	4746	381	38	339	320
350	497	456	411	505	505	486	468	468	2618	5236	421	42	374	352
400	544	500	450	552	552	532	511	511	2863	5726	460	45	409	384
450	580	532	480	588	588	566	545	545	3052	6104	491	48	436	408
500	616	565	509	625	625	602	579	579	3241	6482	521	51	463	432

FOR 2-CAR ATTACHED GARAGES WITH 16' DOOR

Ground Floor Area	Shiplap, Tongue & Groove		Insulation Board Plywood Etc.	Bevel Siding			Drop Siding		Brickwork		8"×16" Conc. Block	Stucco & Cement Plaster	Exterior SF Sidewall Area For Painting	
	1"×4"	1"×6" 1"×8"		1"×6" 1" Lap	1"×8" 1¼" Lap	1"×10" 1½" Lap	1"×6"	1"×8"	4" Veneer	8" Solid			Gable Ends	
Sq Ft	Bd Ft	Bd Ft	Sq Ft	Bd Ft	Bd Ft	Bd Ft	Bd Ft	Bd Ft	Units	Units	Units	Sq Yds	Inc.	Excl.
200	322	295	266	327	327	315	303	303	1694	3388	272	27	242	216
250	371	340	307	377	377	363	349	349	1953	3906	314	31	279	248
300	432	397	358	439	439	423	406	406	2275	4550	366	36	325	288
350	484	444	400	491	491	473	455	455	2548	5096	410	40	364	320
400	535	490	442	543	543	523	503	503	2814	5628	452	45	402	352
450	585	537	484	594	594	572	550	550	3080	6160	495	49	440	384
500	625	572	517	635	635	611	588	588	3290	6580	529	52	470	408
550	677	621	560	687	687	662	636	636	3563	7126	573	57	509	440
600	717	658	593	728	728	700	674	674	3773	7546	606	60	539	464
650	758	695	627	770	770	741	713	713	3990	7980	641	63	570	488
700	798	732	660	810	810	780	750	750	4200	8400	675	67	600	512
750	838	769	693	850	850	819	788	788	4410	8820	709	70	630	536
800	867	795	717	880	880	848	815	815	4564	9128	734	72	652	552
850	908	832	751	922	922	888	854	854	4781	9562	768	76	683	576
900	938	860	776	952	952	917	881	881	4935	9870	793	78	705	592
950	966	886	799	980	980	944	908	908	5082	10164	817	81	726	608
1000	1005	922	832	1020	1020	983	945	945	5292	10584	850	84	756	632

TABLE 52

EXTERIOR SIDEWALL MATERIAL INCLUDING MILLING & CUTTING WASTE WHERE APPLICABLE. . . . GABLE ENDS ARE EXCLUDED
FOR 1-CAR ATTACHED GARAGES WITH 9′ DOOR

Ground Floor Area	Shiplap, Tongue & Groove		Insulation Board Plywood Etc.	Bevel Siding			Drop Siding		Brickwork		8"×16" Conc. Block	Stucco & Cement Plaster	Exterior SF Sidewall Area For Painting	
	1"×4"	1"×6" 1"×8"		1"×6" 1" Lap	1"×8" 1¼" Lap	1"×10" 1½" Lap	1"×6"	1"×8"	4" Veneer	8" Solid			Gable Ends	
Sq Ft	Bd Ft	Bd Ft	Sq Ft	Bd Ft	Bd Ft	Bd Ft	Bd Ft	Bd Ft	Units	Units	Units	Sq Yds	Inc.	Excl.
200	330	303	273	335	335	322	310	310	1736	3472	279	28	261	248
250	383	351	317	389	389	374	360	360	2016	4032	324	32	304	288
300	426	390	352	432	432	416	400	400	2240	4480	360	36	339	320
350	468	429	387	475	475	458	440	440	2464	4928	396	39	374	352
400	510	468	422	518	518	500	480	480	2688	5376	432	43	409	384
450	543	498	449	550	550	530	510	510	2856	5712	459	45	436	408
500	575	527	475	583	583	562	540	540	3024	6048	486	48	463	432

FOR 2-CAR ATTACHED GARAGES WITH 16′ DOOR

Ground Floor Area	Shiplap, Tongue & Groove		Insulation Board Plywood Etc.	Bevel Siding			Drop Siding		Brickwork		8"×16" Conc. Block	Stucco & Cement Plaster	Exterior SF Sidewall Area For Painting	
	1"×4"	1"×6" 1"×8"		1"×6" 1" Lap	1"×8" 1¼" Lap	1"×10" 1½" Lap	1"×6"	1"×8"	4" Veneer	8" Solid			Gable Ends	
Sq Ft	Bd Ft	Bd Ft	Sq Ft	Bd Ft	Bd Ft	Bd Ft	Bd Ft	Bd Ft	Units	Units	Units	Sq Yds	Inc.	Excl.
200	287	264	238	292	292	281	270	270	1512	3024	243	24	242	216
250	330	303	273	335	335	322	310	310	1736	3472	279	28	279	248
300	383	351	317	389	389	374	360	360	2016	4032	324	32	325	288
350	426	390	352	432	432	416	400	400	2240	4480	360	36	364	320
400	468	429	387	475	475	458	440	440	2464	4928	396	39	402	352
450	511	468	422	518	518	500	480	480	2688	5376	432	43	440	384
500	543	498	449	551	551	530	510	510	2856	5712	459	45	470	408
550	585	537	484	594	594	572	550	550	3080	6160	495	49	509	440
600	617	566	510	626	626	603	580	580	3248	6496	522	52	539	464
650	649	595	537	659	659	634	610	610	3416	6832	549	54	570	448
700	680	625	563	691	691	666	640	640	3584	7168	576	57	600	512
750	713	654	590	724	724	697	670	670	3752	7504	603	60	630	536
800	734	673	607	745	745	718	690	690	3864	7728	621	62	652	552
850	766	702	634	778	778	749	720	720	4032	8064	648	64	683	576
900	788	722	651	800	800	770	740	740	4144	8288	666	66	705	592
950	808	742	669	820	820	790	760	760	4256	8512	684	68	726	608
1000	840	771	695	853	853	822	790	790	4424	8848	711	70	756	632

TABLES 53 and 54

2″ × 4″ and 2″ × 6″ Rafters for All Garages
(Board feet, Including Ridge)

These Tables show the number of board feet of rafters, 16″ and 24″ on center for hip and gable roofs of pitches 1/8 to 1/2, cutting and fitting waste included.

HOW TO USE THESE TABLES

1. Determine the *ground-floor* area of your garage.
2. Select the roof pitch nearest that of your roof, the size of rafter (2″ × 4″ or 2″ × 6″) and center to center spacing of rafters.
3. Read the number of board feet directly from either Table 53 or 54 as the case may be and in accord with the *ground-floor* area of your garage. If the *ground-floor* area falls between those in the Tables, interpolate as explained under the Dwelling section, page 20.

Overhang

Table quantities do not allow for any overhang at the eaves or gables. For each 12″ of horizontal overhang at the eaves add 5% to the quantity shown in the Tables.

Hip and Gable Roofs

Hip and gable roofs of the same pitch and covering the same horizontal area require the same board feet of framing for rafters. A minor difference may be where the hip rafters in the hip roof are larger members than the rafters themselves.

Dormer Framing

The board feet of framing for dormers will be almost identical to the board feet of framing in the main roof, as though there were no dormers. The only difference would be if the dormers had a significant overhang.

Trusses

For estimating pre-fab trusses refer to Table 55.

Nails

For estimating purposes, an acceptible average quantity of nails is:

$$2'' \times 4'' \text{ rafters} \ldots 16d \ldots 10 \text{ lbs per } 1,000 \text{ FBM}$$
$$2'' \times 6'' \quad '' \quad \ldots \quad '' \ldots 9 \quad '' \quad '' \quad '' \quad ''$$

BASIC FORMULAS FOR RAFTERS

When it is desirable to determine the FBM for rafters by simple formula instead of using Tables 53 and 54, the same formulas that are used for dwellings (Table 11-12A) may be used. These include ridge pole and apply to either hip or gable roofs. To use Table 11-12A multiply the *ground-floor* area by the factor shown for the size of rafter and pitch of roof. No overhang is included in the Table. Add 5% to the FBM developed for each 12″ of horizontal overhang.

Where the roof extends over areas outside the perimeter of the building, use the horizontal area covered by the roof in place of the *ground-floor* area.

Illustrative Example

A 2-car garage is 24′ × 30′ and the pitch of the roof is ⅓ or 8″ rise-per-foot-of-run. The *ground-floor* area is 720 sq ft, rafters are 2″ × 6″, 24″ on center. The garage has a flush cornice, no overhang.

From Table 11-12A, the formula for the total FBM for rafters 2″ × 4″, 24″ on center, and roof pitch of ⅓, is .66A

$$.66 \times 720 = 475 \text{ FBM}$$

Note that Table 54 produces the same answer. Basic formulas are usually more convenient to use than the Tables to avoid interpolating when *ground-floor* areas are in between those in the Tables.

TABLE 53

2" × 4" RAFTERS FOR ALL GARAGES INCLUDING RIDGE POLE
NUMBER OF BOARD FEET REQUIRED, INCLUDING CUTTING
AND FITTING WASTE

Ground Floor Area Sq Ft	16" Center to Center Roof Pitch							24" Center to Center Roof Pitch						
	1/8	1/6	5/24	1/4	1/3	5/12	1/2	1/8	1/6	5/24	1/4	1/3	5/12	1/2
200	114	116	120	124	132	144	156	78	80	82	86	92	98	108
250	143	145	150	155	165	180	195	98	100	103	108	115	123	135
300	171	174	180	186	198	216	234	117	120	123	129	138	147	162
350	200	203	210	217	231	252	273	137	140	144	151	161	172	189
400	228	232	240	248	264	288	312	156	160	164	172	184	196	216
450	257	261	270	279	297	324	351	176	180	185	194	207	221	243
500	285	290	300	310	330	360	390	195	200	205	215	230	245	270
550	314	319	330	341	363	396	429	215	220	226	237	253	270	297
600	342	348	360	372	396	432	468	234	240	246	258	276	294	324
650	370	377	390	409	429	468	507	254	260	267	280	300	219	351
700	399	406	420	434	462	504	546	273	280	287	301	322	343	378
750	428	435	450	465	495	540	585	293	300	208	323	345	368	405
800	456	464	480	496	528	576	624	312	320	328	344	368	392	432
850	485	493	510	527	561	612	663	332	340	3 50	366	391	417	459
900	513	522	540	558	594	648	702	351	360	369	387	414	441	486
950	542	551	570	589	627	684	741	371	380	390	409	437	466	513
1000	570	580	600	620	660	720	780	390	400	410	430	460	490	540

300

TABLE 54

2" × 6" RAFTERS FOR ALL GARAGES INCLUDING RIDGE POLE
NUMBER OF BOARD FEET REQUIRED INCLUDING CUTTING
AND FITTING WASTE

Ground Floor Area Sq Ft	16" Center to Center — Roof Pitch							24" Center to Center — Roof Pitch						
	1/8	1/6	5/24	1/4	1/3	5/12	1/2	1/8	1/6	5/24	1/4	1/3	5/12	1/2
200	164	170	174	180	192	208	228	114	116	120	124	132	144	156
250	205	213	218	225	240	260	285	143	145	150	155	165	180	195
300	246	255	261	270	288	312	342	171	174	180	186	198	216	234
350	287	298	305	315	336	364	400	200	203	210	217	231	252	273
400	328	340	348	360	384	416	456	228	232	240	248	264	288	312
450	369	383	392	405	432	468	513	257	261	270	279	297	324	351
500	410	425	435	450	480	520	570	285	290	300	310	330	360	390
550	451	468	479	495	528	572	627	314	319	330	341	363	396	429
600	492	510	522	540	576	624	684	342	348	360	372	396	432	468
650	533	553	566	585	624	676	741	370	377	390	409	429	468	507
700	574	594	609	630	672	728	798	399	406	420	434	462	504	546
750	615	638	653	675	720	780	855	428	435	450	465	495	540	585
800	656	680	696	720	768	832	912	456	464	480	496	528	576	624
850	697	723	740	765	816	884	969	485	493	510	527	561	612	663
900	732	765	783	810	864	936	1026	513	522	540	558	594	648	702
950	779	808	827	855	912	988	1083	542	551	570	589	627	684	741
1000	820	850	870	900	960	1040	1140	570	580	600	620	660	720	780

TABLE 55

Pre-Fab Roof Trusses for All Garages

(Board feet Required)

Table 55 shows the board feet (FBM) required for pre-fab roof trusses. It includes trusses that have 2″ × 4″ rafters and 2″ × 4″ cords, and also trusses that have 2″ × 6″ rafters and 2″ × 4″ cords. All trusses are spaced 24″ on center.

HOW TO USE THIS TABLE

1. Determine the *ground-floor* area of your garage.
2. Select the type of truss that is to be used and the roof pitch nearest to that of your roof.
3. Read the number of board feet for the trusses directly from the Table for the *ground-floor* area of your garage. If the *ground-floor* area of the garage falls between those in the Table, interpolate as explained under the Dwelling section, page 20.

Gussets, Metal Connectors and Nails

The estimator should make an allowance for gussets, metal connector and nails to assemble the trusses as the Table 55 does not include these items.

Struts and Braces

The bracing and struts, 2″ × 4″ members, are included in this Table.

Overhang . . . Hip and Gable Roofs . . . and Dormer Framing

For a discussion of these items please refer to the previous Tables 53 and 54.

TABLE 55—PRE-FAB TRUSSES FOR ALL GARAGES   303

BASIC FORMULA FOR TRUSSES FOR GARAGES

The Basic Formulas for prefab trusses for garages are the same as those shown in Table 13A, page 197. The illustrative example under that Table demonstrates the application of the formulas.

TABLE 55

ROOF TRUSSES, 24″ ON CENTER, INCLUDING BRACES & STRUTS
NUMBER OF BOARD FEET REQUIRED FOR RAFTER SIZE & ROOF PITCH SHOWN

Ground Floor Area Sq Ft	2″ × 4″ Rafter and Cord Roof Pitch								2″ × 6″ Rafter . . . 2″ × 4″ Cord Roof Pitch						
	$1/8$	$1/6$	$5/24$	$1/4$	$1/3$	$5/12$	$1/2$		$1/8$	$1/6$	$5/24$	$1/4$	$1/3$	$5/12$	$1/2$
200	210	212	214	218	224	230	250		246	248	252	256	264	276	288
250	263	265	268	273	280	289	313		308	310	315	320	330	345	360
300	315	318	321	327	336	345	375		369	372	378	384	396	414	432
350	368	371	375	382	392	404	438		430	434	440	448	462	483	504
400	420	424	428	436	448	460	500		492	496	504	512	528	552	576
450	473	477	482	490	504	520	563		554	558	567	576	594	620	648
500	525	530	535	545	560	575	625		615	620	630	640	660	690	720
550	578	583	588	600	616	635	688		676	682	693	700	726	760	790
600	630	636	642	654	672	690	750		738	744	756	768	792	828	864
650	683	689	696	709	728	750	813		800	806	820	832	858	900	936
700	735	742	749	763	784	805	875		861	868	882	896	924	966	1008
750	788	795	803	818	840	866	938		922	930	945	960	990	1035	1080
800	840	848	856	872	896	920	1000		984	992	1008	1024	1056	1108	1152
850	893	900	910	926	952	982	1063		1046	1054	1071	1088	1122	1173	1224
900	945	954	963	981	1008	1035	1125		1107	1116	1134	1152	1188	1242	1296
950	998	1007	1016	1036	1064	1098	1188		1168	1178	1200	1216	1254	1310	1368
1000	1050	1060	1070	1090	1120	1150	1250		1230	1240	1260	1280	1320	1380	1440

TABLES 56 THROUGH 61

Roof Decking For All Garages
(Including Milling and Cutting Waste)

These Tables show quantities of various kinds of roof decking for garage roofs with roof pitches shown.

Table	Roof Pitch	Inches Rise-Per-Foot-Of-Run
56	1/8	3
57	1/6	4
58	5/24	5
59	1/4	6
60	1/3	8
61	1/2	12

MILLING, CUTTING AND FITTING WASTE
(See Table 15-20A, page 208)

HOW TO USE THESE TABLES

1. Determine the *ground-floor* area of your garage.
2. Use the Table with the roof pitch nearest to that of the roof of your garage, and select the kind of roof decking desired. Note that the square foot area of the roof is shown in each Table. This allows the estimator to substitute any decking material not shown in these Tables making proper allowance for waste.

Read the Table quantities directly for the *ground-floor* area of your garage. If the *ground-floor* area falls between those in the Tables, interpolate as explained under Dwellings, page 20.

Dormers

The quantity of roof decking for dormers is almost identical to that area taken up by the dormer in the main roof. The only amount to be added would be in the overhang, if there is any.

Hip and Gable Roofs

The surface area of a hip roof is identical to that of a gable roof of the same pitch and covering the same horizontal area.

Nails for Decking

For estimating purposes, an acceptable average quantity of nails for various kinds of roof decking will be found under Table 30-38E, page 261.

SHORTCUT FORMULAS FOR ESTIMATING ROOF AREAS AND QUANTITIES OF ROOF DECKING

These formulas will be found under Table 15-20B, in the dwelling section page 216.

Compute the square foot area of the roof by multiplying the horizontal or *ground-floor* area by the factor shown in Table 15-20B for the appropriate roof pitch. That area as computed is multiplied by the milling and cutting waste factor shown in Table 15-20A depending on the type of decking material to be used.

TABLE 56

ROOF DECKING FOR ALL GARAGES WITH A ROOF PITCH OF 1/8
(Includes Milling and Cutting Waste)

Ground Floor Area Sq Ft	Roof Surface Area Square Ft	Shiplap 1"×6" 1"×8" Board Ft	Shiplap 1"×10" Board Ft	Tongue & Groove Boards 1"×4" Board Ft	Tongue & Groove Boards 1"×6" 1"×8" Board Ft	Tongue & Groove Boards 1"×10" Board Ft	Square Edge Bds. 1"×4" Board Ft	Square Edge Bds. 1"×6" 1"×8" Board Ft	Plywood, Insulation & Particle Board Sq Ft
200	206	252	244	274	252	244	246	236	226
250	258	315	305	343	315	305	308	295	283
300	309	378	366	411	378	366	369	354	340
350	360	440	427	480	440	427	430	413	396
400	412	504	488	548	504	488	492	472	452
450	464	567	550	617	567	550	554	531	510
500	515	630	610	685	630	610	615	590	565
550	567	693	670	754	693	670	676	649	622
600	618	756	732	822	756	732	738	708	678
650	670	820	793	890	820	793	800	767	735
700	721	882	854	960	882	854	860	826	790
750	773	945	915	1028	945	915	922	885	850
800	824	1008	976	1100	1008	976	984	944	900
850	876	1070	1037	1165	1070	1037	1046	1000	960
900	927	1134	1100	1233	1134	1100	1107	1062	1017
950	978	1200	1160	1300	1200	1160	1170	1120	1074
1000	1030	1260	1220	1370	1260	1220	1230	1180	1130

306

TABLE 57

ROOF DECKING FOR ALL GARAGES WITH A ROOF PITCH OF 1/6
(Includes Milling and Cutting Waste)

| Ground Floor Area | Roof Surface Area | Shiplap | | Tongue & Groove Boards | | | Square Edge Bds. | | Plywood, Insulation & Particle Board |
| | | 1"×6" 1"×8" | 1"×10" | 1"×4" | 1"×6" 1"×8" | 1"×10" | 1"×4" | 1"×6" 1"×8" | |
Sq Ft	Square Ft	Board Ft	Board Ft	Board Ft	Board Ft	Board Ft	Board Ft	Board Ft	Sq Ft
200	212	258	250	282	258	250	252	244	234
250	265	323	312	353	323	312	315	305	293
300	318	387	375	423	387	375	378	366	351
350	371	452	438	494	452	438	440	427	410
400	424	516	500	564	516	500	504	488	468
450	477	580	563	635	580	563	567	549	527
500	530	645	625	705	645	625	630	610	585
550	583	710	688	776	710	688	693	670	644
600	636	774	750	846	774	750	756	732	702
650	689	840	813	916	840	813	819	793	760
700	742	900	875	987	900	875	882	854	819
750	795	968	938	1058	968	938	945	915	878
800	848	1030	1000	1128	1030	1000	1008	976	936
850	900	1100	1062	1200	1100	1062	1070	1037	1000
900	954	1160	1125	1269	1160	1125	1134	1098	1053
950	1007	1225	1190	1340	1225	1190	1200	1160	1111
1000	1060	1290	1250	1410	1290	1250	1260	1220	1170

307

TABLE 58

ROOF DECKING FOR ALL GARAGES WITH A ROOF PITCH OF 5/24

(Includes Milling & Cutting Waste)

Ground Floor Area	Roof Surface Area	Shiplap		Tongue & Groove Boards			Square Edge Bds.		Plywood, Insulation & Particle Board
		1"×6" 1"×8"	1"×10"	1"×4"	1"×6" 1"×8"	1"×10"	1"×4"	1"×6" 1"×8"	
Sq Ft	Square Ft	Board Ft	Board Ft	Board Ft	Board Ft	Board Ft	Board Ft	Board Ft	Sq Ft
200	218	266	258	290	266	258	260	250	240
250	273	333	323	363	333	323	325	313	300
300	327	400	387	435	400	387	390	375	360
350	382	466	452	508	466	452	455	438	420
400	426	532	516	580	532	516	520	500	480
450	436	600	580	653	600	580	585	563	540
500	546	665	645	725	665	645	650	625	600
550	600	732	710	800	732	710	715	688	660
600	654	800	774	870	800	774	780	750	720
650	709	865	840	943	865	840	845	813	780
700	763	930	900	1015	930	900	910	875	840
750	818	1000	970	1088	1000	970	975	938	900
800	872	1064	1030	1160	1064	1030	1040	1000	960
850	927	1130	1100	1233	1130	1100	1105	1163	1020
900	981	1200	1160	1305	1200	1160	1170	1125	1080
950	1035	1264	1225	1378	1264	1225	1235	1188	1140
1000	1090	1330	1290	1450	1330	1290	1300	1250	1200

308

TABLE 59

ROOF DECKING FOR ALL GARAGES WITH A ROOF PITCH OF 1/4
(Includes Milling and Cutting Waste)

Ground Floor Area Sq Ft	Roof Surface Area Square Ft	Shiplap 1"×6" 1"×8" Board Ft	Shiplap 1"×10" Board Ft	Tongue & Groove Boards 1"×4" Board Ft	Tongue & Groove Boards 1"×6" 1"×8" Board Ft	Tongue & Groove Boards 1"×10" Board Ft	Square Edge Bds. 1"×4" Board Ft	Square Edge Bds. 1"×6" 1"×8" Board Ft	Plywood, Insulation & Particle Board Sq Ft
200	224	274	264	298	274	264	266	258	246
250	280	343	330	373	343	330	333	323	308
300	336	411	396	447	411	396	400	387	369
350	392	480	462	522	480	462	466	452	430
400	448	548	528	600	548	528	532	516	492
450	504	617	594	670	617	494	600	580	554
500	560	685	660	745	685	660	665	645	615
550	616	754	726	820	754	726	732	710	676
600	672	822	792	894	822	792	800	774	738
650	728	890	858	968	890	858	865	840	800
700	784	959	924	1043	959	924	930	900	860
750	840	1028	990	1118	1028	990	1000	970	922
800	896	1096	1056	1192	1096	1056	1064	1030	984
850	952	1165	1122	1266	1165	1122	1130	1100	1046
900	1008	1233	1188	1340	1233	1188	1200	1160	1107
950	1064	1300	1254	1416	1300	1254	1264	1225	1170
1000	1120	1370	1320	1490	1370	1320	1330	1290	1230

TABLE 60

ROOF DECKING FOR ALL GARAGES WITH A ROOF PITCH OF 1/3
(Includes Milling and Cutting Waste)

Ground Floor Area Sq Ft	Roof Surface Area Square Ft	Shiplap 1"×6" 1"×8" Board Ft	Shiplap 1"×10" Board Ft	Tongue & Groove Boards 1"×4" Board Ft	Tongue & Groove Boards 1"×6" 1"×8" Board Ft	Tongue & Groove Boards 1"×10" Board Ft	Square Edge Bds. 1"×4" Board Ft	Square Edge Bds. 1"×6" 1"×8" Board Ft	Plywood, Insulation & Particle Board Sq Ft
200	240	292	284	320	292	284	286	276	264
250	300	365	355	400	365	350	358	345	330
300	360	438	426	480	438	426	429	414	396
350	420	511	500	560	511	497	500	483	462
400	480	584	568	640	584	568	572	552	528
450	540	657	640	720	657	640	644	620	494
500	600	730	710	800	730	710	715	690	660
550	660	800	780	880	800	780	787	760	726
600	720	876	852	960	876	852	858	828	792
650	780	950	923	1040	950	923	930	900	858
700	840	1022	994	1120	1022	994	1000	966	924
750	900	1100	1065	1200	1100	1065	1073	1035	990
800	960	1170	1136	1280	1170	1136	1144	1104	1056
850	1020	1240	1207	1360	1240	1207	1216	1173	1122
900	1080	1314	1278	1440	1314	1278	1287	1242	1188
950	1140	1390	1350	1520	1390	1350	1360	1310	1254
1000	1200	1460	1420	1600	1460	1420	1430	1380	1320

TABLE 61

ROOF DECKING FOR ALL GARAGES WITH A ROOF PITCH OF 1/2

(Includes Milling and Cutting Waste)

Ground Floor Area	Roof Surface Area	Shiplap		Tongue & Groove Boards			Square Edge Bds.			Plywood, Insulation & Particle Board
		1"x6" 1"x8"	1"x10"	1"x4"	1"x6" 1"x8"	1"x10"	1"x4"	1"x6" 1"x8"		
Sq Ft	Square Ft	Board Ft	Board Ft	Board Ft	Board Ft	Board Ft	Board Ft	Board Ft	Sq Ft	
200	284	346	336	378	346	336	338	326	310	
250	350	433	420	472	433	420	422	410	390	
300	426	520	504	567	520	504	500	490	470	
350	500	606	588	660	606	588	590	570	546	
400	568	690	672	756	690	672	676	652	620	
450	640	780	756	850	780	756	760	730	700	
500	710	865	840	945	865	840	845	815	780	
550	780	950	924	1040	950	924	930	900	860	
600	852	1040	1008	1134	1040	1008	1014	980	940	
650	923	1125	1090	1230	1125	1090	1100	1060	1015	
700	994	1210	1176	1323	1210	1176	1180	1140	1090	
750	1065	1300	1260	1420	1300	1260	1270	1220	1170	
800	1136	1385	1344	1512	1385	1344	1350	1300	1250	
850	1207	1470	1430	1600	1470	1430	1436	1390	1326	
900	1278	1560	1512	1700	1560	1512	1520	1470	1400	
950	1350	1644	1600	1800	1644	1600	1605	1550	1480	
1000	1420	1730	1680	1890	1730	1680	1690	1630	1560	

311

TABLES 62 THROUGH 67

Roofing for All Garages
(Including Cutting and Fitting)

These Tables show the quantities of various kinds of roofing materials for all garages with the roof pitches as follows:

Table	Roof Pitch	Inches Rise-per-Foot-of-Run
62	1/8	3
63	1/6	4
64	5/24	5
65	1/4	6
66	1/3	8
67	1/2	12

CUTTING AND FITTING WASTE

The percentages added to the areas to be covered in these Tables for cutting and fitting, starters, ridge caps, etc., are shown in Table 21-26A, page 217.

HOW TO USE THESE TABLES

1. Determine the *ground-floor* area of your garage.

2. Use the Table with the roof pitch nearest to that of your garage and select the kind of roofing material desired.

3. Read the quantity directly from the Table for your *ground-floor* area. If the *ground-floor* area falls between those in the Tables, interpolate as explained under Dwellings, page 20.

Overhang

These Tables do not include roofing on any overhang at the eaves or gable ends. Add 5% to the Table quantities for each 12″ of horizontal overhang at the eaves.

Dormers

The quantity of roofing on dormers, in most cases, is equivalent to the area in the main roof that is taken up by the dormer. The only amount to be added would be for dormer overhang.

Hip and Gable Roofs

A hip roof and a gable roof have identical roof surface areas where the pitch of the roofs is the same and both roofs cover the same horizontal area.

Nails

An acceptable average quantity of nails for various types of roofing is shown under Tables 21 to 26, page 218.

SHORTCUT FORMULAS FOR ESTIMATING THE AREA OF ROOFS AND QUANTITY OF ROOFING

The formulas for estimating the area of roofs and quantity of roofing from the *ground-floor* area is shown under Tables 21-26, pages 218-219. To determine the sq ft area of the roof, use Table 21-26B. Multiply that area by the factors shown in Table 21-26A, page 217, to obtain the number of sq ft of roofing needed.

TABLE 62

ROOFING FOR ALL GARAGES WITH A ROOF PITCH OF 1/8 INCLUDING CUTTING AND FITTING WASTE

Ground Floor Area	Roof Surface Area	Asphalt Strip Shingles	Wood Shingles				Asbestos Cement Shingles	Clay Roofing Tile	Number of Rolls of Saturated Felt Roofing Paper	
			18" Long		24" Long					
			4" Exposure	5" Exposure	6" Exposure	7" Exposure			15-Lb	30-Lb
Sq Ft	Sq Ft	Sq Ft	Sq Ft	Sq Ft	Sq Ft	Sq Ft	Sq Ft	Sq Ft		
200	206	226	278	226	284	226	226	215	.57	1.14
250	258	283	348	283	350	283	283	270	.70	1.40
300	309	340	415	340	426	340	340	325	.85	1.70
350	360	396	485	396	500	396	396	380	1.00	2.00
400	412	452	555	452	568	452	452	430	1.13	2.27
450	464	510	625	510	640	510	510	485	1.27	2.54
500	515	565	695	565	710	565	565	540	1.42	2.84
550	567	622	765	622	780	622	622	595	1.56	3.12
600	618	678	835	678	852	678	678	650	1.70	3.40
650	670	735	905	735	923	735	735	700	1.84	3.68
700	721	790	975	790	994	790	790	755	1.98	3.97
750	773	850	1040	850	1065	850	850	810	2.12	4.24
800	824	900	1110	900	1136	900	900	865	2.27	4.54
850	876	960	1180	960	1207	960	960	920	2.40	4.80
900	927	1017	1250	1017	1278	1017	1017	970	2.55	5.10
950	978	1074	1320	1074	1350	1074	1074	1025	2.70	5.40
1000	1030	1130	1390	1130	1420	1130	1130	1080	2.83	5.66

TABLE 63

ROOFING FOR ALL GARAGES WITH A ROOF PITCH OF 1/6 INCLUDING CUTTING AND FITTING WASTE

Ground Floor Area	Roof Surface Area	Asphalt Strip Shingles	Wood Shingles 18" Long 4" Exposure	Wood Shingles 18" Long 5" Exposure	Wood Shingles 24" Long 6" Exposure	Wood Shingles 24" Long 7" Exposure	Asbestos Cement Shingles	Clay Roofing Tile	Number of Rolls of Saturated Felt Roofing Paper 15-Lb	Number of Rolls of Saturated Felt Roofing Paper 30-Lb
Sq Ft	Sq Ft	Sq Ft	Sq Ft	Sq Ft	Sq Ft	Sq Ft	Sq Ft	Sq Ft		
200	212	234	286	234	292	234	234	224	.59	1.17
250	265	293	358	293	336	293	293	280	.73	1.46
300	318	351	429	351	438	351	351	336	.88	1.76
350	371	410	500	410	511	410	410	392	1.02	2.04
400	424	468	572	468	584	468	468	448	1.17	2.34
450	477	527	644	527	657	527	527	504	1.32	2.64
500	530	585	715	585	730	585	585	560	1.46	2.93
550	583	644	787	644	800	644	644	616	1.61	3.22
600	636	702	858	702	876	702	702	672	1.76	3.51
650	689	760	930	760	950	760	760	728	1.90	3.80
700	742	819	1000	819	1022	819	819	784	2.05	4.10
750	795	878	1073	878	1100	878	878	840	2.20	4.40
800	848	936	1144	936	1170	936	936	896	2.34	4.68
850	900	1000	1216	1000	1240	1000	1000	952	2.50	5.00
900	954	1053	1287	1053	1314	1053	1053	1008	2.63	5.27
950	1007	1110	1360	1110	1390	1110	1110	1064	2.78	5.56
1000	1060	1170	1430	1170	1460	1170	1170	1120	2.93	5.85

TABLE 64

ROOFING FOR ALL GARAGES WITH A ROOF PITCH OF 5/24 INCLUDING CUTTING AND FITTING WASTE

Ground Floor Area	Roof Surface Area	Asphalt Strip Shingles	Wood Shingles				Asbestos Cement Shingles	Clay Roofing Tile	Number of Rolls of Saturated Felt Roofing Paper	
			18" Long 4" Exposure	5" Exposure	24" Long 6" Exposure	7" Exposure			15-Lb	30-Lb
Sq Ft	Sq Ft	Sq Ft	Sq Ft	Sq Ft	Sq Ft	Sq Ft	Sq Ft	Sq Ft		
200	218	240	294	240	300	240	240	228	.60	1.20
250	273	300	370	300	375	300	300	285	.75	1.50
300	327	360	440	360	450	360	360	342	.90	1.80
350	382	420	515	420	525	420	420	400	1.05	2.10
400	426	480	588	480	600	480	480	456	1.20	2.40
450	436	540	660	540	675	540	540	515	1.35	2.70
500	546	600	735	600	750	600	600	570	1.50	3.00
550	600	660	810	660	825	660	660	630	1.65	3.30
600	654	720	882	720	900	720	720	684	1.80	3.60
650	709	780	955	780	975	780	780	740	1.95	3.90
700	763	840	1029	840	1050	840	840	798	2.10	4.20
750	818	900	1100	900	1125	900	900	855	2.25	4.50
800	872	960	1176	960	1200	960	960	912	2.40	4.80
850	927	1020	1250	1020	1275	1020	1020	970	2.55	5.10
900	981	1080	1323	1080	1350	1080	1080	1026	2.70	5.40
950	1035	1140	1400	1140	1425	1140	1140	1085	2.85	5.70
1000	1090	1200	1470	1200	1500	1200	1200	1140	3.00	6.00

TABLE 65

ROOFING FOR ALL GARAGES WITH A ROOF PITCH OF 1/4 INCLUDING CUTTING AND FITTING WASTE

Ground Floor Area	Roof Surface Area	Asphalt Strip Shingles	Wood Shingles				Asbestos Cement Shingles	Clay Roofing Tile	Number of Rolls of Saturated Felt Roofing Paper	
			18" Long		24" Long					
			4" Exposure	5" Exposure	6" Exposure	7" Exposure				
Sq Ft	Sq Ft	Sq Ft	Sq Ft	Sq Ft	Sq Ft	Sq Ft	Sq Ft	Sq Ft	15-Lb	30-Lb
200	224	246	300	346	310	246	246	236	.60	1.25
250	280	308	375	308	390	308	308	295	.80	1.55
300	336	369	450	369	465	369	369	354	.95	1.85
350	392	430	525	430	545	430	430	413	1.10	2.15
400	448	492	600	492	620	492	492	472	1.25	2.50
450	504	554	675	554	700	554	554	531	1.40	2.80
500	560	615	750	615	775	615	615	570	1.55	3.10
550	612	676	825	676	855	676	676	649	1.70	3.40
600	672	738	900	738	930	738	738	708	1.85	3.70
650	728	800	975	800	1010	800	800	767	2.00	4.05
700	784	860	1050	860	1085	860	860	826	2.15	4.35
750	840	922	1125	922	1165	922	922	885	2.35	4.65
800	896	984	1200	984	1240	984	984	944	2.50	5.00
850	952	1046	1275	1046	1320	1046	1046	1000	2.65	5.25
900	1008	1107	1350	1107	1395	1107	1107	1062	2.80	5.60
950	1064	1170	1425	1170	1475	1170	1170	1120	2.95	5.90
1000	1120	1230	1500	1230	1550	1230	1230	1180	3.10	6.20

TABLE 66

ROOFING FOR ALL GARAGES WITH A ROOF PITCH OF 1/3 INCLUDING CUTTING AND FITTING WASTE

Ground Floor Area	Roof Surface Area	Asphalt Strip Shingles	Wood Shingles				Asbestos Cement Shingles	Clay Roofing Tile	Number of Rolls of Saturated Felt Roofing Paper	
			18" Long		24" Long					
			4" Exposure	5" Exposure	6" Exposure	7" Exposure				
Sq Ft	Sq Ft	Sq Ft	Sq Ft	Sq Ft	Sq Ft	Sq Ft	Sq Ft	Sq Ft	15-Lb	30-Lb
200	240	264	324	264	332	264	264	252	.66	1.32
250	300	330	405	330	415	330	330	315	.83	1.65
300	360	396	486	396	498	396	396	378	.99	1.98
350	420	462	567	462	580	462	462	440	1.15	2.30
400	480	528	648	528	664	528	528	504	1.32	2.64
450	540	494	730	594	750	594	594	570	1.50	3.00
500	600	660	810	660	830	660	660	630	1.65	3.30
550	660	726	890	726	915	726	726	695	1.82	3.63
600	720	792	972	792	1000	792	792	756	1.98	3.96
650	780	858	1053	858	1080	858	858	820	2.15	4.30
700	840	924	1134	924	1162	924	924	882	2.31	4.62
750	900	990	1215	990	1245	990	990	945	2.50	4.95
800	960	1056	1296	1056	1328	1056	1056	1008	2.64	5.28
850	1020	1122	1380	1122	1410	1122	1122	1070	2.80	5.60
900	1080	1188	1458	1188	1494	1188	1188	1134	2.97	5.94
950	1140	1254	1540	1254	1580	1254	1254	1200	3.15	6.30
1000	1200	1320	1620	1320	1660	1320	1320	1260	3.30	6.60

TABLE 67

ROOFING FOR ALL GARAGES WITH A ROOF PITCH OF 1/2 INCLUDING CUTTING AND FITTING WASTE

Ground Floor Area	Roof Surface Area	Asphalt Strip Shingles	Wood Shingles				Asbestos Cement Shingles	Clay Roofing Tile	Number of Rolls of Saturated Felt Roofing Paper	
			18" Long		24" Long					
			4" Exposure	5" Exposure	6" Exposure	7" Exposure			15-Lb	30-Lb
Sq Ft	Sq Ft	Sq Ft	Sq Ft	Sq Ft	Sq Ft	Sq Ft	Sq Ft	Sq Ft		
200	284	310	384	312	392	312	312	298	.78	1.55
250	350	390	480	390	490	390	390	373	.97	1.94
300	426	470	576	468	590	468	468	447	1.16	2.32
350	500	546	672	546	685	546	546	522	1.36	2.72
400	568	620	768	624	784	624	624	600	1.55	3.10
450	640	700	864	700	880	700	700	670	1.75	3.50
500	710	780	960	780	980	780	780	745	1.94	3.90
550	780	860	1056	860	1080	860	860	820	2.13	4.26
600	852	940	1152	936	1175	936	936	894	2.33	4.65
650	923	1015	1250	1015	1275	1015	1015	968	2.52	5.00
700	994	1090	1344	1090	1370	1090	1090	1043	2.70	5.45
750	1065	1170	1440	1170	1470	1170	1170	1118	2.90	5.80
800	1136	1250	1536	1250	1570	1250	1250	1192	3.10	6.20
850	1207	1326	1632	1325	1665	1325	1325	1266	3.30	6.60
900	1278	1400	1728	1400	1765	1400	1400	1340	3.50	7.00
950	1350	1480	1824	1480	1860	1480	1480	1416	3.68	7.36
1000	1420	1560	1920	1560	1960	1560	1560	1490	3.88	7.75

Key to Tables and Formulas

Glossary of Terms

Attached garage. A one-, two- or three-car garage one side of which is attached to a dwelling.

Basement. Lowest habitable floor of a building, usually below ground level.

Basement garage. A one- or two-car garage occupying a portion of a dwelling basement.

Board foot. A piece of wood 12″ square and 1-inch thick or an equivalent volume of wood.

Breezeway. Covered passage between house and garage.

Brick veneer construction. Same as frame construction, but with 4 inches of brick veneer on exterior walls.

Carport. An open sided, roofed-over shelter for automobiles; may be attached to dwelling or detached.

Ceiling heights. Distance from finish floor to ceiling in a room.

Crawl space. A shallow space below the living quarters of a dwelling without basement.

Detached garage. A one-, two- or three-car garage independent of the dwelling; may be joined by a breezeway.

Dormer. A small gable projecting from a sloping roof usually with a window in the gable end.

Estimate. A judgment or approximation of the quantity of material, labor and cost of items of construction.

Exterior surface materials. All construction materials in or applied to the exterior walls of a building except framing.

Exterior walls. Outside walls of a building.

FBM. Feet board measure.

Footing. Supporting base of a building.

Foundation walls. Supporting walls of a building above the footing to the underside of the first floor.

Forms. Wood or metal sides erected to contain concrete when poured in order to maintain the shape or form desired.

Formula. Mathematical form or rule for estimating.

Frame construction. A building constructed principally of wood and above the foundation—framed walls, floors and roof.

Framing. Rough wood timber structure of a building.

Gable area. The square foot area of the portion of a wall contained between the slopes of a double-sloped roof.

Gable area adjustment. Procedure for adjusting gable materials where pitch of the roof is other than 1/4.

Gable roof. A pitched roof ending in a gable or gables.

Ground-floor area. The square feet in that area taken up by the building at ground level including extensions and recessed parts actually within the exterior walls of the building.

Hip roof. A roof on a rectangular building, the roof sloping on all four sides.

Horizontal roof area. The square foot area of a horizontal plane beneath the roof of a building.

Interior surface materials. All materials that are applied to the interior wall and floor surfaces excluding framing materials and exterior masonry walls.

Interpolate. To determine values between known values.

Irregular shaped buildings. Not shaped like a rectangle, usually composed of two or more rectangles.

Length-to-width adjustment. An adjustment to Table quantities when the L:W of a building is other than 2:1. Applies only to footing, foundation and exterior wall materials.

Length-to-width ratio (L:W). The quotient of the length of a building to its width, or its theoretical equivalent in an irregular shaped building.

One- and one-half story dwelling. One that has substantial livable area on a second floor level or at a few feet below the first floor plate line.

One-story dwelling. One that has the major portion of the livable area on one floor. There may be a basement.

Ordinary brick construction. A building constructed similar to frame construction except the exterior walls are masonry; 8″ brick or concrete block.

OSHA. Occupational Safety and Health Administration regulations for the construction industry.

Overhang. That portion of the roof extending beyond the exterior face of a building.

Overhead. Operating costs of a contractor or subcontractor.

Patio. Usually an unroofed, paved recreational area attached to a dwelling.

Perimeter. Lineal feet bounding a plane area.

Pitch of roof. Slope of a roof.

Porch. An open or enclosed room, deck or platform attached to a dwelling.

Profit. Amount in dollars or a percentage of total cost added by a contractor or subcontractor to the estimate as a return on investment.

Rafter. A structural member of a roof.

Rectangle. Parallelogram with a right angle.

Rectangular buildings. In the shape of a rectangle.

Reinforcing. Metal rods or wire mesh imbedded in concrete to provide tensile strength.

Ridge pole (ridge board). A lateral framing member on edge at the roof ridge to join and support rafters.

Rise of roof. The degree in elevation; the height above the plate line to the peak or ridge.

Roofing. Material surfacing the roof to make it watertight.

Run of a roof. Run is equal to 1/2 the span.

Shortcut formula. Simplified rule or form for estimating materials.

Span. Distance between the walls that support the roof rafters or a truss.

Specification. A description of the kind, quantity and quality of materials and workmanship that control construction of a building.

Subcontractor. One who contracts to perform a specific part of a prime contract.

Two-story dwelling. One with two livable floors—full height at the exterior wall.

Truss. A framework of wood (or metal) usually arranged in a triangle to support a roof.

Unit cost. Combined cost of labor and material to install a unit of material or to perform an operation.

Wall height adjustment. Procedure for increasing or decreasing Table quantities for exterior wall heights that are different from Table-based heights.

INDEX

Other Practical References

Construction Estimating Guides

Construction Estimating Reference Data
Collected in this single volume are the building estimator's 300 most useful estimating reference tables. Labor requirements for nearly every type of construction are included: sitework, concrete work, masonry, steel, carpentry, thermal & moisture protection, doors and windows, finishes, mechanical and electrical. Each section explains in detail the work being estimated and gives the appropriate crew size and equipment needed. Many pages of illustrations, estimating pointers and explanations of the work being estimated are also included. This is an essential reference for every professional construction estimator. **368 pages, 11 x 8½, $18.00**

Building Cost Manual
Square foot costs for residential, commercial, industrial, and farm buildings. In a few minutes you work up a reliable budget estimate based on the actual materials and design features, area, shape, wall height, number of floors and support requirements. Most important, you include all the important variables that can make any building unique from a cost standpoint. **240 pages, 8½ x 11, $12.00. Revised annually**

Cost Records for Construction Estimating
How to organize and use cost information from jobs just completed to make more accurate estimates in the future. Explains how to keep the cost records you need to reflect the time spent on each part of the job. Shows the best way to track costs for sitework, footing, foundations, framing, interior finish, siding and trim, masonry, and subcontract expense. Provides sample forms. **208 pages, 8½ x 11, $15.75**

Berger Building Cost File
Labor and material costs needed to estimate major projects: shopping centers and stores, hospitals, educational facilities, office complexes, industrial and institutional buildings, and housing projects. All cost estimates show both the manhours required and the typical crew needed so you can figure the price and schedule the work quickly and easily. **344 pages, 8½ x 11, $30.00**

Estimating Home Building Costs
Estimate every phase of residential construction from site costs to the profit margin you should include in your bid. Shows how to keep track of manhours and make accurate labor cost estimates for footings, foundations, framing and sheathing finishes, electrical, plumbing and more. Explains the work being estimated and provides sample cost estimate worksheets with complete instructions for each job phase. **320 pages, 5½ x 8½, $14.00**

National Construction Estimator
Current building costs in dollars and cents for residential, commercial and industrial construction. Prices for every commonly used building material, and the proper labor cost associated with installation of the material. Everything figured out to give you the "in place" cost in seconds. Many time-saving rules of thumb, waste and coverage factors and estimating tables are included. **512 pages, 8½ x 11, $16.00. Revised annually.**

Electrical References

Electrical Construction Estimator
If you estimate electrical jobs, this is your guide to current material costs, reliable manhour estimates per unit, and the total installed cost for all common electrical work: conduit, wire, boxes, fixtures, switches, outlets, loadcenters, panelboards, raceway, duct, signal systems, and more. Explains what every estimator should know before estimating each part of an electrical system. **400 pages, 8½ x 11, $25.00**

Residential Electrical Design
Explains what every builder needs to know about designing electrical systems for residential construction. Shows how to draw up an electrical plan from the blueprints, including the service entrance, grounding, lighting requirements for kitchen, bedroom and bath and how to lay them out. Explains how to plan electrical heating systems and what equipment you'll need, how to plan outdoor lighting, and much more. If you are a builder who ever has to plan an electrical system, you should have this book. **194 pages, 8½ x 11, $11.50**

Estimating Electrical Construction
A practical approach to estimating materials and labor for residential and commercial electrical construction. Written by the A.S.P.E. National Estimator of the Year, it explains how to use labor units, the plan take-off and the bid summary to establish an accurate estimate. Covers dealing with suppliers, pricing sheets, and how to modify labor units. Provides extensive labor unit tables, and blank forms for use in estimating your next electrical job. **272 pages, 8½ x 11, $19.00**

Manual of Electrical Contracting
From the tools you need for installing electrical work in new construction and remodeling work to developing the finances you need to run your business. Shows how to draw up an electrical plan and design the correct lighting within the budget you have to work with. How to calculate service and feeder loads, service entrance capacity, demand factors, and install wiring in residential, commercial, and agricultural buildings. Covers how to make sure your business will succeed before you start it, and how to keep it running profitably. **224 pages, 8½ x 11, $17.00**

Handbook of Modern Electrical Wiring
The journeyman electrician's guide to planning the job and doing professional quality work on any residential or light commercial project. Explains how to use the code, how to calculate loads and size conductors and conduit, the right way to lay out the job, how to wire branch and feeder circuits, selecting the right service equipment, and much more. **204 pages, 5½ x 8½, $14.75**

Electrical Blueprint Reading
Shows how to read and interpret electrical drawings, wiring diagrams and specifications for construction of electrical systems in buildings. Shows how a typical lighting plan and power layout would appear on the plans and explains what the contractor would do to execute this plan. Describes how to use a panelboard or heating schedule and includes typical electrical specifications. **128 pages, 8½ x 11, $8.50**

Professional Remodeling Guides

Manual of Professional Remodeling
This is the practical manual of professional remodeling written by an experienced and successful remodeling contractor. Shows how to evaluate a job and avoid 30-minute jobs that take all day, what to fix and what to leave alone, and what to watch for in dealing with subcontractors. Includes chapters on calculating space requirements, repairing structural defects, remodeling kitchens, baths, walls and ceilings, doors and windows, floors, roofs, installing fireplaces and chimneys (including built-ins), skylights, and exterior siding. Includes blank forms, checklists, sample contracts, and proposals you can copy and use. **400 pages, 8½ x 11, $18.75**

How to Sell Remodeling
Proven, effective sales methods for repair and remodeling contractors: finding qualified leads, making the sales call, identifying what your prospects really need, pricing the job, arranging financing, and closing the sale. Explains how to organize and staff a sales team, how to bring in the work to keep your crews busy and your business growing, and much more. Includes blank forms, tables, and charts. **240 pages, 8½ x 11, $17.50**

Remodelers Handbook
The complete manual of home improvement contracting: Planning the job, estimating costs, doing the work, running your company and making profits. Pages of sample forms, contracts, documents, clear illustrations and examples. Chapters on evaluating the work, rehabilitation, kitchens, bathrooms, adding living area, re-flooring, re-siding, re-roofing, replacing windows and doors, installing new wall and ceiling cover, re-painting, upgrading insulation, combating moisture damage, estimating, selling your services, and bookkeeping for remodelers. **416 pages, 8½ x 11, $18.50**

Paint Contractor's Manual
How to start and run a profitable paint contracting company: getting set up and organized to handle volume work, avoiding the mistakes most painters make, getting top production from your crews and the most value from your advertising dollar. Shows how to estimate all prep and painting. Loaded with manhour estimates, sample forms, contracts, charts, tables and examples you can use. **224 pages, 8½ x 11, $19.25**

Plumbing & Piping References

Plumbers Handbook Revised
This new edition shows what will and what will not pass inspection in drainage, vent, and waste piping, septic tanks, water supply, fire protection, and gas piping systems. All tables, standards, and specifications are completely up-to-date with recent changes in the plumbing code. Covers common layouts for residential work, how to size piping, selecting and hanging fixtures, practical recommendations and trade tips. This book is the approved reference for the plumbing contractors exam in many states. **240 pages, 8½ x 11, $16.75**

Estimating Plumbing Costs
Offers a basic procedure for estimating materials, labor, and direct and indirect costs for residential and commercial plumbing jobs. Explains how to interpret and understand plot plans, design drainage, waste, and vent systems, meet code requirements, and make an accurate take-off for materials and labor. Includes sample cost sheets, manhour production tables, complete illustrations, and all the practical information you need to accurately estimate plumbing costs. **224 pages, 8½ x 11, $17.25**

Plumber's Exam Preparation Guide
Lists questions like those asked on most plumber's exams. Gives the correct answer to each question, under both the Uniform Plumbing Code and the Standard Plumbing Code — and explains why that answer is correct. Includes questions on system design and layout where a plan drawing is required. Covers plumbing systems (both standard and specialized), gas systems, plumbing isometrics, piping diagrams, and as much plumber's math as the examination requires. Suggests the best ways to prepare for the exam, how and what to study and describes what you can expect on exam day. At the end of the book is a complete sample exam that can predict how you'll do on the real tests. **320 pages, 8½ x 11, $21.00**

Basic Plumbing with Illustrations
The journeyman's and apprentice's guide to installing plumbing, piping and fixtures in residential and light commercial buildings: how to select the right materials, lay out the job and do professional quality plumbing work. Explains the use of essential tools and materials, how to make repairs, maintain plumbing systems, install fixtures and add to existing systems. **320 pages, 8½ x 11, $17.50**

Builder's Office Manuals

Computers: The Builder's New Tool
Shows how to avoid costly mistakes and find the right computer system for your needs. Takes you step-by-step through each important decision, from selecting the software to getting your equipment set up and operating. Filled with examples, checklists and illustrations, including case histories describing experiences other contractors have had. If you're thinking about putting a computer in your construction office, you should read this book before buying anything. **192 pages, 8½ x 11, $17.75**

Builder's Office Manual
This manual will show every builder with from 3 to 25 employees the best ways to: organize the office space needed, establish an accurate record-keeping system, create procedures and forms that streamline work, control costs, hire and retain a productive staff, minimize overhead, and much more. **208 pages, 8½ x 11, $13.25**

Contractor's Year-Round Tax Guide
How to set up and run your construction business to minimize taxes: corporate tax strategy and how to use it to your advantage, and what you should be aware of in contracts with others. Covers tax shelters for builders, write-offs and investments that will reduce your taxes, accounting methods that are best for contractors, and what the I.R.S. allows and what it often questions. **192 pages, 8½ x 11, $16.50**

Builder's Guide to Construction Financing
Explains how and where to borrow the money to buy land and build homes and apartments: conventional loan sources, loan brokers, private lenders, purchase money loans, and federally insured loans. How to shop for financing, get the valuation you need, comply with lending requirements, and handle liens. **304 pages, 5½ x 8½, $11.00**

Construction References

Wood-Frame House Construction

From the layout of the outer walls, excavation and formwork, to finish carpentry, and painting, every step of construction is covered in detail with clear illustrations and explanations. Everything the builder needs to know about framing, roofing, siding, insulation and vapor barrier, interior finishing, floor coverings, and stairs. . .complete step by step "how to" information on what goes into building a frame house. **240 pages, 8½ x 11, $11.25. Revised edition**

Rough Carpentry

All rough carpentry is covered in detail: sills, girders, columns, joists, sheathing, ceiling, roof and wall framing, roof trusses, dormers, bay windows, furring and grounds, stairs and insulation. Many of the 24 chapters explain practical code approved methods for saving lumber and time without sacrificing quality. Chapters on columns, headers, rafters, joists and girders show how to use simple engineering principles to select the right lumber dimension for whatever species and grade you are using. **288 pages, 8½ x 11, $14.50**

Roof Framing

Frame any type of roof in common use today, even if you've never framed a roof before. Shows how to use a pocket calculator to figure any common, hip, valley, and jack rafter length in seconds. Over 400 illustrations take you through every measurement and every cut on each type of roof: gable, hip, Dutch, Tudor, gambrel, shed, gazebo and more. **480 pages, 5½ x 8½, $19.50**

Contractor's Guide to the Building Code

Explains in plain English exactly what the Uniform Building Code requires and shows how to design and construct residential and light commercial buildings that will pass inspection the first time. Suggests how to work with the inspector to minimize construction costs, what common building short cuts are likely to be cited, and where exceptions are granted. **312 pages, 5½ x 8½, $16.25**

Stair Builders Handbook

If you know the floor to floor rise, this handbook will give you everything else: the number and dimension of treads and risers, the total run, the correct well hole opening, the angle of incline, the quantity of materials and settings for your framing square for over 3,500 code approved rise and run combinations—several for every 1/8 inch interval from a 3 foot to a 12 foot floor to floor rise. **416 pages, 8½ x 5½, $12.75**

Reducing Home Building Costs

Explains where significant cost savings are possible and shows how to take advantage of these opportunities. Six chapters show how to reduce foundation, floor, exterior wall, roof, interior and finishing costs. Three chapters show effective ways to avoid problems usually associated with bad weather at the jobsite. Explains how to increase labor productivity. **224 pages, 8½ x 11, $10.25**

Home Builders Guide

The "how to" of custom home building explained by a successful professional builder: How to anticipate problems, eliminate bottlenecks, keep the work going smoothly, and end up with a finished home that is a credit to your skill and professionalism. Explains working with subcontractors, lenders, architects, municipal authorities, building inspectors, tradesmen and suppliers, avoiding design problems, getting financing, making sure your building permit is issued promptly, work scheduling and more. **359 pages, 5½ x 8½, $7.00**

Building and Remodeling for Energy Savings

The practical handbook of what you can and should be doing to meet the needs of your energy-conscious clients: How to build energy efficiency into every job, plan the site to save up to 30% on heating and cooling costs, when to use and when to avoid storm sash and thermal glass, how to use windows, skylights and clerestories to light room interiors, what every builder must know about insulation, weatherstripping and condensation. Hundreds of practical tips and pages of reference data are included. **320 pages, 8½ x 11, $15.00**

Construction Superintending

Explains what the "super" should do during every job phase from taking bids to project completion on both heavy and light construction: excavation, foundations, pilings, steelwork, concrete and masonry, carpentry, plumbing, and electrical. Explains scheduling, preparing estimates, record keeping, dealing with subcontractors, and change orders. Includes the charts, forms, and established guidelines every superintendent needs. **240 pages, 8½ x 11, $22.00**

Rafter Length Manual

Complete rafter length tables and the "how to" of roof framing. Shows how to use the tables to find the actual length of common, hip, valley and jack rafters. Shows how to measure, mark, cut and erect the rafters, find the drop of the hip, shorten jack rafters, mark the ridge and much more. Has the tables, explanations and illustrations every professional roof framer needs. **369 pages, 8½ x 5½, $12.25**

Building Layout

Shows how to use a transit to locate the building on the lot correctly, plan proper grades with minimum excavation, find utility lines and easements, establish correct elevations, lay out accurate foundations and set correct floor heights. Explains planning sewer connections, leveling a foundation out of level, using a story pole and batterboards, working on steep sites, and minimizing excavation costs. **240 pages, 5½ x 8½, $11.75**

Spec Builder's Guide

Explains how to plan and build a home, control your construction costs, and then sell the house at a price that earns a decent return on the time and money you've invested. Includes professional tips to ensure success as a spec builder: how government statistics help you judge the housing market, cutting costs at every opportunity without sacrificing quality, and taking advantage of construction cycles. Every chapter includes checklists, diagrams, charts, figures, and estimating tables. **448 pages, 8½ x 11, $24.00**

HVAC Contracting

Your guide to setting up and running a successful HVAC contracting company. Shows how to plan and design all types of systems for maximum efficiency and lowest cost — and explains how to sell your customers on the designs you propose. Describes the right way to use all the instruments, equipment and reference materials essential to HVAC contracting. Includes a full chapter on estimating, bidding, and contract procedure. **256 pages, 8½ x 11, $24.50.**

Blueprint Reading for the Building Trades

How to read and understand construction documents, blueprints, and schedules. Includes layouts of structural, mechanical and electrical drawings, how to interpret sectional views, how to follow diagrams; plumbing, HVAC and schematics, and common problems experienced in interpreting construction specifications. This book is your course for understanding and following construction documents. **192 pages, 5½ x 8½, $11.25**

Builder's Guide to Government Loans

This comprehensive guide will help you take advantage of the many government loan programs. Everything is explained in step-by-step instruction and actual sample forms are included: HUD and FHA loan insurance and guarantees for operative builders, interest subsidies, rent supplements, public housing programs, turnkey projects, VA loans, FmHA rural housing programs, and Small Business Administration loans for builders. **416 pages, 5½ x 8½, $13.75**

Finish Carpentry

The time-saving methods and proven shortcuts you need to do first class finish work on any job: cornices and rakes, gutters and downspouts, wood shingle roofing, asphalt, asbestos and built-up roofing, prefabricated windows, door bucks and frames, door trim, siding, wallboard, lath and plaster, stairs and railings, cabinets, joinery, and wood flooring. **192 pages, 8½ x 11, $10.50**

Construction References

Roofers Handbook

The journeyman roofer's complete guide to wood and asphalt shingle application on both new construction and reroofing jobs: How professional roofers make smooth tie-ins on any job, the right way to cover valleys and ridges, how to handle and prevent leaks, how to set up and run your own roofing business and sell your services as a professional roofer. Over 250 illustrations and hundreds of trade tips. **192 pages, 8½ x 11, $9.25**

Masonry & Concrete Construction

Every aspect of masonry construction is covered, from laying out the building with a transit to constructing chimneys and fireplaces. Explains footing construction, building foundations, laying out a block wall, reinforcing masonry, pouring slabs and sidewalks, coloring concrete, selecting and maintaining forms, using the Jahn Forming System and steel ply forms, and much more. **224 pages, 8½ x 11, $13.50**

Builder's Guide to Accounting

Explains how to set up and operate the record systems best for your business: simplified payroll and tax record keeping plus quick ways to make forecasts, spot trends, prepare estimates, record sales, receivables, checks and costs, and control losses. Loaded with charts, diagrams, blank forms and examples to help you create the strong financial base your business needs. **304 pages, 8½ x 11, $12.50**

Concrete and Formwork

This practical manual has all the information you need to select and pour the right mix for the job, lay out the structure, choose the right form materials, design and build the forms and finish and cure the concrete. Nearly 100 pages of step-by-step instructions cover the actual construction and erecting of nearly all site fabricated wood forms used in residential construction. **176 pages, 8½ x 11, $10.00**

Carpentry

Illustrates all the essentials of residential work: form building, simplified timber engineering, corners, joists and flooring, rough framing, sheathing, cornices, columns, lattice, building paper, siding, doors and windows, roofing, joints and more. One chapter demonstrates how the steel square is used in modern carpentry. **219 pages, 8½ x 11, $6.95**

Excavation and Grading Handbook

The foreman's and superintendent's guide to highway, subdivision and pipeline jobs: how to read plans and survey stake markings, set grade, excavate, compact, pave and lay pipe on nearly any job. Includes hundreds of practical tips, pictures, diagrams and tables that even experienced "pros" should have. **320 pages, 5½ x 8½, $15.25**

Concrete Construction & Estimating

Explains how to estimate the quantity of labor and materials needed, plan the job, erect fiberglass, steel, or prefabricated forms, install shores and scaffolding, handle the concrete into place, set joints, finish and cure the concrete. Every builder who works with concrete should have the reference data, cost estimates, and examples in this practical reference. **571 pages, 5½ x 8½, $17.75**

Operating The Tractor-Loader-Backhoe

Explains how to get maximum productivity from this highly versatile machine. Describes how experienced operators plan the job before work begins, cut wasted movement to a minimum, work effectively in tight quarters and handle the really difficult jobs safely and efficiently. Covers cutting, filling, compacting, trenching, working around utility lines, craning, tunneling, footings, truck loading, grading, demolition, even stump removal and brush cleaning. Each task is illustrated with diagrams and photographs. If you own or rent a hoe, you need this practical manual. **192 pages, 8½ x 11, $23.75**